GUNSLINGERS

GUNSLINGERS

by

Carl W. Breihan

Introduction by

Harold Preece

Published by

Leather Stocking Books

Pine Mountain Press, Inc. Publishing Group

P.O. Box 13604

Wauwatosa, WI 53226

Cover Illustration: Eugene E. Ruble

Manufactured in USA.

ISBN:0-89769-020-6

DEDICATED TO OUR GRANDCHILDREN

Susan A., Michael R. and
Rebecca M. Willey
and
Eric Jon and Marc Chadwick Breihan

Ethel & Carl W. Breihan

CONTENTS

INTRODUCTION

A foremost Western scholar, Joe Snell, has commented that Carl W. Breihan "knows more about Jesse James than any man living." Carl shares posthumously with Jesse James the fact of being a Missourian. Six of his thirteen published books have dealt with that Midwest desperado who has been called "the Prince of American Outlaws."

Naturally, his interests have included research and picked up folksay of men who heisted banks and boarded trains, so that a growing number of Western fans have come to regard him as the final authority on early day lawbreakers — to lawbreakers Carl has also faced personally as a lawman who branched out into literature.

Carl has worn the badge as a constable, a deputy sheriff, and a member of the St. Louis County, Missouri, Police Board. He has faced up to more than one brush with some fellow trying to call a bluff on justice. In one of his many letters to me, he tells of one grim set-to with a lawbreaker. Carl wrote:

> *This fellow was an ex-marine and an expert shot with a .45 automatic, so we took along tear gas rather than take heroic chances with him. Our group of lawmen wanted him for robbery and for beating up a family in the house where he was holed up. Funny though that one of the tear gas shells struck the window sill outside so that the gas came right back at us. I would suffer from a terrible headache and sore eyes for a week to come.*
>
> *Finally, we made it through the gas to the back of the house. There we broke in and collared him after a fierce struggle. I was carrying a sawed-off shotgun loaded with .00 buckshot. As it*

turned out, I didn't have to use the weapon, but I would have done so without hesitation had I been compelled.

Missouri had been the colorful mother state of the Old West. From the dramatic folklore of his native terrain Carl Breihan, at an early age, became immersed in its robust outlawry legendry.

The James Boys and their allies — the Younger Brothers — The Daltons, kin to the Youngers — Johnie Ringo — and other riders of the back trails all had their beginnings in Missouri. Actually, the word "Missourian" carried the same fearful connotation as "Texan" during the raw days of the West.

From his background interest in the native outlawry of his home state, Carl's interests branched out to include pistol enforced wrong-doing throughout the West. Name some gunslinger from Texas or Arizona or wherever, Carl can fascinate you with tales that make you hear the hum of the rails, the shootouts between lawmen and outlaws, the cursing of exasperated possemen losing the trail of some hoodlum pack — and their rejoicing in apprehending trigger trash destined for the penitentiary or the gallows.

Nor does Carl just rewrite what other authors have written before him. He seeks out descendants of men who live the old times to note down transmitted memories of some uncle or cousin who may have ridden with or run from posses. He seeks out dimming records stowed in forgotten corners of courthouses and archives to resurrect happenings that are vital events of Western and American history. In long buried collections, packed away and seldom remembered, he finds yellowed reward posters and sometimes revealing correspondence and diaries. That same patient, endless effort is reflected in this latest Breihan classic, GUNSLINGERS.

Combining skill with words and insight into the complex forces motivating Western society, Carl portrays five noted gunslingers. These subjects are Tom Horn, who lost his badge in Wyoming to die on the gallows like a common criminal for suspected murder of a rancher's child; Doc Holliday, the emigree Georgia dentist who drilled men rather than drilled teeth out in Arizona; and Frank Canton, a law dodger in Texas while wearing his birth handle of Joe Horner to become adjutant general of Oklahoma under the monicker he died wearing.

Rounding out the quintet is Texas' grotesque John King Fisher who gave up outlawing when the Rangers made cow rustling too hazardous an occupation, and who strutted around, a pathological egomaniac, in tiger skin britches — and that's not a Texas tall tale. Completing this fine book is "Bearcat" Henry Starr, the educated Cherokee Indian with big hopes in his field of larceny, but hope bringing only slim pickings. The Starr sequence is a reprint of a very rare pamphlet written by the luckless young Cherokee as such.

It is part of Carl's gift at narration that he does not stereotype his characters. All were men of the gun, but each was an individual in his own right. Where there were extenuating circumstances in the life of each, the author reveals them.

Tom Horn ran away from Missouri at age fourteen to escape further beatings from a brutal father. The West was full of drifting kids, escaping drudgery with the hoe and heavy punishment with the strap. They were to be found from the cattle ranges of Texas to the mines of Nevada and Wyoming. More than one went the way of Tom Horn.

Doc Holliday's own physical condition made it difficult for him to earn his living at dentistry. People, as Carl points out, were reluctant to risk their own health by consulting a practitioner afflicted with tuberculosis. So the gambling table became his livelihood and the gun his defiance of fate.

These things Carl Breihan understands as a man who has dealt with all kinds of odd characters. He has had the good fortune to know people who have some strong inherited traditions of Doc Holliday though they are reluctant to discuss him publicly. But one tale of these is repeated in his chapter on the prodigal dentist.

Many authors have written of the off-and-on attachment between Holliday, brought up decently, and a tough saloon harridan recalled as "Big Nose" Kate Elder. These two continually fought and "made up" in what was a sleazy sort of relationship. However, only Carl Breihan has revealed from highly confidential sources a very tender, youthful romance between the high-strung young Georgian and a girl named Melanie who was his first cousin. A devout Catholic, she became a nun, perhaps out of both family and religious considerations.

Did this sad denouement contribute to the moral downfall of the man who became a dentist without working very hard at it? Did it have to do with dying Dr. Holliday converting to Catholicism a few months before his dath in Glenwood Springs — though by that time Melanie's sacred vows would have prevented marriage? It seems that the two continued correspondence that Carl has seen, but is not at liberty to print. By contrast, Kate Elder, as the author points out, accused him of robbing a stagecoach after one quarrel though Carl points out she was the only "witness." Nothing came of the charge. Doc Holliday made all the money he needed from gambling without having to stick up stagecoaches. Does all of this mean that a book on Holliday — the most authentic one on him every written — could be incubating in that talented creativity of Carl Breihan? A lot of his informed fans could hope so.

By contrast, the author shows King Fisher as a colorful egotist very much in love with himself. Fisher, as he points out, had been a South Texas rustler baron before pinning on a lawman's badge for the sake of protection. Texas has produced many *bandidos,* but none more generally braggart and showoff than this man who finally got what he had been courting in that famous showdown at San Antonio.

Skillfully Carl guides his readers toward their own points of view about his characters. Usually he presents the facts and lets you take it from there. He does understand the historic background of Western outlawry and of the West itself as the last region of America to be settled. He knows how to interpret it.

His style is fluent. It glides along like an easily trailed lasso. His work never violates reality. He does not invent to magnify that high, natural drama of the Old West. Actually, it was Carl Breihan who some years ago did more than anyone else to expose an old bushwhacker claiming to be "Jesse James" no less. Carl took the witness stand in a Missouri court to torpedo an action brought by this ex-carnie to have himself declared the actual Jesse so long dead. This underscores Carl's prodigious investigation and research. He digs into library collections and official archives to trace the most minute facts. He carries on a tremendous correspondence with descendants of or admirers of Western characters. When necessary, he checks out given sources with still others.

I knew Carl Breihan first as seller of books. Then, over these years I watched him emerge as a writer of books. I recall his in-depth works on the James brothers and agree with Joe Snell that Carl Breihan knows more about Jesse than anybody around. But more, too, about many other long riders.

After reading this work, GUNSLINGERS, in manuscript, I can say that it measures up in every respect to the usual Breihan quality. It is vivid; it is highly entertaining, making you feel that you are in Wyoming watching Tom Horn die on the scaffold, seeing King Fisher strutting in his tiger skin pants, or observing Doc Holliday sitting at a salon table brooding over his memories of that long ago woman. You see the bullying Ben Thompson finally getting his comeuppance from an unseen assailant and view, with some sadness, the desperate attempts of Henry Starr to go straight, but never quite making it. You may also consider Carl's statement, partially based on his experience as an officer, that "Many criminals are made mostly by environment and circumstance. And once a criminal is started on that path, he cannot turn back even though he wants to . . ."

The author comments:

> *One minute incident can work a gigantic psychological change in the minds of people, especially in those of young boys; and one which sometimes causes them to become social outcasts. It is our duty and obligation to try and help these people, not to readily condemn them at all times."*

In private life Carl Breihan is a devoted husband and

father of three children, and an upstanding citizen of St. Louis County and represents the 6th District on the St. Louis County Council, the Legislative Branch of that Government.

I believe this book by Breihan is one of his best. Buy it!

Harold Preece
Edmond, Oklahoma

CHAPTER I

FRANK CANTON

GUNSLINGER & LAWMAN

It was 1864. Civil War raged through the land as great armies under Generals Lee and Grant fought for control of the South. And in Missouri it was springtime, the time of the farmer.

Fourteen-year-old Joe Horner wiped the sleep dirt from his eyes as he lazily sat on the edge of his bunk-type bed. It had been a fearful night for the lad, the screaming of the panther had awakened him numerous times, and the thunder-like noise had kept booming until past midnight.

The bright sunlight caused Joe to blink rapidly as he peered from the upstairs window of the modest Horner cabin in Christian County, near Ozark, Missouri. To his surprise he saw no puddles of water in the barnyard, no beads of water dripping from the trees. He could smell the scent of honeysuckle, the dogwood in full bloom, and the flowers on the fruit trees in the back yard of their home.

Joe slipped into a well-worn cotton shirt and a pair of older overalls, using wooden pegs to hold up the bib rather than buttons. Things were rough for the frontier families in Missouri with the war going on and all.

Barefooted, he climbed down the homemade wooden ladder from his loft room to the kitchen.

"Mother, I'm surprised to see no rainwater. I heard it thunder like crazy during the night," Joe remarked.

"That was no thunder, son, from what I heard early this morning the noise was from Colonel Porter's cannon over near Springfield. I guess his men had a run in with McNeill's troops."

"When will it all end?" asked the boy.

"Things are going badly for the Confederacy, son, and I expect the war could be over within a year. Pray that it will. I hear that General Price is supposed to come up from Arkansas to try one more swoop through Missour. Don't know when, but soon, I guess, one never knows during times like these."

"Pray that your brother John returns since we need his help to survive. You have done a good job, Joseph, but the farm is too much for the two of us. And your father was killed tending the wounded Confederate soldiers at Gettysburg,"

Tears came to the eyes of Joe's mother as she recalled her husband and his good deeds. The good doctor had practiced in Iowa, Kansas, Arkansas, Indiana, and Missouri. The family had come from Virginia to Missouri, from that part of Virginia which became West Virginia in 1861 when the State divided itself. The people of West Virginia wanted to remain in the Union, the others did not. Even so, many soldiers from the newly created State fought with the Confederacy. Dr. Joseph Horner and his family had left a number of relatives in Wetzel and Tyler Counties, Virginia.

Joe and his mother had made a living farming their acreage with corn and soybeans and raising a few hogs and chickens. Every Saturday the boy would walk bare-footed into the little town of Ozark to exchange eggs and some vegetables for the staples of life, such as coffee, sugar, flour and other kitchen items. Fortunately, they did not live in one of the counties which had been burned by order of General Ewing at Kansas City after Quantrill's raid on Lawrence, Kansas.

April passed. May brought with it new grass and blooming shrubs of jack-oak, the chirping birds in the trees, and the smell of freshly turned earth. The heat of the summer was preceded by the rich rains which steamed the corn and painted the grass. The budding berries provided dessert for Joe and his mother, a luxury they seldom enjoyed.

Young Joe Horner had become an expert in the use of firearms, as had other frontier lads who were responsible for placing meat on the supper table. Many times Joe, usually accompanied by his faithful redbone hound Beauregard, would hunt rabbits, quail and wild turkey.

Early one morning Joe heard Beauregard making a racket to indicate some animal had been treed.

"Mother, I guess Beauregard has another 'coon treed. Guess I'll mosey out to see."

Picking up his rifle and a hunting knife, the lad trudged off into the forest, following the sound of the dog's baying. After walking about a half mile he discovered that his dog had treed a full-grown panther. It took all the courage he could muster to get close to the tree. Before he could fire his rifle the animal caught sight of him and leaped. The redbone hound attacked the panther at the same time.

There was such a turning and rolling in the struggle that the boy was afraid to shoot because he might hit his faithful ally. The brave lad drew his knife and lunged at the panther. Joe made a sudden stab through the panther's heart, leaped back, and shouted at Beauregard to do the same. The lad was no worse off than having his trousers torn from the waist down. The animal had caught the overalls at the waist with one of his paws and had ripped it to the ground.

The panther was too heavy for Joe to lift, so he hurried back home and told his mother about it. She did not believe him at first, but when she and several neighbor boys went to the spot, there was the dead panther.

Late in July of 1864 a group of horsemen rode into the

yard of the Horner home, bringing their mounts to a dust-filled skidding stop before the porch of the cabin.

Mrs. Horner stepped from the house and asked the men their business.

"Madam, I am Bill Anderson of Quantrill's command," said the apparent leader of the group, as he raised his hat. "We are riding through some counties recruiting men for General Price's upcoming push through Missouri. We know who you are and that your son and your husband both fought for the Confederacy; your son probably still is, and we know of Dr. Horner's death."

Joe gawked as he stood on the porch, leaning against one of its supporting posts. He looked at the speaker. Bill Anderson was a man of light build, medium height, rather dark complexion, with large, restless black eyes. His hair was worn long and hung in glossy ringlets from beneath his black slouch hat, which was adorned with a long black plume.

"So this was Bloddy Bill, the silent, brooding devil who never spared a Union soldier," thought Joe. "He sure doesn't look all that dnagerous to me."

"If you have any food for my men, we will appreciate it," said Anderson to Joe's mother.

"We have plenty bread and beans to which you are welcome."

Joe studied the guerrillas as they ate their food. They were a non-descript lot. Some wore the butternut of the Confederacy; some wore old Union coats and trousers, others whatever they could put their hands on. All of them wore four to six loaded Navy Dragoon pistols, ready for instant use. Their horses were fitted with good saddles and bridles. Some saddle scabbards held a rifle or a shotgun for use at close quarters.

Young Horner remembered the stories about Quantrill and his men, Jesse James, Cole Younger and others. From long continued practice they had acquired a skill that was almost incredible. They went into battle at full gallop, and when within range of the enemies' guns, they set up a terrible rebel yell, and increased their speed until within forty or fifty yards, when they opened fire probably shooting with both hands. Joe also had heard that nearly all of their victims had been shot in the head.

On October 27, 1864, Anderson was killed from ambush by Union soldiers near Orrick, Missouri, in the southwest corner of Ray County.

About a month after Lee's surrender at the McLean House at Appomattox John Wesley Horner returned home. It was a heart-rending scene as mother and son embraced. The poor mother had not been sure that she would ever see her older son again. Joe spent hours on end listening to the war stories his brother told.

"All right, Joe, this is the first and last time I am going to speak about these things. I would not be doing it now except I believe you and mother should know them." That ended any more questions.

One day in 1866 John Horner called his mother and his brother Joe in for family conference.

"Mother, I believe it would be best if we went to Texas to live with Sis and her family for a time. You know that Missouri is being overrun with carpetbaggers and men who'll steal you blind at every opportunity. Perhaps Texas is just as bad, but I think it would be the best move."

Both Mrs. Horner and young Joe agreed. That year the family of three moved to Denton County, Texas, to live with an older daughter of Mrs. Horner.

Texas. It still was a house divided. There were the diehards who always resented the loss of the Texas Republic; the opposite side of the political fence found bitter opponents to the Lone Star State. With the disbanding of the Texas Rangers by the reconstruction governor and the State Police taking charge, it was virtual hell for the ex-Confederates and their friends.

All wars have their aftermath of reconstruction, pioneering, mass movements. The Mexican War was responsible to some degree for the great migratory movement that quickened Americans to a national consciousness that focused attention on California, Texas, Oregon, New Mexico, and the Indian Nations Territory. Even many of the Quantrillians moved to Texas, mostly in the area of Sherman to escape the reprisals of the Missouri Enrolled Militia, supposedly enforcing the reconstruction laws.

Pioneers flocked to Texas, building small towns within a short distance of the United States Military forts. This afforded them some protection from the Comanches and also provided a trading post facility.

When the forts were finally abandoned by the military, the people took them over, using the buildings for homes and stores. Thus, even today, some towns in Texas bear the names of the forts which once stood there: Fort Worth, Fort Griffin, Fort Davis, Fort Stockton, and Fort Elliott, with the name Mobeetie.

These post Civil War times also spawned hundreds of outlaws, badmen, and famous lawmen. The Texas terrain afforded a natural hideout for outlaws, gunslingers Wild Bill Longley, John Wesley Hardin, John Selman, and even a neighbor of the Horner family, one Sam Bass from Indiana. After the Texas Rangers had been reinstated these outlaws were run to earth in one manner or another, but for a number of years Texas fought a fierce battle to overcome the ever-threatening element of outlawry.

Joe Horner, now twenty years old, decided it was time that he went out on his own.

"Mother, I'm going to go on a cattle drive for Burk Burnett to Abilene. Don't worry about me since I'll make out all right. I have had a lot of experience now and John taught me many things."

It was no easy task herding over fifteen hundred head of cattle from Denton, Texas, to Abilene, Kansas, for rainstorms and dust storms battered them half the way. A few head of cattle had been lost to swollen rivers and marauding Indians but not one man had been lost.

"What the hell them Indians up ahead want?" asked Joe.

"They want us to pay a toll for the right to cross their land. They try this trick on all the drovers."

"What tribe is that? You gonna pay 'em?"

"Hell no, Joe. Them's Osage though. Remember what they did to Colonel Harrison and his crack unit of twenty Confederate officers on their way to rob the mint at Denver?

Only one got away."

After Burnett had refused to pay the toll to the Indians, the war party ran off nearly all their saddle mounts. As a result the cowboys were forced to trudge the remaining miles to Abilene. The stampede had been brought under control and only a few head of cattle had been lost to the Indians.

There seems no record of Horner getting into any trouble in Abilene, although he was there a week and was dead broke by that time. Trail drivers were an easy prey for the saloon keepers, gamblers, and the bawdy house madams. These places were called "the red light district" because when the railroad men frequented them they left their red lanterns burning on the steps of these places.

During the early part of September, 1869, Horner went on another cattle drive, this time to North Platte, Nebraska. At one point in the drive several hundred head of cattle were rustled near Blue River. With several other men Horner tracked down the rustlers, but an accidental gunshot scared them off. In their haste they left behind an army mule which was later claimed by the military at Fort McPherson.

From this point on until his participation in the invasion of Wyoming by the cattlemen, Horner's life is sketchy. He served in many capacities, however, and in 1871 he served under Sheriff Lee Crutchfield of Jacksboro, Texas, as a deputy. At one time he was hired as a guard to transport three Kiowa Indian chiefs who were awaiting trial for border atrocities. Santank, one of the chiefs, was killed while trying to escape.

According to old records Horner filed a claim in 1872 for a piece of land near Graham, Texas, and while working in the area of Young and Jack Counties it was claimed that both he and his brother had been Texas Rangers. However, this report is not substantiated in the archives of that august body of lawmen.

During the year 1874 a rash of warrants were issued against Joe Horner for stealing cattle. No doubt the warrants were in order since Joe and a friend named Bill Cotman suddenly had a large herd of cattle which they sold to the military at Fort Richardson for a ridiculously low price. By now Horner was a bad man to mess around with, he was a tough gunslinger with nerves of steel. While on a bender in Fort Richardson in October of 1874, Joe was accosted by several soldiers who demanded that he buy them drinks.

"Hell with you blue-bellies. Your kind killed my father and gutted Missouri to no end," replied Joe, spitting in disgust at the sawdust-covered floor.

"Easy, Joe,: said the excited bartender. "Don't make trouble in here, please."

"They let me alone, I'll do the same."

The soldiers kept badgering Joe until it was too late.

"Buy us some drinks or we'll shoot your butt off."

With that Joe's right hand snaked down and came up working the deadly .45. The saloon rocked with its roar. When the smoke had cleared the sergent was dead and Private George Smith of I Troop, 10th Cavalry, was seriously wounded.

"Good Lord, man! Don't stand there, get moving," said the frightened bartender. "You just killed a Union soldier."

"Hell, so what? Gimme another drink and I'll be on my way."

The bartender did not argue. Joe gulped down another whiskey, then reeled out to his horse, muttering, "Them damned Yanks deserved killing."

This incident had a profound effect upon Joe for he was not heard from again for over two years. By that time his name was fairly well known, and warrants for bank robbery, rustling, and what not, were issued against him.

During a sudden raid on a saloon in Mererick, Texas, Joe Horner and John King Fisher were arrested. Texas Ranger Lee Hall brought both desperate men to Eagle Pass, Maverick County, where outstanding warrants of all sorts were still pending against both men. Fisher managed to be released on bond. How Horner escaped from the Eagle Pass jail has never been revealed, nor did he ever explain it. Perhaps he used some means of bribery to which he did not wish to admit.

At any rate, Joe Horner now realized that Texas was too hot for him, so he took cover by posing as a cowboy with a trail drive enroute to Ogallala, Nebraska. It was there that Joe Horner became Frank M. Canton.

The Stock Growers Association hired Canton as an inspector and a range detective when he showed up in Wyoming's Carbon County sometime in 1877. His first assignment took him to Miles City, Montana, where he met W. D. Smith and Joe LaFors. LaFors later would become famous as an expert tracker of Butch Cassidy and the Sundance Kid and for tricking Tom Horn into confessing he killed a lad named Nickell.

At the base of the Big Horn Mountains Frank Canton commenced to stock a large acre tract he had homesteaded. At the same time he worked on occasion for the cattle association. It was during his stay at the ranch that he was elected sheriff of Johnson County, Wyoming, and given about eighteen deputies to keep the peace in a county thousands of square miles.

One day Sheriff Jeff Carr of Cheyenne visited Canton.

"Frank, I need your help in the matter of arresting Big Nose George Parrott (real name was Lathrope) and his gang of cutthroats. They have been running wild with their train robberies."

"All right with me, Jeff, soon as you are ready let me know."

The time came in August, 1878, when Parrott and his men decided to rob the Union Pacific train a short distance east of the little mining town of Carbon, Wyoming. They used the same trick as did Jesse James when he robbed the train at Adair, Iowa, in 1873. They pulled spikes on a downhill curve, and a length of wire was attached to the rail. It was their intention to pull and spread the rail from their place of concealment and pitch the train down a ravine.

However, Parrott's scheme was doomed to failure since the loose rail was spotted by section foreman Erick Brown, who put two and two together and sensed the proposed robbery. Luckily he was not spotted by the outlaws and hurried into Carbon, where the news was flashed to Rawlins, sixty miles away. A posse headed by Deputy Sheriff Robert Widdowfield and the railroad detective named Tip Vincent was soon on its way to the scene.

The outlaws decided that the train was late for some

reason or another, so Parrott sent one of his men into Carbon to see if he could learn the reason for the delay. It was not long before the man returned and hurriedly told his chief that the train actually was late due to a washout of the track; also that their presence was known and a posse was on its way.

"We have plenty of time before the posse gets here from Rawlins," mused Parrott. "We'll just mosey to Elk Mountain and give them lawmen a surprise."

The outlaws rode to Rattlesnake Canyon near Elk Mountain and waited for the posse to put in its appearance. When it did so, the outlaws ambushed the men, killing Vincent and Widdowfield. The date was August 19, 1878.

Nothing had been heard from Parrott for two years when he was arrested in Montana. Frank Canton and Jeff Carr went to Helena and brought Parrott back to Wyoming, lodging him in jail at Rawlins. On the evening of March 22, 1881, an angry mob stormed the jail and lynched the doomed man from a telegraph pole in the street. Dr. John E. Osborne made a death mask of Parrott, as well as removing the skin from the dead man's chest and fashioning it into a medicine bag. More of Parrott's skin got around. A tanned piece of it was in the possession of Professor Reed of the University of Wyoming at Laramie for many years. The skin from Parrott's thighs was removed, tanned, and fashioned into a pair of shoes, these being in the possession of the Rawlins National Bank at this time. The top of Parrott's skull was presented to Lillian Heath, Dr. Osborne's assistant, later Mrs. Lou Nelson of Rawlins, and she presented it to the Union Pacific Museum at Omaha.

On May 12, 1950, the bones of Big George were uncovered in a whiskey barrel in which they were buried. Workmen digging a foundation for a new store building in downtown Rawlins made the find. A bottle of vegetable compound and a pair of shoes with glass nails were found with the bones.

It was odd that Frank Canton, once Joe Horner, was now pursuing outlaws and arresting them for the same kinds of crimes he himself once committed. One of his finest arrests was the apprehension of Teton Jackson, a noted outlaw and rustler from the Jackson Hole area. Most officers were reluctant to tackle Jackson since he was a member of a band led by Bill Hickman, a group who were called "The Destroying Angels of Brigham Young." He had run fancy free even though warrants for Jackson existed in Utah, Wyoming, and Idaho.

One day word was brought to Canton that Jackson was gathering stolen stock and herding them into the Big Horn Basin with the aid of an unsavory character named Tom Lucas. Canton decided to take two of his deputies, Ed Loyd and Chris Gross, and ride all night in order to reach the Lucas cabin early in the morning.

One can imagine the surprise felt by Jackson and Lucas when Canton and his two men burst into the cabin, .45's drawn and ready for use. Both outlaws surrendered without a shot being fired.

"Good show, men, this is the way I like to do business, "grinned Canton. "You two take the cattle back to where they belong. I'll take Jackson on to Buffalo. No need to worry about Lucas since we have no warrant for him, and he'll not give us any trouble."

While there were murder charges pending against Jackson, he was first taken to Blackfoot, Idaho, to stand trial on charges of horse theft. Convicted, he was quickly rushed to the state prison at Boise, since the people of Blackfoot feared an attack on their town by Hickman and his riders. Jackson managed to escape from prison, and to drop into total obscurity.

Apparently Frank Canton did a good job as sheriff since he was re-elected and served another two-year term, but on his third try he was defeated.

In 1885 Frank Canton married Annie Wilkerson. She was a girl from Illinois whose family had come west and had settled near Big Horn, Wyoming. As time passed, Canton appeared to be a happily married man with two fine children, but the lack of activity began to gnaw at his soul.

It was odd that in 1888 Canton took employment again with the Wyoming Stock Growers Association since he was a small rancher, and all such were considered rustlers by the association. The small ranchers, in turn, accused the association members of stealing their own cattle in order to place the blame on the little fellows. At any rate, it was the prelude to the fast approaching black record that was to blot the history of Wyoming . . . the Johnson County War.

The first act of horror committed by the cattlemen occurred during the summer of 1889. Whether or not Canton participated in this outrage is a moot question. Some said he was there; others said he was not. The story begins with a man named Jim Averill.

Jim Averill had built the first general store on the old Oregon Trail near Independence Rock, where the Sweetwater River flowed through wide, rich bottomland. It was an ideal location and soon a post office was added to the site. Later Averill married a Missouri pioneer girl named Ella Watson, and it was in the cabin behind the store that their son was born. He was named Tom Averill.

Those were desperate days in Wyoming. What could the settlers do? Fences were torn down and great herds of cattle stampeded over the crops. Even as the news of disaster neared their home, the Averills refused to budge from the spot. Averill was not a coward and he was an expert with the revolver and the rifle; he could draw his pistol with the striking speed of a rattler and place the bullet where he wanted to nearly every time.

The neighbors respected the Averill family, not entirely because Jim was a fast gunfighter, but because he had taken the time to become well-read and knew the complex homestead laws backwards and forward. He was hoping these laws would soon apply to the vast territory that was Wyoming so that settlers who had proved their claims could live in peace. But between him and this dream was an organization hungry for the land they owned; a bloated creature which recognized no law but its own.

The powerful cattlemen, under the impressive titles of The Cattlemen's Association or the Board of Livestock Commissioners, sat in judgment and decreed that the West was not for the homesteader. Normally, each settler had a legal claim to his 160 acres, but such claims meant nothing to those self-appointed judges of the destiny of the territory.

Most of the settlers were ignorant of the case the shrewd cattle barons were building up against the settlers. However, Jim Averill received newspapers from New York, and he read with disgust and amazement the absurd accusations which the cattle people were heaping upon the homesteaders. The newspaper accounts branded each settler a thief and a renegade; that they had come West just to get out of it what they could in any way, shape or form. Of course, Jim Averill, being a sensitive and just man, sent letters of protest to the leading newspapers in several of the larger eastern cities. Some of the clippings came back to Averill; all of them found their way into the hands of the cattlemen.

Jim Averill was a marked man after that. Apparently he was aware of this, and he planned meetings with the homesteaders in an effort to meet the coming crisis. Many of the settlers were ready to pull up stakes and move out in order to protect their wives and children. Others said they would remain until literally forced off their land. These men were not cowards. They had brought their families over the weary trail miles and through hostile Indian country to settle in this new land. Yet they realized they could not cope with hundreds of hired gunslingers on the payroll of the cattle barons. Jim Averill naturally was chosen their spokesman and he wrote letters to the eastern newspapers, as well as to the officials in Washington, pleading the case of the settlers.

Several days after the meeting young Tom Averill was seated on the cracker barrel in his father's store when a man strode through the doorway. The boy noted the man's skin tight trousers, his dusty leather vest, and his low-slung hip weapon. Tom could see his father stiffen when he saw the man enter, and his right hand moved nearer to his own revolver. Expecting a quick shotout, the boy jumped from his perch and raced back to the door and waited.

"I'll take a pint of rye, Jim," the tall man stated.

Averill took the bottle from a box under the counter, never letting his eyes leave the other man's face.

"A little off the beaten path, aren't you, Mike?"

Young Tom recognized the man at that point. Men called him "Black Mike" because of his swarthiness, his cruelty, and because he always wore black clothes. Some said he was the leader of the band of gunslingers hired by the cattlemen to run the settlers off the range. Frank Canton was another name he had heard.

"I'm heading for Split Rock, heard they need hands up that way," Mike replied to Averill's question.

At that moment an Indian entered the store and asked for a bottle of whiskey.

Averill's glance flicked to the window, then back to the Indian's face. Tom Averill peered over the counter and through the window. There, standing near the hitch rack, each with a rifle in the crook of his arm, stood three of Black Mike's henchmen.

Black Mike had stepped sideways a little, his eyes cold under shaggy brows, and his mouth now a mere slit. Averill's hand remained close to his weapon.

"Sorry, no liquor to Indians; you know better than that, Mike."

"C'mon, Jim, he cooks for us, a little snort won't hurt."

"Just the chance you want to have me arrested for selling liquor to an Indian. Sorry, Mike, you plan's backfired."

Young Tom expected fireworks after that. But before Mike could draw his revolver, two pistols leaped into the hands of Jim Averill.

"Get out," he told the Indian. "You, too, Mike. I want no trouble today. You got your men outside in case a shot is fired in here. If that does not work, you want to charge me with whiskey-selling to Indians."

"You're crazy, Averill," said Mike, glowering.

"Get, Mike. There'll be no brawl in here unless you start it, and if you do, I'll put a slug through your mangy head."

Black Mike backed out of the store and conferred with his cronies; then they all mounted and rode away.

Averill turned around at the counter and saw his son.

"You still here, Tom? I thought you were with your mother."

With that Tom dashed to the barn and found seclusion in a small cave he had dug out near the one end of the building. There he pondered over what he had just seen. It was some experience, he thought, seeing his father almost kill a man in their own store; it would be a thrilling story to tell his friend Johnny Marsh. But he never got the chance to tell Johnny about it.

The next morning James Marsh, Johnny's father, came riding up to the store on a lathered horse.

"They burned me out, Jim!" he cried. "Just before dawn, barn, house, everything!"

"Did you recognize any of them?"

"No, they were dressed like Indians and fired flaming arrows into the buildings."

"Well, they are not going to scare me out," declared Averill.

"I'm loading what I got left into a wagon and heading for Oregon," Marsh replied.

That same afternoon a covered wagon drawn by four horses rattled to a stop in front of the Averill home. It was the Marsh family.

"If there's any mail for me, Jim, hold it until you hear from me," yelled James Marsh.

Young Tom saw a tear in the eyes of his pal Johnny as the boy waved a final goodbye.

Homesteaders from Devil's Gate and other places began to pass the Averill place, and no amount of talking could change their minds about leaving.

"What are you going to do, Jim?" a man asked.

"I'm going to stay right here and damned to those rustlers."

"It's getting worse, Jim; now they are accusing the homesteaders of being rustlers and are hanging them. Only a short time ago they hanged three men up near the Seminole Hills."

Other settlers rode by, up from the Pathfinder country, where the Sweetwater joined the North Platte. They all told the same stories of horror as they hurried to get out of the territory.

One summer night in 1889 the cattlemen set fire to the Averill home, but the family managed to escape. Averill wanted to take his wife and child out of the danger zone, but she would not consent to it, stating they could rebuild the house.

The Averills did begin to rebuild. Homesteaders who had heard the news came by to help; freighters with the creaking wagons brought in logs, hand-hewn planks, and poles. Averill always told them the fire had been caused by a bad flue.

Jim Averill had a small herd of eighty cattle. One day his two riders failed to return so a search party was sent out to look for them and the cattle. The two men had disappeared and the cattle were found in a draw, shot to death.

One of the most frequent visitors at the store in those days was Nathan Ellidge, a name well known in Wyoming history. At the time he was freighting to old Fort Fittmer and stopped at the Averill store with supplies and mail.

"Well, Jim, I crossed the trail of Black Mike today. He's working for the Association."

"I figured he would be. Well, we'll be ready for him if he turns up here. I understand that Frank Canton also has thrown in his lot with the cattlemen again."

"Yep, heard that, too. Never know what'll happen these days. You take care now, hear?"

Fewer and fewer people traveled by the Averill store, and one day in July Tom saw a huge cloud of dust in the distance. The boy realized that only a fast-moving stagecoach or a troop of cavalry could kick up that much dust.

As the dust cloud came closer and three riders emerged from it, Tom could see they were not soldiers but ordinary cowboys. Quickly fifteen of the riders dashed to the front of the store, dismounted and headed inside the building, leaving several of their members to hold the horses. Tom walked to the store in the wake of the riders, where he saw his father standing behind the counter, hands within easy reaching distance of his weapons.

"We give you plenty of warning, Jim Averill, now we have come to take you," said Black Mike James.

"For what?" demanded Jim Averill.

"For rustling!"

"That's a lie, and you know it. You have no proof."

"What about a trial?" Averill went on.

"You and your wife have already been tried," one of the men muttered.

Averill was helpless; every man in the store held a gun on him. His hesitation in deciding to parley or fight had given Black Mike's men the extra second they needed.

"Run!" cried Averill. "Ella! Ella! Take Tommy and run!"

At that instant Mrs. Averill appeared in the doorway, a rifle in her hand. It was to no avail, four men leaped upon her and disarmed her before she could pull the trigger.

Young Averill did not run. He dived into the mass of humanity, kicking, yelling, biting. He bit one hairy hand and carried away a piece of the man's flesh. Black Mike strolled up to the boy and knocked him sprawling under the counter.

"Run, boy, run!" pleased his mother.

Tom ran to the porch, mulling over in his mind where he could hide from these awful men. Still the lad decided it was his duty to try and help his parents, not realizing what awful things these men had planned when they rode into the Averill homestead.

Two men pushed Jim Averill through the doorway, his hands roped behind his back. When he saw this, Tom yelled wildly and commenced kicking everything in sight. Black Mike saw Tom, and before the boy could duck around the building, he reached over and grabbed the boy by the collar. He then pulled him up and pressed him tightly against the saddlehorn.

The group rode across the valley, Jim and his wife being pulled behind as they stumbled along. Mrs. Averill kept begging for the men to free her son, but Jim Averill did not raise his voice.

Soon the party came to a cottonwood grove just over the hill from the Averill home. Here the men halted and Black Mike dumped Tom on the ground. The boy scrambled to his feet and started off on a run, only to be stopped by an expertly tossed lariat in the hands of the villain Black Mike.

"Try that again and I'll yank your head off!"

Black Mike then forced the boy to walk to the front of the crowd. There, before the eyes of young Tom, was enacted a scene of utter horror, sadism, and depravity.

The boy's mother was lifted to the back of a horse, and slowly a horseman rode alongside her and placed a hangman's noose over her head. Suddenly the boy began to realize the awful truth of what was taking place. Coiling the rope carefully, the horsemen then tossed it over the lower limb of a cottonwood tree. Another man seized the dangling end of the rope and attached it to the horn of his saddle, tugging the end to make it tight.

Jim Averill pleaded with the men to hang him instead of his wife, but to no avail.

"Pull away!" ordered Black Mike.

The rider who had tied the one rope end to his saddle put spurs to his mount and the rope tightened. Another man struck the animal on which Mrs. Averill was seated, and the horse lunged forward. The rope horse, trained to block, swung sideways and braced all four feet. Tom managed to look up. He saw his mother dangling in the air, face black and swollen; it was a sight that haunted him until his dying day.

The block horse slackened the rope and the body of Mrs. Averill struck the earth with a dull thud. A minute or two later the body of Jim Averill was dangling from the same limb from which his wife had been hanged.

Black Mike never took his eyes off the body until the last movement of life was stilled. Then, like a crazed person, he turned and looked at Tom Averill. The boy squirmed and kicked, and Mike grabbed his ankles and swung the boy's body around like a pendulum. Tom took one last look at the bodies of his parents, expecting to have his head dashed against the trunk of the same cottonwood tree.

"Mike! Not that! Ain't you satisfied?"

"I'll kill the bastard if I want to, bust his head like a melon."

The other man seized the boy's shoulders and refused to let go.

"Dammit, Mike, let go or I'll . . ." and the boy heard the click of a revolver.

"All right, Joe, he's yours, but what are you going to do, let him around to witness against us?"

"No, we'll ditch him somewhere far from here where no one will believe a word he says. What are you going to do with the others?"

"The buzzards can take care of them," said Mike.

The following days found the gunmen far into the Dakotas, and there Tom was tied securely and pushed into a small cave on the hillside. Black Mike fired several shots into the cave to make certain Tom Averill never talked to anyone about what he had seen. He figured that way he could also maintain the satisfaction of his men. Mike had also instructed his men to drive the large staple at the end of the animal trap chain into a log to make certain Tom could not move.

"Now, you young whelp, yell your head off. Only ones to hear you will be Indians and they'll take care of you in short order," grinned Mike.

The bullet which Mike had fired struck the boy in the chin and he felt a red hot pain in his throat. He fell into unconsciousness.

After some time he regained consciousness and began calling for help.

Finally the boy's cries were heard by friendly Indians who removed his chains and nursed him back to health. Tom felt safe in the Sioux village. Later he joined the Buffalo Bill Wild West Show, using the name of Buffalo Tom Vernon. Until he reached the age of twenty-one he was under the guardianship of Annie Oakley, an arrangement suggested by Buffalo Bill Cody.

In later years such men as "Deadwood Dick" Clarke, "Pawnee Bill" (Major Gordon Lilliё, and Tom Grant, along with Bill Cody and Annie Oakley, were able to prove the identify of Buffalo Tom Vernon as Tom Averill. However, the records in the files of the Department of the Interior in Washington now show that the homestead of James Averill and Ella L. Watson was cancelled on February 28, 1891.

Some reports have claimed that an invalid young boy was present when the lynchings occured, and that he had been poisoned by the men who had hanged Jim Averill and his wife.

The cattle ring, now brazen and bold due to lack of prosecution in the Averill matter, hanged another settler named Art Waggoner on June 4, 1891. Three gunslingers had gone to his home, using false papers to make the arrest. It was not until June 12th that Waggoner's body was found hanging from a tree in what now is called "Dead Man's Canyon."

In an attempt to kill Nathan D. Champion and Ross Gilbertson at the cabin of W. H. Hall, on November 1, 1891, the would-be assassins were put to rout when Champion began firing at them from pistols he had hidden under his pillow. Champion recognized one of the attackers as Joe Elliott, who was arrested and then released on bond. Due to the subsequent murder of Champion the case never came to trial . . . no witnesses.

On the evening of November 28, 1891, Orley E. Jones, also known as "Ranger Jones," had gone to Buffalo, Wyoming, to arrange for a load of lumber for a new home since he was about to be married. Fifteen miles from town, while crossing Muddy Creek, Jones was shot three times by someone in ambush under the bridge. Whoever killed Jones released the horses and ran the buckboard and Jones' body into a deep gully.

Two days after the murder of Jones, John A. Tisdale, who lived some sixty miles from Buffalo, had gone into town to purchase some supplies. While talking to some friends at the Cross H Ranch, Sidale had remarked that he was in fear of his life.

"I overheard Fred Hesse (a leader of the gunfighters) and Frank Canton talking in town. Canton told Hesse that he was after me and would kill me. I even bought a double-barreled shotgun in case of trouble."

Tisdale never got the chance to use the new shotgun.

A contemporary report of the incident was told in this manner:

Tisdale still showed his uneasiness at the Cross H Ranch, and that night had the window blinds all closed and told one of the boys there that he thought the cowmen were going to kill him. He started the next morning on his journey home. Three miles on his murderer was lying in a gulch withing twenty feet of the road, waiting for his

Cattle raiders of Johnson County.

University of Oklahoma

Frank Canton seated to right of woman. *University of Oklahoma*

Frank Canton Sheriff of Johnson County.

University of Oklahoma

Frank Canton in later years.

University of Oklahoma

Stable of the TA Ranch where Frank Canton and hired Texas gunfighters made their stand against Sheriff Red Angus and Araphahoe Brown.

Frank Canton

University of Oklahoma

Frank Canton, Adjutant-General of Oklahoma.

University of Oklahoma

Iron Tail of Oglala Dakota tribe. Born 1850.

Smithsonian

victim to approach. Slowly but surely Tisdale, with his heavy load, was going to meet his death at the hands of the cowardly fiend. He approached, passed, and when twenty-five feet by, the murderer's rifle belched forth its deadly contents. The first shot, from appearances, struck the handle of his six-shooter, which he had under his coat on the left side, and glanced off. He had evidently tried to cock his shotgun then, for one of the shells was indented slightly, as though he had drawn the hammer back part way, and it had then slipped from his thumb, he having received a death shot in the side, before he had time to fully cock it, and the poor fellow fell back on his load shot to death.

The killer drove the wagon and its contents about a mile down the road, killed the horses and left them and the wagon in an underbrush.

Charles Basch, who had been riding in the vicinity, witnessed the last act by the killer, and he raced into Buffalo and ran to the office of Sheriff Angus.

"Sheriff, I just saw Frank Canton murder John Tisdale on the trail."

"You sure, Charlie? Seems it could have been Fred Hesse."

"Hell, sheriff, I know them both; it was Canton."

Canton was arrested and given a hearing before Judge Paramalee. During the two days of the trial that followed witnesses claimed that Canton was no where near the scene of the murder. And while the accusations of corruption in the court and direct accusations against Canton, it was never proved that he had killed Tisdale.

Frank Canton and Fred Hesse both left Wyoming after Canton's trial. It is known that Canton went to Chicago to visit his wife and children. There he found his two girls suffering from diptheria. One of the girls died while he was there. Canton remained in Illinois all that winter, caring for his family as best he could under the circumstances.

While Canton was in Chicago new evidence was presented to the court with regard to the Tisdale matter. However, Governor Barber refused to extradite Canton to

Wyoming, so nothing was done until Canton's return to Wyoming in March of 1892. In Cheyenne he was served with papers and arrested. Taken to Laramie City, Canton was released by Judge Blake under $30,000 bond.

April, 1892. A date of infamy in the history of the State of Wyoming. Nothing has been recorded in the annals of American history so cold-blooded and murderous as the cowardly invasion of that State by the Wyoming Stock Growers Association.

One scorching matter lingered in the minds of all the people. Why did Acting Governor Amos W. Barber officially override the law and authorize the military to call out the militia instead of doing it himself, as prescribed by the laws of Wyoming?

This order was issued on March 23, 1892, and on April 5 the invasion of Johnson County began, a bad choice since Johnson County was under the able protection of Sheriff W. G. Angus, a lawman respected and feared by everyone.

The gunfighters and killers who had been hired to carry out the murderous work for the Cattlemen's Association were recruited by such men as George W. Baxter, R. M. Allen, Frank M. Canton, Tom Smith and a few others. The wages were flattering and had enticed the right calibre of men for this dastardly job. One George Dunning, a member of the hired killer band, stated the men were to be paid $5.00 a day and all expenses. This included a horse, pistols, and a rifle. Each man was also to receive $50 for each man killed by the mob.

The band of hired killers met at Denver, Colorado, on the first day of April, 1892, where they were met by committee of the cattlemen. It was believed that the gunslingers were to go to Buffalo, kill Sheriff Angus and his deputies; then kill as many citizens as possible and raid the outlying settlements and ranches. Spotters had been planted in Natrona, Converse, and Weston Counties to locate the men whose name appeared on the death list of the invaders. It was believed that once the invasion began hundreds of families would gather what belongings they could and flee the State. All telegraph wires had been cut to prevent the news from reaching other parts of the country.

On April 5, 1892, a special train carrying the hired killers steamed into Cheyenne. At six o'clock that evening a trainload of murderers and their supplies headed for Casper, two hundred miles to the northwest.

Just before daylight the next day the train stopped near the stockyards in Casper. There wagons were loaded and the horsemen mounted. Soon the cavalcade of destruction began its move across the open prairie, led by guides summoned for that purpose. Accompanying the mob were reporters from the *Cheyenne Sun* and the *Chicago Herald*, as well as a number of prominent members of the association who went along for the ride.

Major Frank Wolcott was supposed to be in charge of the entire operation, with Frank M. Canton supervising the Wyoming gunmen and Tom Smith captain over the Texans he had recruited.

While in the vicinity of the Tisdale Ranch the invaders were informed by Mike Shonsy, a henchman, that some rustlers were at a nearby ranch. Therefore, it was decided to await the supply wagons before advancing to the Nolan K. C. Ranch on the North fork of the Powder River. Friday night was spent at the Tisdale place, with plans to advance to the K. C. Ranch and blow up the house with dynamite. Daylight broke before this could be done, so the gunmen concealed themselves in such spots so as to surround the house.

"Don't shoot into the house yet," said Wolcott. "There is a covered wagon there, and it may be some of our friends."

In a little while two men emerged from the house. One of them went to the creek for a bucket of water, while the other made his way to the barn. Both men proved to be trappers who had stopped at the Champion place to spend the night. They were captured and held prisoners for the time being. Later they were released.

The next man to leave the cabin was Nick Ray, a young cowboy from Missouri, who had, in some manner, incurred the hatred of the cattlemen. A number of shots rang out, and Ray fell backwards against the cabin. Nathan D. Champion, a native of Round Rock, Texas, rushed to the door, firing his pistol as fast as he could. He laid down his gun and helped Ray back into the cabin.

Until noon volley after volley was fired into the house. Near three o'clock Jack Flagg and his stepson rode up on horseback, being careful to keep themselves concealed from the mob. Flagg was able to give the alarm, even though he and his stepson had been followed by seven of the attackers, these men gave up the pursuit when they noted Flagg and his stepson had rifles.

The attackers loaded a wagon with hay and wood, then backed it up against the house. A torch was applied to this fuel and in seconds the house was a mass of devouring flames.

Nat Champion, pistol in hand, raced from the south end of the burning house. A number of shots were fired at him, but he managed to reach a ravine several hundred yards from his house. There he was fired upon by a dozen men. Even as he raised his pistol to return their fire, Nat Champion was dead.

A blood-soaked memorandum book was found in the dead man's pocket, a bullet hole through it. In it was found the following message written with a dull pencil; it was dated April 9, 1892:

> *Me and Nick was getting breakfast when the attack took place. Two men here with us — Bill Jones and another man. The old man went after water and did not come back. His friend went to see what was the matter and he did not come back. Nick started out and I told him to look out, as I thought there was some one at the stable and would let them come back.* Nick is shot, but not dead yet. He is awful sick. I must go and wait on him. It is now about two hours since the first shot. Nick is still alive; they are still shooting and are all around the house. Boys, there is bullets coming in like hail. Them fellows is in such shape I can't get at them. They are shooting from the stable, the river and back of the house. Nick is dead; he died about 9 o'clock. I see smoke down at the stable. I think they have fired it. I don't think they intend to let me get away this time.
>
> It is now about noon. There is someone at the stable yet; they are throwing a rope out at the door and drawing it back. I guess it is to draw me out. I wish that duck would get out

further so I could get a shot at him. Boys, I don't know what they have done with them two fellows that stayed here last night. Boys, I feel pretty lonesome just now. I wish there was someone here with me so we could watch all sides at once. They may fool around until I get a good shot before they leave. It's about 3 o'clock now. There is a man in a buckboard and one on horseback just passed. They fired on them as they went by. I don't know if they killed them or not. I seen lots of men come out on horses on the other side of the river and take after them. I shot at the men in the stable just now; don't know if I got any or not. I must go and look out again. It don't look as if there is much show of my getting away. I see twelve or fifteen men. One looks like (name scratch out). I don't know whether it is or not. I hope they did not catch them fellows that run over the bridge toward Smith's. They are shooting at the house now. If I had a pair of glasses I believe I would know some of those men. They are coming back. I've got to look out.

Well, they have just got through shelling the house like hail. I heard them splitting wood. I guess they are going to fire the house tonight. I think I will make a break when night comes, if alive. Shooting again. I think they will fire the house this time. It's not night yet. The house is all fired. Goodbye, boys, if I never see you again.

NATHAN D. CHAMPION

Sam T. Clover, the reporter from the *Chicago Herald*, wrote the following account of the affair; however, it appears that it had been edited by either Canton or Wolcott.

The roof of the cabin was the first to catch on fire, spreading rapidly downward until the north wall was a sheet of flames. Volumes of smoke poured in at the window from the burning wagon, and in a short time through the plastered cracks of the log house puffs of smoke worked outward. Still the doomed man remained doggedly concealed, refusing to reward them by his appearance. The cordon of sharpshooters stood ready to fire upon him the instant he started to run. Fiercer and hotter grew the flames, leaping with mad impetuosity from room to room until every part of the house was ablaze and only the dugout at the west end remained intact.

"Reckon the cuss has shot himself," remarked one of the waiting gunmen. "No fellow could stay in that hole a minute and be alive."

These words were barely spoken when there was a shout. "There he goes." A man clad in his stocking feet, bearing a Winchester and a pistol, emerged from a volume of black smoke that issued from the rear door of the house and started off across the open space surrounding the cabin into a ravine, fifty yards south of the house, but the poor devil jumped square into the arms of two of the best shots in the outfit, who stood with leveled Winchesters around the bend waiting for his appearance. Champion saw them too late, for he overshot his mark just as a bullet struck his rifle arm, causing the gun to fall from his nerveless grasp. Before he could use his revolver a second shot struck him in the breast and a third and fourth found their way to his heart.

Nate Champion, the king of cattle thieves, and the bravest man in Johnson County, was dead. Prone upon his back, with his teeth clenched and a look of mingled defiance and determination on his face to the last, the intrepid rustler met his fate without a groan and paid the penalty for his crimes with his life. A card bearing the significant legend, "Cattle thieves, beware" was pinned on his blood-soaked vest, and there in the dawn, with his red sash tied around him and his half-closed eyes raised toward the blue sky, this brave but misguided man was left to die by the band of regulators who, having succeeded in their object, rapidly withdrew from the scene of the double tragedy.

Jack Flagg and his stepson had ridden into Grabing, about thirty miles from the Chmpion house, and they secured the assistance of three men to try to rescue Champion, not knowing, of course, that the man had been killed. A dozen more recruits were obtained at the Carr Ranch; there it was learned that one Terrance Smith had informed Sheriff Angus at Buffalo of the proceedings.

The fight at Champion's cabin had delayed the invaders to such an extent that their mission now was impossible. Enough time had been given for Sheriff Angus and others to muster a contingent of fifty men, who later surrounded the invaders at the T. A. Ranch on April 11. While Wolcott's forces had been camped near Carr's Ranch on Crazy Woman Creek, word came that a posse were on their trail. Canton was outvoted in his objections about staying at the T. A. Ranch to fight it out.

"We'll be trapped like rats in a trap. This whole mess has turned sour, and I am washing my hands of the whole matter," Canton told Wolcott.

"Good, but you'll have to remain with us nevertheless, Canton; you have no where else to go without getting shot," grinned Wolcott.

Several hundred determined and revenge-seeking citizens surrounded the gunfighters in the log buildings of the ranch. Araphoe Brown and E. U. Snider took command until the arrival of Sheriff Red Angus. They realized that the fortifications were impregnable to small arms, and they also feared interference by the State Militia forces.

"We'll build a moveable breastwork and run it close enough to the buildings to toss dynamite near the structures," said Brown.

"A damned good idea," agreed others. "Just like the Confederates did at Lexington with moveable breastworks made of bales of cotton."

One correspondent sent the following item to his editor:

The idea of building a moveable fort or breast work originated with Araphoe Brown and E. U. Snider. The running gear of the two captured Arp & Hammond wagons, two pair, were placed side by side several feet apart and then fastened together by a frame of logs. The rear of the wagons was the front of the fort and was comprised of two thicknesses of eight-inch logs fastened together by wire. This formed a breastwork of over six feet high, with five portholes in it, also protected by eight-inch pieces. If necessary baled hay could be placed inside, making the protection still stronger. Five men could move it easily, and it would protect forty men. The plan was to move the ingenius contrivance upon the invaders near enough to throw giant powder into their fort. It was in working order and had been moved about 100 yards when the soldiers came in sight. All proceedings at once ceased and the men who for 48 hours had held the fighting cattlemen at bay cheered the troops lustily as they advanced to the rescue.

On April 12, the second day of the siege, an urgent message had been sent to Governor Barber over the repaired telegraph lines. It informed him that an illegal band of armed men had invaded Johnson County, killing Nick Ray and Nathan Champion, and were resisting arrest by Sheriff Angus' posse. The wire asked that toops be sent to the scene of battle.

Governor Barber was on the spot. His sympathies were with the Wolcott-Canton invasion forces; yet, when a runner from the besieged forces slipped through the lines and asked for his help, he had to make a move. He quickly sent the following message:

Cheyenne, Wyoming, April 12, 1892

William Henry Harrison,
President, Washington, D.C.

An insurrection exists in Johnson County, in the State of Wyoming, in the immediate vicinity of Fort McKinney, against the government of said state. The Legislature is not in session and cannot be convened in time to afford any relief whatever or take action thereon. Open hostilities exist and large bodies of armed men are engaged in battle. A company of militia is located at the City of Buffalo, near the scene of action, but its continued presence in that city is absolutely required for the purpose of protecting life and property therein. The scene of action is 125 miles from the nearest railroad point, from which portions of the state militia could be sent. No relief can be afforded by state militia, and civil authorities are wholly unable to afford any relief whatever.

United States troops are located at Fort McKinney, which is 13 miles from the scene of action, which is known as the T. A. Ranch. I apply to you on behalf of the State of Wyoming, to direct the United States troops at Fort McKinney to assist in supressing the insurrection. The lives of large numbers of persons are in imminent danger.

Amos W. Barber,
Acting Governor

President Harrison acted immediately with the following:

Washington, April 12, 1892
11:05 P.M.

The Governor of Wyoming, Cheyenne, Wyoming:
I have, in compliance with your call for aid of the United States forces to protect the State of Wyoming against domestic violence, ordered the Secretary of War to concentrate a sufficient force at the scene of the disturbance and to cooperate with your authorities. You should have a competent and authorized representative at the place.

Benjamin Harrison

Shortly thereafter Brigadier General John R. Brooke at Omaha notified Colonel J. J. Van Horn at Fort McKinney to act in the matter as quickly as possible.

On the morning of April 13, Colonel Van Horn rode into camp with his troops from Fort McKinney. Had he been a few hours later no doubt Wolcott and his entire band of killers would have been destroyed.

Sheriff Angus and Captain Parmalee called for the surrender of the besieged forces.

"Yes, to your troops, Captain, but to Sheriff Angus, never!" yelled Wolcott.

Within two hours the prisoners were being taken to Fort McKinney. Most of the citizens seemed satisfied with the turn of events and were glad to return to their homes. However, some of them were disgruntled because Wolcott and Canton had gotten off so easy, and it was feared that some groups might try to lynch them. In any event, the prisoners were taken to Cheyenne as a further precaution. They then were taken to nearby Fort D. A. Russell, where they spent sixty days, presumably under military guard. However, many of the so-called prisoners visited Cheyenne at will or visited the homes of their friends in the area. Major Wolcott was paroled and traveled to Chicago and Omaha, where he contacted influential persons seeking advice on how to secure the release of his friends.

Since William W. Walker and Benjamin Jones, the two trappers who had been at the scene of the Ray Champion killings, were the only witnesses who could testify against the cattlemen, every effort was made to get them out of Wyoming. Sheriff Angus could not arrest them since he had no charges against them, but Deputy Sheriff E. H. Kimball, at Douglas, issued a warrant against them for stealing two pistols. It was just a move to hold them as witnesses against Wolcott and his invaders.

On the other hand, the invaders employed O. P. Witt, a stable keeper of Douglas, to rid the country of Walker and Jones at any cost. The two trappers outwitted their would-be assasin and hurried to Harrison. When boarding the train there they were taken into custody by Witt and a man named Harvey, along with five or six other hoodlums.

At Crawford City Marshal Morrison had been wired a message to apprehend and hold Walker and Jones. However, he did not know them and accidentally arrested them, along with Witt, when the two trappers began to yell that they were going to be killed. Deputy Sheriff Kimball later stated that when he arrived at Crawford to return the two trappers to Wyoming on a writ of *habeus corpus,* they had already gone on to Chardon on a special train.

Taken to Omaha, the prisoners were charged with selling whiskey to the Indians, a trumped up charge in order to hold them. However, this time it was done by the enemy under the directions of Attorneys F. H. Harvey of Douglas and H. Donzleman of Cheyenne. Later, the prisoners were whisked into the office of the United States marshal, where Donzleman had also gone. What went on is anyone's guess, but shortly thereafter, the prisoners were taken to the West Side station, where a Missouri Pacific night express was boarded. The witnesses never were seen again after that.

Judge J. W. Blake, Second Judicial District, Johnson and Albany Counties, granted the invaders a change of venue from Johnson County to Cheyenne, on the grounds that too much publicity had been given the matter to insure a fair trial in Johnson County.

On August 7, 1892, the cattlemen and their cohorts were arrained before Judge Scott, District Court for Laramie County, at Cheyenne.

"They'll never be tried," said one disgusted citizen. "No witnesses, for one thing. Besides the skids have been greased to dismiss the whole damned thing."

He was right. All prisoners were released on their own recognizances, most of them returning to their own homes or to their domiciles in other states. On January 21, 1893, when the case was called, all the prominent cattlemen appeared; the hired gunmen did not. Prosecuting Attorney Alvin Bennett of Johnson County made a motion to enter a *nolle prosse,* to which the attorneys for the defense objected. However, the judge accepted the motion and the prisoners were discharged, the same motion applying to the men who did not appear.

So ended the legal fiasco which followed the infamous Johnson County War or the Invasion of Wyoming.

Existing conditions in Wyoming forced Frank Canton to leave the territory, for he fully realized there now was no safe place for him to hide. The most probably place for him to find security for a time was with his family in Chicago so he returned to the Windy City to visit his wife and daughter. Inactivity again preyed upon him and he accepted a position in Nebraska City. His job as superintendent at a meat packing plant did not appeal to him, however, and he felt more at home when he was packing a pistol. Now forty-five years old and with the frontier fast closing its doors to gunslingers, Frank Canton had only one more place to go where such men were in demand. That place was Oklahnoma Territory, a spot infested with outlaws such as Bill Doolin, the Dalton gang remnants and others of like ilk.

Early in 1894 Frank Canton rode into Pawnee, Oklahoma Territory. As he rode his horse slowly down the main street, his keen eyes darted from side to side, always on the alert for some danger.

Hell," he thought, "all these damned frontier towns look alike."

And I suppose they did . . . with their false fronts, long

rows of tents and few permanent buildings. In a flash he saw the customary barber shop, the bitters palace, the saloons and gambling dens, the mercantile, the bawdy houses and what not.

The building, such as it was, that caught his eye was the one with the familiar sign, "Sheriff's Office." In front of the place stood an impressive-looking man, a sixgun at his side, a gleaming badge pinned to his leather coat.

When Sheriff Frank Lane saw Canton riding toward his office, he walked into the street to greet him.

"Frank, remember me?" he asked.

Canton stroked his chin, giving the sheriff a quick onceover.

"Of course, you served under me in Wyoming. Believe the name is Frank Lane. I'll be damned, never expected to see one of my deputies a sheriff of a county way down here."

"Was easy, Frank, no one wants the job, too risky. How about pinning a deputy badge on your shirt and working for me, a kinda reverse situation." Both men laughed.

"Sounds good to me. I need the job."

That was how Frank Canton was introduced into Oklahoma Territory, and he was to serve with such distinction that the State later made him Adjutant General.

"Tell you what, Frank, I'm going to appoint you chief deputy of Pawnee County and also introduce you to United States Marshal Evett Dumas Nix."

Of course, Marshal Nix saw in Canton a man who could serve the Territory with wide authority rather than be shackled to only one county.

"Canton, you should be a Deputy United States Marshal and not just a deputy sheriff," Nix told him at their very first meeting.

"Dammit, Evett," said Sheriff Lane, "I get him broke in for Pawnee County and already you want to steal him from me. But that's up to Frank."

Canton saw the advantages of being a Federal officer so he accepted the offer of Marshal Nix. His appointment came at a time when such men as Deputy Marshals Bill Tilghman, Chris Madsen, Heck Thomas, and Bud Ledbetter, were waging a constant war upon many outlaws in the area, including those who remained of the Dalton gang and others.

Most of his fellow workers hated Frank Canton, and he never enjoyed the respect of his peers. As one of them commented later on, "No one except Bill Tilghman had any use for Canton, and Bill was too kind-hearted a man, even to put up with Canton. Canton was belligerent, mean, abusive, and thought he was better than everyone else. In spite of that he was a good officer and reckless and fearless as hell, no question about that."

Other unsavory characters also ran businesses in Pawnee. One such family was that of John, Dal, Bill, and Bee Dunn, who owned a meat market in that town. Many people believed they were cattle rustlers who butchered the animals and sold the meat at their market. The Dunn ranch was also known to be a haven for outlaws looking for a place to rest and to hide from the law.

One day Canton confronted the Dunn brothers.

"I've a proposition for you," said Deputy Marshal Canton. "If you'll agree to betray your outlaw friends into our hands, I'll see to it that you are granted immunity from prosecution for your illegal acts. I mean Bill Doolin as well."

"That's a hell of a thing to say," said Bee Dunn. You got nothing on us to arrest us for."

"No, not right now," grinned Canton, "but I could in short order, don't you think?"

"We'll have to think on it," said John Dunn. "This is just the sort of stunt you'd pull, Canton; no wonder everybody hates your guts."

"That does not concern me right now, letting personal feelings into the matter won't solve a thing."

A few days later, while Canton was waiting for a reply from the Dunn brothers, a man came into his office and reported that Lon McCool was hiding out a man wanted in Kansas. Canton simply went to the McCool home, broke down the door, and arrested the fugitive without a shot being fired. Just as Canton was leaving, McCool appeared on the scene.

"Damn you, Canton, you entered my cabin illegally and

you have no right to arrest this man. You had no papers to do so."

"McCool, you're lucky this time. I'll break into your place any time the spirit moves me, especially when you are harboring a criminal. Keep your damned trap shut or I'll arrest you too."

"You no-good damned manhunter, Canton, you ought to die right now!" cried McCool, as he slapped Canton in the face and went for his gun. It was a bad move on his part, an almost fatal one. Canton shoved McCool away, drew a .41 calibre Derringer and shot his would-be killer in the forehead.

The giant hulk of McCool collapsed, apparently dead. When Canton learned that the bullet had not penetrated the man's skull, he threw away the Derringer in disgust.

"That McCool must have a head made of iron," Canton told Bill Tilghman later on. "Another thing, I'll never use a damned Derringer again, not reliable."

Bill said little about the matter; he never got too excited over such incidents.

Lon McCool later admitted that slapping Canton in the face was not a very bright idea. He also said he had the worst headache of his entire life.

On April 29, 1895, Bill Dunn gave Canton the information he wanted.

"Four members of the Doolin gang are headed for our ranch," he said, "and they should be there within a few days."

Bill Tilghman and Heck Thomas found no outlaws, so they waited. The Dunn ranchhouse was a two-story building with two large rooms downstairs, divided by a hallway. The upper room was furnished with bunks to accommodate twenty men or more. The building faced south and had doors and windows in use on all sides except the east. On this blind side the lawmen dug a shallow pit a short distance from the house. heck Thomas, Bee Dunn, and one of the possemen entered the pit, while Bill Tilghman, Will Dunn, and the remaining posse members stationed themselves inside the house.

The bad weather had apparently delayed the outlaws. On May 2, however, just as dusk was falling, Bitter Creek George Newcomb and Charley Pierce rode toward the house from the north. As the two bandits neared the house, Heck Thomas called to them to surrender. Instead, the two Doolin gang members leaped from their horses, running at full speed toward the excavation which protected the lawmen, firing their pistols as they ran. Belch-Winchesters sent a barrage of lead at the approaching figures. Both fell, mortally wounded.

Another story was told which has the two outlaws killed with not a peace officer around. Bee and John Dunn claimed they had shot and killed the two outlaws as they slept in the upstairs room of their house. Evidence seems to point in that direction since there were shotgun buckshot wounds on the bottom of the feet of both men, indicating they had been shot while lying down asleep.

The Dunn brothers brought the corpses into Pawnee to claim the posted rewards. There the bodies were viewed by hundreds of the morbidly curious before being claimed by relatives. Bitter Creek's father lived at Fort Scott, Kansas, where he was a prominent businesman, and he came to Guthrie to claim his son's body. The bodies had been taken to Guthrie since it was the center of activities for the lawmen. The body of Pierce was claimed by a brother from Paris, Texas.

Instead of getting the rewards they had expected, the Dunn brothers got a shocking surprise. They were greeted by Frank Canton who had a warrant for Bee's arrest. Canton charged Dunn with aiding and abetting the outlaws. However, Bee Dunn was later released from custody.

Of course, one can readily see what a deadly hatred now existed between Frank Canton and Bee Dunn after Canton's aboutface action. Nothing really occurred for a while, and it took the death of outlaw Bill Doolin to bring the matter to a climax. According to most accepted versions of Bill's death on August 24, 1896, he was killed by a blast from Heck Thomas' shotgun. However, Canton was circulating another story . . . that the shotgun slugs which killed Doolin had been fired by Bee Dunn. This statement placed Canton at odds with Dunn, as well as with Heck Thomas. Careful research of the matter by this author and data supplied by Bill's son indicate that what follows is what really happened.

During the night of August 24, Doolin rode up to the

Ellsworth home near Lawson, Oklahoma, and hid in the barn. That morning he told Ira and Frank Ellsworth and his wife, Edith, that he was preparing to leave the territory that same evening.

"Edith, I am taking you and Jay this evening and heading for West Texas or New Mexico. I hope we can make it and start life over. This outlaw business is not worth it."

Heck Thomas was in Chandler when he received a telegram from one of his spies, stating that Doolin was at the Ellsworth place. With Deputy Rufus Cannon and his son, Albert, Thomas hurried to Bee Dunn's place. There he was joined by Henry Cotts, Dal Bee, George, and John Dunn. At Lawson they picked up the two Noble brothers. Thomas posted his son and Cannon on one road leading into Lawson. George Dunn and Cotts were assigned to guard another road. He then took the remainder of his posse to the west road, one which Doolin generally used when in that area.

West of the Ellsworth house and a little east of Eagle Creek, Thomas posted his men in the cane patch. Tom and Charles Noble were hidden first, and down the hill waited the Dunn brothers and Heck Thomas, stationed next to Bee Dunn. Bill and Bee Dunn were armed with shotguns, while the others carried Winchester rifles. Bee had Dr. W. R. Call's eight-gauge shotgun loaded with buckshot. It was no doubt the same weapon he had used in the killing of Newcomb and Pierce.

At sundown Doolin went to the barn and saddled his horse. He was going to check the trail for an ambush while his wife and child were readying themselves to take the wagon trip west. Bill stalked slowly down the dark road, his .40-.82 Winchester cradled in his left arm. As he drew near the cane field on the south side of the road Heck Thomas yelled, "Halt, Bill! This is Heck Thomas!"

Doolin turned and fired into the darkness, his bullet nearly striking Thomas and Bee Dunn. At the same instant Bee let go with the shotgun, later saying it went off accidentally. Bill Dunn also fired his shotgun, others chiming in with the sharp crack of the Winchesters. All the shots went wild except the buckshot from the two shotguns. Heck Thomas had fired twice, one of the bullets striking Doolin in the right side.

In light of the buzzing gossip concerning the death of Doolin, something was bound to happen, and it did. Dunn was the first to make amove. It might also be noted that Bee Dunn had agreed to relay to Canton the whereabouts of Doolin; instead, one of his men had wired the information to Heck Thomas. Also, Deputy Canton was now pressing old charges in Pawnee County against Bee.

Things came to a head on the afternoon of Friday, November 13, 1896, in Pawnee. Dunn was standing near the butcher shop on Main Street when Canton passed by.

"Damn you, Canton, I understand you have it in for me!" cried Bee Dunn, going for his gun at the same time, the weapon sticking momentarily in its holster. That gave Canton the advantage he needed, and he shot Dunn dead. An account of the affair appeared in the November 19, 1896, issue of the *Kingfisher, Oklahoma, Free Press:*

> *Last Friday afternoon Deputy F. M. Canton, one of the best officers in the territory, shot and killed Bee Dunn, one of the worst characters in the territory. Dunn was standing in front of the butcher shop on Main Street in Pawnee when Canton passed. Dunn stopped Canton and remarked, "Canton, I understand you have it in for me, by God." With those words Dunn went for his gun. Canton was too quick for him, however, and shot the tough. Dunn's gun caught on his suspender. Canton fired one shot and killed Dunn instantly. Canton gave himself up to Sheriff Lake, but was simply placed under guard. Dunn is the slayer of the Slaughter Kid and Bill Doolin. He was considered one of the worst men in the country and had just been given a commission as deputy by United States Marshal Nagle. Public sentiment is entirely with Canton. Canton's trial will come up next week. Dunn's brothers arrived and threatened to fire the town and kill Canton.*

A report which read as follows was handed down by the coroner's inquest, and it appeared in the November 20, 1896, issue of the *El Reno News:*

The grand jury now in session at Pawnee has decided that the killing of Bee Dunn by Marshal F. M. Canton was justifiable and failed to return an indictment. Canton was released.

Frank Canton was still in an uproar about the remaining Dunn brothers, who now were being used by Heck Thomas as possemen. Canton asked that the Dunns be delivered to him and Thomas refused.

"You are deliberately obstructing justice, Heck, and you damned well know it," Canton told his brother officer.

"I'll not turn them over to you for execution, Canton, we know your reputation too well," was Heck's response.

One can only wonder what the outcome of such a figbht between Canton and Thomas might have been. As it was, the remaining Dunns, Dal, John, and George skipped out and were not heard from again.

At that time Canton felt his presence in Oklahoma no longer was needed so in 1897 he set out for the Yukon, a wild place where gold had been discovered a year earlier. A man of Canton's temperament could enjoy such a God-forsaken spot.

Without bothering to inform his wife of his intentions, Canton began his journey to Circle City, Alaska, where a Deputy United States Marshal appointment awaited him. An early freeze caused his journey to be delayed for the winter months. Near Minook Creek the passengers disembarbed and prepared to spend the harsh winter.

With the party was a young man named Rex Beach, with whom Canton did some unsuccessful prospecting to kill time. In later years Rex Beach wrote a famous novel called *The Spoilers,* with the central character of the novel being patterned after Frank Canton. Some have also claimed that Owen Wister used Canton's life as a pattern for his book, *The Virginian.* This could be true since Canton and Wister had been friends in Wyoming; also, Canton had been born in Virginia. Writers who strive to debunk Canton have, of course, scoffed at this idea.

In April of 1898 Canton assumed his duties as a deputy marshal at Circle City. This work was slow and dragging, leaving Canton with extra time. To keep himself busy he accepted employment with the North American Trading Company. This he held until his work as a peace officer became too time-consuming.

Canton had a difficult territory to cover; it extended over 300 square miles of Alaskan wilderness, and it was a Herculean task to make all the arrests he was asked to make. It was during this time that Canton resorted to his own old fashioned style of gunplay, probably for the last time.

In the spring of 1898, while he was looking through some wanted posters, Canton noticed the photo of a man whom he had seen around Circle City. While engrossed in this work he had a visitor, the captain of the ship which brought passengers to the place.

"Cap'n, ever see this fellow around here? Know him?" asked Canton, handing the captain the poster.

"Never, marshal," lied the man, displaying no emotion whatsoever. However, he lost no time in warning this friend of his.

Several ineffective shots were fired at Canton before he could arrest the young man, a fugitive from Idaho, and on whom a $2,500 reward had been posted.

"Damn, that's a long way to go for $2,500," muttered Canton. "Yet, that's a heap of money."

Before he could leave for the states, however, Canton had another visitor. The man was a Catholic priest.

"Marshal, you have arrested a young man who is sort of a hero. Some time back he rescued a woman and a child from an ice floe at considerable risk to his own life."

"Is that so?"

"Yes, it is; besides, the charges in Idaho are not that bad."

"I know that. Leave the matter to me."

In a few days Canton released the young man and told him to leave the territory.

In February of 1899 Canton and several deputies traveled to Fort Yukon to bring back three fugitives. On the return trip Canton lost his snow glasses, and he soon developed snow blindness. He then returned to the states for treatment.

Now fifty years old, Frank Canton decided to return to Buffalo, Wyoming, after an absence of seven years. It was like a repeat performance. However, the area did not appeal to him as it once had so in less than a year he returned to Pawnee, Oklahoma, of all places. As it had happened before, now it happened again. Canton was appointed a Deputy United States Marshal by Marshal Charles F. Colcord, Fourth District, Perry, Oklahoma.

At the height of his new popularity in Oklahoma Canton got a bright idea. He returned to Texas, the scene of his many crimes while using the name — his real name — of Joe Horner. Although he went to Texas on the pretext of becoming chief investigator for the Texas Cattle Raisers' Association, Canton really went there to clear the name of Joe Horner.

As a peace officer Canton had become a good friend of Texas Governor James Hogg, who had pardoned an old friend of Horner's named John Wesley Hardin. Canton marched into the office of the governor and stated his purpose.

"Governor, I want a written pardon for Joe Horner."

"Joe Horner!" exclaimed Governor Hogg. "We haven't heard from him for twenty years or more. No need for a pardon, the man's probably dead by now anyhow."

"Well, I'd appreciate it anyway, all you have to do is sign the documents."

The governor drew up the necessary documents and signed them. Joe Horner had been pardoned!

Canton read the documents carefully, then fixed his gaze upon Governor Hogg and said, "By the way, Jim, I'm Joe Horner!"

"What the hell, this some kind of a joke?" asked the governor. "But I've never known you to be one much for a joke of any kind."

After Canton had finally convinced the governor that it was no joke, that chief executive burst into a roar of laughter.

"I'll be damned! Best I've heard for many a year," he said, wiping his eyes. "Anyhow, Frank, you and I are still friends, right?"

"Right!"

Canton's wife now tried to persuade him to use his real name, but he refused, stating that his daughter Ruby should not have to live with the past. He never changed his mind on the matter. Years later when he wrote his autobiography, Canton made no mention whatsoever of Joe Horner.

When the adventures of this man Canton seemed to be at an end, another matter cropped up to attract his attention. On June 17, 1900, the Boxer Rebellion broke out in Peking, China. Several Americans and British residents were among those killed, so a relief expedition of American, British, French, Japanese, Russian, and German troops fought its way into Peking and captured the city on August 14, 1900. Frank Canton also was there. He served as chief packer with two pack trains of the Ninth United States Infantry.

Later, Canton returned to Oklahoma, as though drawn by a magnet. He also resumed his role as a lawman, and when Charles N. Haskell was voted Oklahoma's first governor, the first thing he did was to appoint Frank Canton Oklahoma's first Adjutant General. Canton moved his family to Guthrie, then the State Capitol, where he served for nine years under three governors. Even at the age of sixty his search for adventure never stopped.

In 1908 Canton single-handedly suppressed the "Crazy Snake Rebellion" in McIntosh County. Crazy Snake was a name used by Chitto Harjo, an Indian who did not like the idea that Indian Territory now was the State of Oklahoma. He threatened an armed insurrection by his Indian followers.

Many people on the frontier parts of Oklahoma had good reason to fear such an Indian attack so they petitioned the governor to call out the State Militia. Frank Canton just laughed.

"Let me handle this. I'll go after Crazy Snake alone."

The governor could not believe him, yet he did not interfere when Canton stated he was going to do just that. After a long talk with Crazy Snake it appeared there would be no more trouble from the Indians. At any rate, there was none for nearly a year.

The Sooner State was thrown into another panic when Crazy Snake started his "Smoked Meat Rebellion." Efforts were made by veteran lawmen such as Bill Tilghman and Chris Madsen, to no avail. Finally Canton called in a hundred or so of his best guardsmen, and the Crazy Snake matter was closed once and for all.

Canton, however, never lost his persistent habit of going in alone. When he was sixty-three years old, Canton once again pulled off a solitary exploit that many others in number might have ignored. Alone, Canton went to Delaware County to settle a county seat fight between two feuding towns.

The new county seat of Delaware County was a town named Jay. Bill Creekmore had platted a new townsite he called New Jay. He had seized all the county books and records, proclaiming his town of New Jay the county seat. Before another fight such as the celebrated "County Seat Wars" of Kansas could commense, Canton rode into New Jay alone. With him he carried his guns and a proclamation from the governor. His hair and his mustache white, Canton still exhibited a gunfighter's background and his deadly reputation. Creekmore was easily convinced that the county seat should be at Jay. The records were returned to that town and have remained there ever since.

Many writers who wish to defame frontier lawmen and gunfighters usually state they became pathetic alcoholics. The same thing was said of Canton, yet he found time and made the effort to fill five thick tablets in writing his memoirs.

On Tuesday, September 27, 1927, Joe Horner, alias Frank Canton, died at the home of his daughter in Edmond, Oklahoma. Of him former Marshal Charles F. Colcord said: "No braver man ever lived than Frank Canton, and no man done more than he to establish law and order. In my opinion Frank Canton brought more criminals and outlaws to justice than any other peace officer in the Southwest."

Frank Canton was buried at Rose Hill Cemetery in Edmond, Oklahoma, on September 29, 1927. Less than a year later his daughter Ruby was also buried in the Canton family plot. His wife Annie survived her husband by twenty-one years.

Perhaps all the wrongs he did while using his real name of Joe Horner cannot be erased by the good he did on the side of law and order. All will agree that Frank Canton was a man among men!

BIBLIOGRAPHY

Baber, Daisy F., The Longest Rope, *Caxton Printers, Ltd., Caldwell, Idaho, 1940.*

Bancroft, Hubert Howe, History of Nevada, Colorado and Wyoming, *Historical Press, San Francisco, 1890.*

Canton, Frank M., Frontier Trails, *Houghton Mifflin Co., New York, 1930.*

Clover, Samuel Travers, On Special Assignment, *Lothrop Publishing Co., Boston, 1903.*

Gard, Wayne, Frontier Justice, *University of Oklahoma Press, Norman, 1949.*

Henricks, George David, Bad Man of the West, *Naylor Co., San Antonio, Texas, 1941.*

Huckabay, Ida Lasater, Ninety-four Years in Jack County, *The Steck Co., Austin, Texas, 1949.*

LeFors, Joe, Wyoming Peace Officer, *Laramie Printing Co., Laramie, Wyoming, 1953.*

Linford, Velma, Wyoming, Frontier State, *Old West Publishing Co., Denver, Colorado, 1947.*

McPherren, Ida, Trail's End, *Prairie Publishing Co., Casper, Wyoming, 1938.*

Mercer, Asa Shinn, Banditti of the Plains, *Grabhorn Press, San Francisco, 1935.*

Mokler, Alfred James, History of Natrona County, *R. R. Donnelley and Sons, Chicago, 1923.*

Rainey, George, The Cherokee Strip, *Cooperative Publishing Co., Guthrie, Oklahoma, 1933.*

Oklahoma, *Guide to the Sooner State, WPA Project, University of Oklahoma Press, Norman, 1941.*

Rollinson, John K., History of Wyoming Cattle Trails, *Caxton Printers, Caldwell, Idaho, 1948.*

Walker, Tacetta B., Stories of Early Days in Wyoming, *Prairie Publishing Co., Casper, Wyoming, 1936.*

CHAPTER II

DOC HOLLIDAY, THE DEADLY DENTIST

He was a man to be reckoned with, this Doc Holliday from Georgia. In 1875 he was twenty-four years old, fast with a gun, vicious and mean, caring for no one but his beloved cousin Mattie Holliday. At the time he was average height, pale, very thin, with piercing blue eyes that sometimes turned gray, with blond hair that seemed gray at times. He seemed always in a sorrowful mood, spoke with a soft southern accent, and wore the clothing of the day, always neat and presentable.

Yes, this was John Henry Holliday, son of Henry and Alice Jane Holliday of Griffin, Georgia. The man who was destined to become the great gunfighter Doc Holliday was born on August 14, 1851, on Tinsley Street, and was baptized on March 21, 1852, at the Griffin Presbyterian Church.

John's father joined the Georgia Twenty-Seventh in September of 1861. He was off to war as a captain in the quartermaster corps. By the end of the Battle of Malvern Hill in 1862, the captain, now a major, was totally unfit for military duty. His resignation was accepted by the Confederate command and he returned to Griffin, a beaten man, with no more in his pockets than a thousand dollars in Confederate bills.

Shortly after his return from the battlefield, Major Holliday moved his family to Valdosta, Georgia, to seek his fortune anew. The Hollidays were prominent citizens of the war-ravaged town, where they set about to bring things back to normal. A blow struck the family when John's mother died on September 16, 1866.

It was in Valdosta that John, now eighteen years old, met his lovely first cousin, Mattie Holliday, a devout Catholic girl. It was love at first sight, regardless of the conflict of their religious beliefs and their being related. The two young people attended many social functions at Stewart's Hotel in Valdosta, unmindful of the gossip that spread about their being first cousins.

It was also in Valdosta that John supposedly shot and killed some black boys who were swimming in a river on the Holliday property. However, this has never been satisfactorily proven.

In 1870 John Holliday went to Philadelphia, where in 1872 he graduated from the Pennsylvania College of Dental Surgery. Shortly thereafter he practiced his profession briefly in the office of Dr. Arthur Ford in Atlanta, Georgia. Leaving Atlanta, Holliday opened an office in Griffin, Georgia, where he developed a serious cough. The cough lingered on until a lung hemorrhage forced him to consult a physician.

"I'm sorry, John, but you have a bad case of consumption. Perhaps you have a year or two at the most to live. Try to find a state with a dry climate and take things easy," the good doctor told him.

John Holliday was stunned. He told his father the news. His sad and last goodbye to his beloved Mattie must have been a sorrowful one. He told her he would not saddle her with a consumptive invalid, with the possibility that she might contract the disease. She fully knew in her heart that she would never see him again. They did correspond from time to time, however.

From that day on Doc Holliday was a fatalist; he knew that he was dying, so he decided it might just as well be in the blazing glory of a one-minute gunfight. Throughout the remainder of his life, it is believed that Doc never wantonly killed a man, but he was game for a fight any time, and he had the edge on his opponent because the other men naturally held their lives in high regard, while Doc didn't care which way the chips fell.

So, while Doc Holliday was trying to bolster his physical and nervous system with liquor and dealing cards in foul-smelling barrooms, Mattie Holliday entered the Sisters of Mercy at St. Vincent's Academy in Savannah, Georgia. Perhaps she thought this would serve as a chance to do penance so that Doc might live longer. It was a place of seclusion where she would pray for his soul.

Mattie Holliday entered the convent on October 1, 1883, and her name was changed to Sister Melanie. She took her final vows on February 9, 1886. When Doc Holliday died in Glenwood Springs, Colorado, on Tuesday, November 8, 1887, no one except Sister Melanie was notified of his passing. Before he died Doc had embraced the Roman Catholic Faith and was baptized. Perhaps he thought this was one parting gesture of his great love for Mattie. Mattie, then a nun in the order of the Sisters of Christian Charity, was stationed at St. Joseph's Hospital in Atlanta. There she spent the rest of her long life, working with the sick and the poor. She died on April 19, 1939, and is buried in Atlanta. When Doc died one of the Sisters in Glenwood Springs wrote Mattie and stated that Doc looked like an Indian who had been dead for a week.

My grandmother was a close friend of Bat Masterson and he often spoke to her about Doc Holliday. He stated that the fight at the O.K. Corral was just a case of plain murder and never should have been labeled "The Greatest Gunfight in the Annals of Western History."

Bat stated that Doc had a good side that was very seldom illustrated. His only compassion was for women and children; that Doc had shot three men that he knew of over the mistreatment of women, and that two of them had died. Just how many men Doc killed during his short and wild life has never been truly established, and probably never will be; but, whatever number is given at this time is probably highly inflated.

He said Doc was a cold-blooded killer who felt no more compunction in killing a man that he felt in killing a snake. He drank a quart or more of whiskey each day, enough to kill an ordinary man, but he never saw him when he couldn't whip a gun into action with the speed of light, and was deadly accurate at close range with a sixgun. He never knew him to have an equal, unless it was Wyatt Earp. He always extolled the exploits of Earp, so such a remark could be expected from Bat Masterson.

Bat gave the following description of Doc Holliday:

"Doc was an aristocrat by birth, a professional man by education, a gambler by choice, a dentist whom necessity made a gambler, the nerviest, speediest, deadliest man with a sixgun I ever met, except, of course, Wyatt. Doc was a sophisticated, egotistical, immaculately dressed individualist, he respected no man on earth except Wyatt Earp, a gentleman whom disease made a frontier vagabond, a philosopher whom life made a caustic wit, a long, lean ash blonde fellow nearly dead with consumption, a man who packed more violence and color into his wild, young life than any man on the wild frontier. No men he ever knew among the outlaws would face Doc in a headon gun fight, and of the lawmen he knew, none would have stood a chance unless it was Wyatt Earp."

One old buffalo hunter in Dodge City, Kansas, made the following remark about Doc, "He was the most vicious man I ever knowed, like a rattler, the type I steered clear of."

It was in 1873 that Doc Holliday went to Dallas, Texas, and worked in the office of Dr. John A. Seegar, another dentist from Georgia. It was there, too, that he took to drinking heavily to erase the thought of his disease or to kill the pain that accompanied it. His patients didn't wish to be exposed to the dread disease so Holliday had very little business. He then started to frequent the gambling houses in town, and soon became quite an expert at the Faro and Poker games. He also found that he could make a much better living doing this than by extracting teeth from unwilling customers.

Using whiskey as a crutch, Doc sometimes sat at the gaming tables for forty hours at a stretch, especially when he was in a winning streak. Oddly enough, instead of living in the climate that would aid his health, Holliday confined himself to the smoke-filled saloons and drank quantities of whiskey enough to kill an ordinary man. Yet he outlived the Georgia doctor's prediction by fifteen years.

Doc was a pitiful figure of a man by now, and he saw the face of death each time he looked into his mirror. Because of his health and because he wanted to get himself killed, Doc Holliday became one of the most fearless gunslingers of his era, and a skilled gambler by profession. He hated all men and women except Wyatt Earp and Mattie Holliday. His life was one violent incident after the other. He did nothing all day except sit at the gaming tables, his life a constant game of chance. He carried a Colt's revolver as well as a sheath knife, which he strapped around his neck. His usual silent manner misled many a man into thinking Doc was a harmless little gambler.

While in Dallas, Texas, Doc had a shooting match with a man named Auston, although neither man hit the other. This happened on New Year's Day, 1875. The next day the city fathers of Dallas firmly requested that Doc Holliday leave their town for good.

He then rode into Jacksboro, Texas, where he became involved in several gunfights and was forced to leave town. He started out for Denver with a man named Polecat Adams.

Adams did not own a horse so he rode one of Doc's animals, and although he was a giant of a man, he was not a man of violence. A few days out of Jacksboro, while they were engaged in eating their supper meal, into their camp rode two tough-looking trail weary characters on lathered and spent horses which indicated they were in one hell of a hurry. They unwisely took Doc to be a preacher by his immaculate black clothing and they addressed him as such. Adams was not armed, Doc had a gun in a shoulder holster which they did not notice.

"Damn you, preacher, we're taking your horses," they told Doc.

"You kin have ourn," said the other man. "They'll be as good as yorn when they be rested."

Doc said nothing, waiting for human nature to react. The two men spotted a bottle of whiskey Doc had left exposed. They helped themselves to the liquor, paying no attention to Doc and Adams. Doc then went into action, shooting one man through the head, the other through the heart. He then walked over to the one with the chest wound and said, "You'll take nothing from this camp but this," and he shot and killed the man.

He searched the men and came up with nearly four hundred dollars and told Adams to drag the bodies into the brush. Doc said they had no doubt robbed a bank or a stage, and that he wasn't in the habit of robbing dead men, but could see no reason to leave it for someone else. They broke camp, leaving the dead men for the buzzards and beasts and turned the horses loose.

When they reached Mesa, Texas, hundreds of cattle were bunched and Doc said, "This means money. We'll rest here for a spell."

Doc was soon in a game of Poker, accepting the joshing and ridicule about his dress while he took their money. After several hours Doc announced that he was going to rest that he would return later and resume the game.

"Hell you will!" cried one of the players. "We want a chance to get even. Just sit tight, fancy pants."

Much to their surprise the ranchers found themselves looking into the business end of a cocked pistol.

"Just keep your seats, gentlemen, and no one will get hurt," Doc told the players. "I usually quit playing when I decide to quit, not when you decide for me to quit."

As Doc neared the saloon batwings the fat bartender brought up a shotgun and Doc shot and killed him. Only by Doc's cunning did he manage to escape with a whole skin. He led the ranchers into believing he was headed in another direction. He later told Adams that he had managed to live thus far by taking advantage of human nature by figuring what most men would do, or were going to do, either in a game of chance or in a gunfight, such as the two men they had left in the brush.

In Denver Doc got into an argument with a gambler named Bud Ryan and supposedly slashed the man's face from forehead to chin with his sheath knife, and Ryan carried a vicious-looking scar for the rest of his life. However, this apparently was just another of someone's fabrications, probably Bat Masterson's. The only record of a knifing which concerned one Bud Ryan occurred on June 22, 1887, after he had been arrested by officers for causing a disturbance in a saloon on Larimer Street. Apparently some patron brushed against Ryan when he was being taken from the saloon and Ryan pulled a small pocketknife and cut the man's neck slightly.

At Fort Griffin, Texas, Doc met a fancy girl named "Big Nose" Kate Elder, who was his off-and-on woman for the next few years. It was also in Fort Griffin that Doc first met Wyatt Earp and relayed some information to him as how he could capture Dave Rudabaugh, a notorious New Mexico outlaw who had escaped from the Las Vegas jail.

Doc got into it again with a man named Ed Bailey when he became annoyed at the man's constant habit of peeking at his discard pile.

"Do that again and I'll take in the pot as an automatic win," warned Doc.

However, Bailey refused to take Doc at his word and continued his look-see practice. Without a word Doc raked in the pile of chips and Bailey dove for his pistol. Doc's hand flashed to that deadly sheath knife and in one long sweep, he cut Bailey's stomach open from side to side.

Doc surrendered himself to the local authorities, but a vigilante group decided to take no chances of losing Doc Holliday. They decided to take matters into their own hands. Doc was held in a guarded room at the hotel since the town had no jail. Big Nose Kate then went into action. She set fire to the backside of the hotel, then held up Doc's guard long enough for him to escape. They raced to some nearby willows, where they did out until Polecat Adams brought them some clothes and horses. They mounted up and headed for Dodge City, Kansas, some four hundred miles away.

In Santa Fe Doc gambled while Adams and Kate lived a life of ease. Kate went about town visiting the shops while Adams cared for the animals and camp supplies. He said that Doc was very generous with his money and paid well for every service rendered him.

Later in the week a young boy approached Doc on the street and yelled, "Goddamn yore stinkin' hide, Holliday, you-all shot my father and I'm gonna kill you!"

Doc promptly shot the boy in the leg.

"Listen kid, I don't know who your father was, but if I killed him, he deserved dying or he tried to kill me. Go home, next time I'll put a bullet in your head."

A month later a rancher named Ramick grabbed at Doc during a game, claiming he was being cheated. Doc quickly peeled out of the coat, leaving Ramick standing there, coat in hand. When the dumbfounded man saw Doc's shoulder gun he went into action. For his stupidity he got himself killed.

The sheriff, not impressed by Doc's plea of self-defense, promptly locked him in jail to await trial for murder. Ramick was a well liked rancher and Doc a gunslinging stranger and gambler, hence he realized his changes for a fair trial were very slim indeed, especially now that his reputation had preceeded him wherever he traveled.

When Adams came to visit, Doc conspired with him to aid him in breaking out of the flimsy built jail building. Adams, as planned, during a town celebration, hitched a team of mules to a back jail window and pulled out half the wall.

Doc escaped but poor Adams did not. He went to jail for his part in the jailbreak, but the sheriff wanted Doc.

"Goddamn him, I wanted that wizened little bastard put in prison for life!" exclaimed the sheriff, in total disgust.

So it was, everyone wanted to do away with the little man whom trouble seemed to plague.

Finally reaching Dodge City, Kate took up housekeeping, but she and Doc were at each other's throats constantly. Kate would pack up and leave Doc at the slightest excuse and he cared little about it. Doc went to Leadville, Colorado, on a gambling spree, but this did not appeal to him so he returned to Dodge City. It was at this time that he was credited with saving Wyatt Earp's life. Although none of the newspapers carried any space about the matter, it was stated that Doc had shot a man who was getting a bead on Earp while the marshal was trying to arrest two prominent cattlemen named Ed Morrison and Tobe Driscoll.

In later years Earp made the following comment when questioned about the supposed incident:

"It wasn't long after I returned to Dodge City that Doc Holliday's quickness saved my life. He saw a man draw on me behind my back. He shouted a warning to me, but while the words were coming out of his mouth he had jerked his pistol out of his pocket and shot the other fellow before the latter could fire. On such incidents as that are built the friendships of the frontier."

Doc left Dodge City after a brief stay and wandered into Raton, New Mexico; Durango, Colorado; even going into Wyoming at one point. His existence during that time is not an open book. On his return to Dodge City in 1880 or latter part of 1879 he learned that his friend Earp had gone to Tombstone, Arizona. Doc Holliday decided that if the place was good enough for Wyatt Earp, it was good enough for him.

It was now 1880 and Earp was living with his wife Mattie on Allen Street in Tombstone. Mattie lived with Earp in spite of his affairs with other women. In 1882 she left Tombstone, however, and went to live with Wyatt's parents in California. She committed suicide in Pinal, Arizona, on July 3, 1888.

Doc and Kate settled in Chris Bilicke's Hotel, just a block from where Earp lived.

Tombstone came into being after United States Army Scout Ed Schieffelin had discovered silver in the mountainous country around Camp Huachuca, a newly established army post in the Hualapai country of Arizona. His friend Al Sieber had told him all he would find was his tombstone if he kept prospecting in the Indian-infested mountains.

Schieffelin thought it was a good joke when he named his silver mine "Tombstone" when he recorded it in Tucson on August 25, 1877.

Soon the roaring town of Tombstone, Arizona, sprung up, but the Schieffelin brothers took no part in the building of it. They had come into the Dragoons almost paupers and went out millionaires. Ed died in May of 1897 in his cabin in the Oregon wilds. He was later buried near Tombstone, beneath a mass of rough stones, the grave being visible for miles across the mesa.

Tombstone mushroomed into a boom town almost overnight. Into this magic city of the desert poured outlaws, stage robbers, gamblers, crooked lawmen, merchants and men of other professions. Over the Mogollon Plateau came the canvas-topped wagons drawn by oxen, mules or horses. Through the Texas Canyon, Mustang Pass, they were drawn as through by a magnet to the land of promised riches. Some did not reach their destination as the Apaches swooped down upon them and left them dying on the hot and lonely sands of the *Camino del Diablo.*

The crowds of get-rich seekers swarmed into Tombstone and in a short time the population had swollen to over 15,000 people. More people milled around in the fabulous new town than lived in any other city in the Arizona Territory. In two years the population surpassed that of Tucson, Prescott, and Phoenix, cities which had been established for years.

In Tombstone, Allen was the main street. Two business thoroughfares were named Tough Nut and Fremont Streets. Allen Street was the Fifth Avenue of the town, with the O. K. Corral at one end and the Bird Cage Opera House at the other. The Bird Cage was a sturdily built structure of adobe, frame, and brick, as were other buildings in the town. Today the Bird Cage is a cocktail lounge and museum. The sidewalks were sheltered from the blazing sun by wooden awnings, and along those walks swarmed people of all sorts . . . laborers, cowboys, gunmen, outlaws, capitalists, Mexicans, peace officers, and women and children of all ages.

Although Tombstone was a combination of Deadwood, Hays, Abilene, and Dodge City, it little resembled the rough boom towns except in toughness and killings. It is claimed that a man was shot and killed in Tombstone every day before breakfast. Bars like the Crystal Palace, the Oriental, and the Alhambra (now a grocery store), boasted rich oil paintings, sparkling crystal and spotless mirrors. The many gambling halls were richly carpeted and frequented by men of money and reputation. They rubbed elbows with some of the toughest gunmen who ever wore sixguns or who ever took a drink of whiskey. Now these same gunslingers were drinking champagne, probably for the first time in their lives, for some, the last time.

Doc Holliday took up gambling at the Meagher and Melgren Alhambra Saloon, where he spent most of his time. Earp had an interest in the Oriental Saloon, and of course Doc spent some time there as well. At that time Virgil Earp was working in the Tombstone police force; James Earp, the eldest, was working as a Faro dealer, and Wyatt Earp was working as a shotgun messenger for the Wells Fargo Company. Morgan Earp, the youngest of the Earp brothers, was living with Virgil and his wife.

The owner of the Oriental Saloon, Lou Rickabaugh, was being pressured into allowing a gambler named Johnny Tyler to take over part of the gambling concessions at the saloon. He and his men started a ruckus so Wyatt Earp tossed him out into the street. He returned in a little while with a revolver.

"You son-of-a-bitch, Earp, come out and I'll have it out with you!" He then noticed Doc standing in one corner of the saloon. "You, too, you mangy-looking bastard!"

Doc grinned. He liked nothing better than a fight.

"Go to it, sonny, I'm ready. We can settle things right here and now."

Tyler had not counted on this. He looked at Doc, saw the sickly grin on his emaciated face; no bluff was there.

"Never mind," said Tyler, walking to the door and disappearing into the street.

With the crowds of people also came the newspapers, four of them: *The Nugget,* the political voice of Sheriff Behan, was Tombstone's first newspaper and was established in the latter part of 1879 by A. E. Fay and Thomas Tully. The

Epitaph first appeared on May 1, 1880; its owner was John C. Clum, later mayor of the town. The Epitaph was the champion of the Earps, and there was a constant war between it and the Nugget. Then there were the *Expositor* and the *Evening Gossip*, two fine papers which also kept the citizens of Tombstone informed of what was going on.

At the north end of town, on an unfenced, windswept, desolate slope was Tombstone's Boot Hill Cemetery. There rest some of the most deadly men of the west as well as some of the town's finest citizens.

Into this den of inequity came men of lawless reputation; men who scorned the Tombstone law and who roamed the streets at will. One of these men was Curly Bill Brocius, a robber and a desperate killer. Another such man was John Ringo, said to have been related to the notorious Younger Brothers of Missouri, and also to have attended William Jewell College at Liberty, Missouri. To this day there are a number of families in Missouri named Ringo.

Frank Leslie was also a noted gunslinger of Tombstone, although he usually managed to remain neutral in any squabbles concerning Sheriff Behan and Earp-Holliday factions. Frank Leslie killed Mike Killeen as the result of an argument about Mike's wife. He also killed Billy Claiborne who thought Leslie had killed John Ringo. It was a fair fight so Leslie was not arrested. Later, in a drunken stupor, Frank Leslie killed his second wife and also wounded a young ranch hand of his named Jim Neal. Leslie served time in the Yuma Territorial Prison and disappeared after his release.

Doc Holliday was arrested a number of times in Tombstone, once for alleged participation in a stage holdup and the murder of two men thereon. He was acquitted. Doc was also getting tired and losing patience with the guys who talked too much about his being protected by the infamous Earps.

"I'll kill the next son-of-a-bitch who mentions my name in connection with any stage robbery, come what may!" he told Earp. The news spread. Not much more was said about it after that.

A break came for the Earps when Cochise County was

Doc Holliday.

Wyatt Earp (seated) and Bat Masterson in Dodge City photo taken in 1876 when Earp was 28 and Masterson 23.

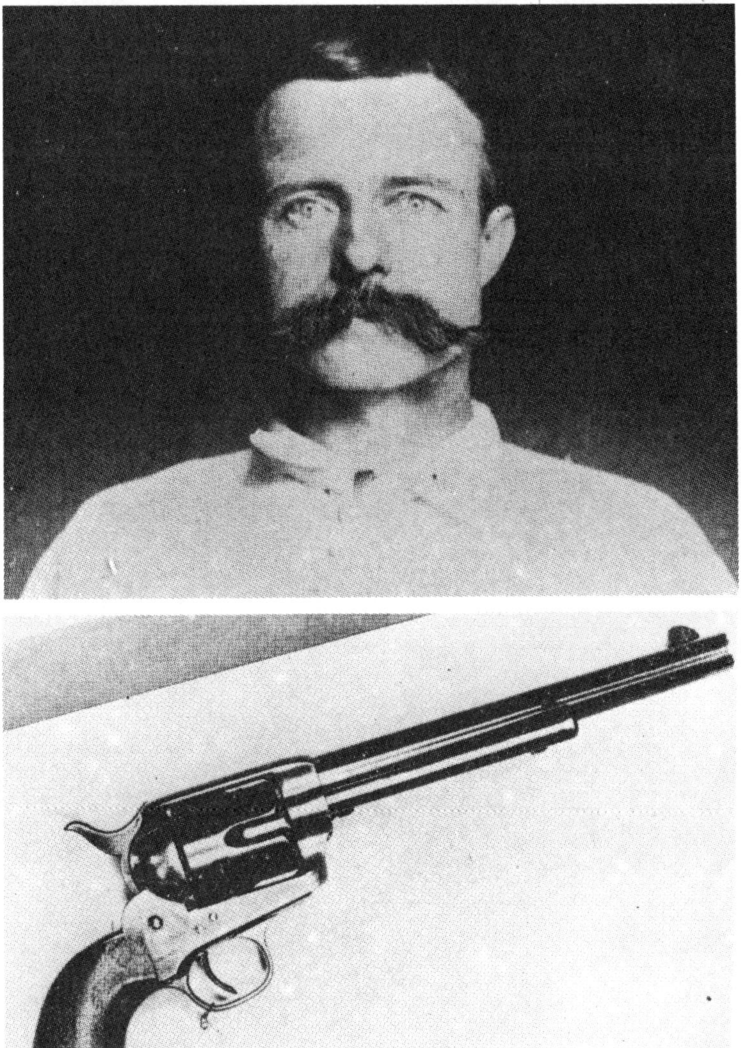

Buckskin Frank Leslie and Colt Peacemaker.

"Big-Nose" Kate Elder, paramour of Doc Holliday.

Frank McLaury who was killed at the OK Corral.

Larry Deger, 300-pound marshal of Dodge City.
Boot Hill Museum, Dodge City, Kansas

John Slaughter, famous sheriff of Cochise County, Arizona.

cut off from Pima County, with Tombstone the county seat. Wyatt Earp felt he should have been appointed sheriff of the new county by the governor; instead, John Behan was appointed to the job. In June of 1881 City Marshal Ben Sippy left town and did not return for some reason. The town council and Mayor Clum appointed Virgil Earp marshall of Tombstone. Wyatt was appointed a deputy United States Marshal by Arizona Marshal Crawley P. Dake.

Had not Earp stayed his hand Doc Holliday probably would have cleaned Tombstone of a number of outlaws. There was a bitter hatred between the outlaw element of Tombstone and Doc Holliday. When the gun law was passed, whereby a man was prohibited from carrying a gun on the streets, except when coming to or leaving town, Doc was appointed an unpaid policeman. This allowed him to pack a gun, while the outlaw element went unarmed. Had Doc appeared on the streets unarmed, his life wouldn't have been worth a plugged nickel. This caused much hell-raising among the outlaws, who claimed that Doc was as bad as they were or worse; nevertheless, he wore his gun.

In March the stage to Benson was attacked by robbers, resulting in the killing of the driver, Bud Philpot, and a man named Peter Roerig. Big Kate, seldom sober, was living with Doc at the time in an old adobe building. Sheriff Behan arrested her and told her he had evidence that Doc had robbed the Benson stage. Kate agreed that he could have done it. In August Kate left Tombstone.

The Clantons wanted to rule the outlaw mob in the area. It was necessary and natural that a showdown between their forces and those of the Earps should materialize one day. It did.

At 2:00 o'clock on the afternoon of October 26, 1881, near the O. K. Corral, this shootout occurred. The corral ran parallel between Allen and Fourth Streets, the Fremont entrance being flanked by Fly's Photo Shop and Bauer's Butcher Shop. Here is an eye-witness account as given by John Montgomery.

"Lined up along the west wall of the corral were six deadly outlaws, grimly awaiting the arrival of the Earp party.

As the Earps came into view, Wesley Fuller became panicky and bolted away from the corral entrance, leaving five men to comprise the Clanton faction. Wyatt Earp and Doc looked them over. They were Ike Clanton, Billy Clanton, Tom and Frank McLaury, and Billy Claiborne.

"The Earps carried sixguns and Doc carried his famous sawed-off shotgun hidden under his coat, as well as his revolver. Doc took a position at the corral entrance, while Virgil Earp was a few feet in the lead, with Wyatt and Morgan Earp following close behind.

"Sheriff Behan darted into Fly's Studio. Tom McLaury stood about ten feet from the street entrance; next to him was his brother Frank. On their right stood Ike and Billy Clanton, the latter a mere boy. At the far end stood Billy Claiborne, a young would-be killer with sixguns strapped low at his sides.

"The Earps claimed that Frank McLaury reached for his gun and that the other outlaws followed suit. They later said that Frank McLaury and Billy Clanton fired at Wyatt Earp. These shots opened the so-called fight at the O. K. Corral. Both shots missed. The ensuing firing lasted less than a minute.

"Billy Claiborne threw down his guns and dashed into Fly's place. Wyatt fired and wounded Frank McLaury in the stomach. I think Tom McLaury was unarmed and jumped behind a horse tied at the corral entrance. The Earps said he fired at them from that vantage point but I did not see him do so. Billy Clanton saw that the Earps meant to kill them all, no matter, so he snapped a shot at Morgan Earp and missed. I saw that the Earps were determined to kill them all. Billy Clanton fired several times and missed. Morgan Earp shot the boy in the right arm, causing him to use his left hand for further action. Morgan said Tom McLaury took another shot at him and the bullet struck him in the right shoulder, plowed across the base of his neck and came out at the left shoulder.

"Wyatt finally nicked the horse where Tom McLaury was hiding and the animal darted away. Doc killed Tom with a blast from his shotgun.

"Ike Clanton got out of the fight by running into Fly's place to join Sheriff Behan and Billy Claiborne. Frank

McLaury fired at Doc Holliday and wounded him in the thigh, while Doc's bullet tore through McLaury's heart. I saw Billy Clanton try to get to his feet, but he fell back, dead."

The rumor that Tom McLaury had not been armed seems substantiated by a report of the Coroner's office. Some folks wanted to know why, if the Clanton outfit had wanted to ambush and kill the Earps and Holliday, were their Winchester rifles still in the saddle scabbards after the fight.

The Coroner's office listed the following personal effects taken from the dead men: Nov. 8, 1881 . . . "From the body of Thos. McLaury I recovered in certificates of deposit in the Pima County Bank, checks and cash in the sum of $2,923.45. From the body of Frank McLaury one Colts six shooting pistol, with belt and cartridges. From the body of William Clanton, one Colts six shooter, with belt and cartridges, and one nickel watch and chain." (There is no mention of a firearm being taken from the body of Tom McLaury.)

On October 30, 1881, the *Daily Nugget* reported the following:

> *Daily Nugget*, October 30, 1881: Yesterday warrants for the arrest of Wyatt, Virgil, and Morgan Earp and J. H. (Doc) Holliday, were placed in the hands of the sheriff, but as Morgan and Virgil Earp were confined to their beds as a result of the shooting at the O.K. Corral, the warrants were not in their cases, served, and only Wyatt Earp and Holliday placed under arrest. When those parties were taken before Justice Spicer, he denied bail as a matter of right, but upon showing of facts by affidavits, bail was granted and fixed in the sum of $10,000 each, being justified in the sum of $20,000 for each of the defendants.

The final curtain was drawn on the matter of the O.K. Corral fiasco when in November Justice-of-the-Peace Wells Spicer gave his findings in the matter.

"After a full review of all the evidence in the matter of the O. K. Corral and the evidence presented by the Earps,

Sheriff Behan, Issac Clanton, and others, I have the less reluctance in announcing this conclusion, because the Grand Jury of this county is now in session, and it is quite within the power of that body, if dissatisfied with my decision, to call witnesses before them, or use the depositions taken before me, and which I shall return to the District Court, as by law required, and to thereupon disregard my findings and find an indictment against the defendants if they think the evidence sufficient to warrant a conviction.

"I conclude the performances of the duty imposed upon me by saying in the language of the statute: 'There being no sufficient cause to believe the within named Wyatt S. Earp and John H. Holliday guilty of the offense mentioned within, I order them to be released.'"

Of course, this is just the conclusion of the report rendered by Judge Spicer, since thousands of words were spoken and recorded, material really not relative to the story at hand.

On March 17, 1882, Morgan Earp was shot and killed while he played a game of pool in Hatch's billiard parlor. James Earp returned to his home town of Colton, California, where he died in 1926 at the age of eighty years. Warren Earp was a special officer for the Arizona Cattlemen's Association in 1900, and was killed by two cowboys. Virgil Earp died of pneumonia at Goldfield, Nebraska, on October 19, 1906, at the age of 65. Wyatt Earp died at his home in Los Angeles on January 13, 1929, age 80.

Doc and Wyatt were released on November 30, 1881, and in a couple days Doc was again in jail for discharging firearms within the city limits of Tombstone.

Anxious to escape further hounding by Sheriff Behan and his warrants, Doc and Wyatt left Tombstone for good. They went to Colorado where they split up. Wyatt went to Trinidad, Colorado, where Bat Masterson was operating a successful gambling house. Doc went to Denver where he was arrested on an Arizona warrant charging him with the murder of one Florentino Cruz. On Friday, May 26, 1882, Governor Pitkin was urged not to honor the warrant since Doc would have no chance for justice in Arizona.

Bat Masterson claimed that Doc Holliday returned to Tombstone from Colorado and killed Johnny Ringo. Others claim this would not have been physically possible, since Doc was supposed to have been in jail in Pueblo on a "charge" of stealing money from someone. It was another indictment to keep him out of Arizona. Wyatt Earp went to see Governor Pitkin and told him he alone had killed Cruz, and that Doc had had no hand in it whatever. Doc was not in jail at the time Ringo was killed. He had been released on a $300 bond, returning in the District Court on July 18, 1882. The bond was set on June 1, and John Ringo was slain around noon on July 12th.

On June 1, 1882, the Pueblo *Chieftain* reported that Doc Holliday appeared before Justice McBride on the swindle charges. He waived examination and was bound over to appear before the District Court. This same paper reported that on July 19, 1882, Doc Holliday was again in District Court on July 18, charged with larceny.

Around the first of July Doc disappeared for a while. He took no one into his confidence. He knew that Wyatt would make every effort to stop him had he known his plans. It was a damned fool thing to do, of course, after all the trouble others had been put to to keep Doc out of Arizona. He went back on his own, in secret, knowing the chances he took.

When Doc reached the Tombstone area he moved in with a family of Mexicans he had once befriended, and who, he knew, would not make his presence known in the Turkey Creek Canyon area.

He watched the road for several days from his place of concealment. He saw Johnny Ringo several times, but he was always accompanied by others. Soon after he saw Buckstin Frank Leslie, and Ringo dismount and rest under a huge five-trunk oak tree. The distance was too great for an effective shot, so Doc waited. He saw Leslie ride off shortly afterward, leaving Ringo drinking his fill of rotgut whiskey. Ringo was asleep when Doc rode slowly across the creek, cocked gun in hand.

Ringo did not move until Doc's feet touched the ground. When he opened his eyes and saw Doc he yelled in surprise,

"You dirty son-of-a-bitch!"

Those were his last words as he clawed for his own gun. Doc walked closer and shot him dead. After he was certain that Ringo was dead, Doc rode back to the home of his Mexican friends, and soon was on his way back to Pueblo. Who really knows? Wyatt Earp himself said he had killed Ringo; others said that Leslie or Johnny-Behind-The-Deuce O'Rourke had done it. Doc told several of his acquaintances that he had killed Ringo.

Doc Holliday was suspected of killing many men; in fact, every murder committed in Colorado was laid at Doc's door, no matter where the crime had been committed. When Masterson was asked if he thought Doc had ever shot a man in the back, this was his reply.

"Not to my knowledge, but I wouldn't have put anything past Doc in those days. Doc couldn't have bested a fourteen-year-old boy in any contest, except with a gun, which he claimed made all men equal."

There were also some good points about Doc Holliday.

When Mattie Boreland came to Tombstone she decided to open a women's ready-to-wear shop there, a store well stocked with the latest fashionable goods. One morning she was going to open her store and found the building raised on house jacks. The man informed her that she had bought the building and not the ground, and unless she came up with two hundred dollars more, he was going to move the building elsewhere.

Mattie wept bitterly when he said he was sorry but there was nothing he could do about it. As she wept, a man, who by his dress appeared to be a preacher, approached and asked if he could be of any service. Mattie, thinking she was addressing a minister, unburdened her woes on him.

Doc asked her to walk a little distance from the scene, informing her she would not want to hear what he had to tell this man.

"Mister, you new in this town?" Doc asked the man.

"Yep, shore am."

"You'll be new in hell if you don't replace that building; then catch the next stage out of Tombstone. Either that or I'll put a bullet between your eyes, and they'll tote you out in a box."

To make his point clear, Doc shoved a cocked pistol into the man's ribs.

The frightened man did as he was told. That was the last Tombstone ever saw of the man. Mattie ran this store for many years, and never again was she questioned as to the ownership of the property.

"Thanks to Doc Holliday, who to me was a fine gentleman, the investment of my life's savings was secured," Mattie later said. Later she was accused of withholding evidence regarding the O. K. Corral matter, incriminating Doc, of course, when she, as an eyewitness to the affair, said she could not identify the man with the pearl-handled revolver.

Doc was the only gunman in Tombstone who carried a pearl-handled revolver. The judge had said that due to Doc's physical appearance, a person should have been able to identify him two blocks off, and Mattie was just across the street, yet she failed to identify him. She stuck to her guns in her testimony. Doc was not called to testify in the trial of Wyatt Earp and others, including himself, nor was another eye-witness, John Montgomery. He had been the only person to witness the beginning of the fight, other than those involved, of course.

Another fine woman of Tombstone was Nellie Cushman, who ran the respectable Russ House and who was called "The Angel of Tombstone." At her small hotel at Sixth and Tough Nut Streets she administered her nursing skills to many a cowpoke who had caught a bullet during the course of an argument, or men who had been injured in some other manner. The town was mighty sad when Nellie left for Alaska. She reportedly passed away in the 1920's.

In 1882 Doc had a horse go lame. He rode the lame horse twenty miles in an effort to find another he could purchase. On his way he ran across the meager home of a poor homesteader. As he reached the back yard of the house he was stopped by a bloodcurdling scream. He dismounted and peeked around the corner of the house. There he saw a young mother in the yard calling to a small child. He also saw something else . . . two rattlers in the shade of a nearby bush. Apparently the sound of their rattlers had attracted the child's attention. Doc stalked closer. He then rested his gun against the house for it was a long and difficult shot. The mother had not yet seen Doc in the yard.

Doc's gun boomed. The mother, frightened by the unexpected sound, fainted dead away. Doc saw one rattler jump. The second shot disposed of the other sidewinder. The child, scared out of his wits, crawled to his mother's side as fast as he could.

The father, who had been sleeping through all the yells by his wife, awakened with a start when he heard the shots. He grabbed his shotgun and ran into the yard. When he saw Doc with a smoking gun in his hand and his wife on the ground he naturally thought that Doc had shot her. Doc later stated that if the woman had not regained consciousness in time, the man surely would have blasted him with his shotgun.

"He'd have shot me sure as hell," said Doc. "Even though I was expecting to leave this world unprepared, I did not expect it at the hands of a homesteader. If I'm shot dead it probably will be done by a coward, and in the back."

Bat Masterson gave my grandmother the name of a man who lived on a ranch north of Denver, a man Doc had befriended when the rancher was just a small boy.

"I doubt that he'll tell you the story, though. He never would tell it to me, nor to anyone else," Bat further commented on the matter.

This man was finally contacted but was not very communicative at first. Finally, he said Doc was responsible for his success, and that he wasn't ashamed of the fact.

"I told Doc I'd never tell anyone this story. Doc also said my being the adopted son of Doc Holliday would cause me more harm than good.

But this gentleman was kind enough to give me a brief version of the Doc Holliday matter, with the explicit agreement that his name would not be mentioned, nor the photo he gave me be used.

"When I was four years old my mother deserted me, leaving me with an old aunt, who cared nothing about my welfare. When I was seven years old I was forced to go out on my own.

"In the early winter of 1886, on a very cold night, I was trying desperately to sell my remaining newspapers on a Denver street. I was approached by a well-dressed man who bought all of my papers and who told me to get inside where it was warm. This man asked about my circumstances when he noticed my poorly clothed body. I was ten years old at the time. I related my story to him and he listened.

"When I had finished he said, 'I am going to give you some money, and if you spend it wisely and go to school, later on I'll send you more, but if you don't spend it wisely, you'll get no more.'

"He told me to go to a certain bank in the area, where I was to see Mr. so-and-so, and that he would give me the money on a certain day of each month. He gave me a note to identify myself to this banker, and he took my address. For many months I called at the bank as directed and was given money. Perhaps I met this kind man about four times. Once shortly before he died, he sent for me to visit him at Glenwood Springs, Colorado, where he was confined in a hospital.

"He knew that he was dying and told me so. He weighed about seventy pounds at the time, nothing but skin and bones. When I left he gave me a check, and told me to get all the education I could get. I did, and attended college for two years, where I studied animal husbandry. Doc had already been buried when I learned of his death so I was unable to attend his funeral. I have visited his grave many times and left flowers, little in return for what he did for me, and it depresses me when I think of it.

"I married a girl whose father left her a small ranch; since then we have added two sections."

That was the extent of the story as related. He told his listener that it was not for publication and this request has been respected down through the years until permission was granted to do so by this man's daughter.

In 1940 I visited this ranch. His daughter informed me

that her father had been killed by a bucking horse. She knew nothing of the Doc Holliday story, at least, very little. However, she showed me some letters, letters to Doc from Mattie Holliday, the cousin who loved him so much.

Doc and Mattie had planned to be married, but his illness prevented that. All her life she remained true to a ghost named John H. Holliday. Mattie died in 1939.

I was allowed to read only part of one letter given to the newsboy by Doc. Doc had asked the boy to destroy them, since he did not want them to fall into the wrong hands. However, the boy had been so impressed by the beauty of the letters that he kept them. These letters are still in the possession of this family. It is hoped they will see fit one day to publish them. If you were to walk into the living room of this ranchhouse you would see a large painting of Doc Holliday displayed on a prominent wall of that room.

After the death of John Ringo, Doc Holliday left Pueblo after appearing before the District Court there on July 18, 1882. Charged with larceny, he got his case continued until it was dropped from the court's docket.

Doc's next move was to Leadville, Colorado, 10,200 feet above sea level. He thought this climate might be beneficial to him. Leadville was a wide-open town, filled with gamblers, card sharks, gunfighters, prostitutes, and con-men, all eager to get their hands on easy money. It was the climate Doc enjoyed most. He checked in at the Clarendon Hotel, next door to the Tabor Opera House, the most elite hotel in town. Doc was really too sick to enjoy the luxurious decorations. There he met some of his old cronies from Tombstone.

Next day Doc ran into a man he had known in Tombstone. While shaking hands, this man said, "Doc, did you know that your buddy Johnny Tyler is here?"

"That dirty son-of-a-bitch!" cried Doc. "Can't I go anywhere without trouble following me or getting there ahead of me, damn! Where is that no good bastard?"

"He's dealing at the Casino. Still tells about how he hates your guts for how you treated him in Tombstone."

Doc next checked in at a rooming house at 106 East Second Street, and began to work for Cy Allen, the owner of the Monarch Saloon at 320 Harrison Avenue. It was not long before Johnny Tyler was plotting to get even with Holliday. He and some of his friends complained to Cy Allen that Doc was short-tempered and was losing customers for the Monarch Saloon. One of Tyler's friends picked a fight with Doc, and he flew into a rage. As a result, Doc was fired. Since he was unable to pay his rent, Doc moved to a room over the Hyman Saloon on Harrison Avenue. The owner of the saloon, Mannie Hyman, felt sorry for Doc and allowed him to use this room at no cost.

Johnny Tyler's hatred for Doc knew no bounds. Doc had been the only man to embarrass him in front of a crowd, and he determined to get even. Tyler, on learning that Doc had borrowed five dollars from Billy Allen, former chief of police, then acting as bartender at the Monarch Saloon, suggested that Allen demand immediate payment of the debt.

On August 19, 1884, Doc met Allen in Hyman's Saloon, where Allen demanded the five dollars he paid him. Doc drew his short-barreled .44 and fired a shot at Allen. The bullet missed and struck the door frame. Doc's second shot struck Allen's right arm from the rear about half way between the shoulder and the elbow, passing out in the front. Henry Kelleman grabbed Doc and prevented him from firing another shot. Doc was then placed in the custody of the police and locked in the county jail.

There was a lot of testimony given at the trial, both pro and con. The outcome was that Doc was acquitted and told to leave town permanently. One must suppose that Johnny Tyler was satisfied with that.

Arizona had not forgotten Doc Holliday. The Denver *Tribune-Republican*, dated March 27, 1885, carried the following:

> *The trial of Doc Holliday, the man with a bloody record, on the charge of shooting Billy Allen, on August last, with intent to murder, began in the Criminal Court before Judge Goldthwaite this morning. A jury was impanelled and the evidence commenced, but the wrangling among the lawyers delayed it materially. The*

difficulty grew out of an old dispute in Tombstone, Arizona, in which Holliday was the ringleader on one side and John Tyler, who is now dealing for a faro bank here, was on the other.

Holliday and Tyler both left Tombstone after the latter had refused to fight a duel with the former at ten paces, and met in Leadville. Tyler was a Pacific and Holliday an Easterner. There was an inextinguishable rivalry and animosity existing between the factions. The old imbroglio was rankling in their breasts here and Tyler and his friends did everything to prejudice the public against Holliday. Billy Allen was among those who sympathized with the Tyler crowd and Holliday put him down as an enemy.

Some financial difficulty aroused between Allen and Holliday, the manner assuming the shape of a quarrel. Allen is alleged by Holliday's friends to have said that he would 'do him up,' while Allen asserts that he said he would whip him. At any rate, on the day of the tragedy a number of Holliday's friends went to his room and represented that Allen was seeking him with a revolver.

About noon he went across the street to Hyman's, and said laconically to the proprietor, 'The time's up.' He then returned to his room where he remained until 5 o'clock. He then sent his revolver by a friend to Hyman's, where it was placed behind one end of the bar. Holliday soon came over and took his stand within reach of the weapon, and near the cigar lighter.

Allen, having overlooked the action behind the bar, put on his coat and assured Mr. Allen, who remonstrated with him, that there would be no trouble, he went to Hyman's and had scarcely crossed the threshold when Holliday levelled his revolver and fired, the bullet striking below the muscle of the right arm and emerging near the shoulder. Holliday sprang behind the bar again, and fired a second time, the bulletin grazing Allen's head. He was then overpowered and disarmed, while Allen was removed to his apartments, recovering shortly afterwards.

Every effort was made to compromise the matter before it reached the courts, but Allen stood firm in favor of prosecution.

Doc went to Denver, registering at the Metropolitan Hotel, but his stay there was not long. He became listed on the police records as a vagrant, an undesirable, so he was asked to leave town. Where did he go? Of all places, he returned to Leadville! He gambled at Hyman's to such an extent that he won a great deal of money. Now his thoughts turned to trying to get well so he could enjoy spending it. It was a little late for that.

Doc next ventured to Glenwood Springs, Colorado, the spot supposed to have curing vapors of mineral smoke and water. It was the summer of 1887 when galloping consumption took over his frail body. Prior to that the disease had been confined to his lungs; now it attacked every sinew of his body. Doc was thirty-five years old.

Doc, still as practical as ever, wrote Mattie and thanked her for remaining faithful to him and for her prayers. He told Father Downey, a Catholic priest, that he had been baptized a Catholic, and he told Rev. S. W. Rudolph, a Presbyterian minister, that he had been raised as a Presbyterian.

At ten o'clock on the morning of November 8th, Doc Holliday died. The next morning's issue of the Glenwood Springs newspaper carried the following:

> *J. A. Holliday, or Doc Holliday as he was better known came to Glenwood Springs from Leadville last May, and by his quiet and gentlemanly demeanor during his short stay and the fortitude and patience he displayed in his last two months of life, made many friends. Although a young man he had been in the west for twenty-five years and from a life of exposure and hardship had contracted the consumption, from which he had been a constant suffered for many years. Since he took up his residence at the Springs the evil effects of the sulphur vapors arising from the hot springs on his weak lungs could readily be detected, and for the last few months it was seen that dissolution was only a question of a little time, hence his death was not entirely unexpected. From the effects of the disease, from which he had suffered half his life, Holliday, at the time of his death, looked like a man well advanced in years, for his hair had silvered and his form emaciated and bent, but he was only thirty-six years old.*
>
> *Holliday was born in Georgia, where relatives of his still reside. Twenty-five years ago, when but eleven years of age, he started for the west, and since that time he has probably been in every state and territory west of the Mississippi River. He served as sheriff in one of the counties of Arizona during the troublous times*

in that section, and served in other official capacities in different parts of the west. Of him it can be said that he represented law and order at all times and places. Either from a roving disposition or while seeking a climate congenial to his disease, Doc kept moving from place to place, and finally in the early days of Leadville came to Colorado. After remaining there for several years he came to this section last spring. For the last two months his death was expected at any time; during the past fifty-seven days he had only been out of bed twice; the past two weeks he was delirious, and for twenty-four hours preceding his death he did not speak.

He was baptized in the Catholic church, but Father Ed Downey being absent, Rev. W. S. Rudolph delivered the funeral address, and the remains were consigned to their final resting place in Linwood Cemetery, at 4 o'clock on the afternoon of November 8th, in the presence of many friends. That Doc Holliday had his faults none will attempt to deny; but who among us had not, and who shall be the judge of these things?

He had only one correspondent among his relatives . . . a cousin, a sister of Charity, in Atlanta, Georgia. She will be notified of his death, and will in turn advise other relatives he may have living.

A maudlin article and certainly one containing errors as to Doc's early life and his coming to the West. Nevertheless, Doc had become a legend of the West, a figure who will endure. Each year many tourists visit his grave at Glenwood Springs. Perhaps Doc's bones do not even occupy the grave today. After a terrible flood some time back, bones were gathered and placed in the spot where Doc's original grave had been. Are they Doc's bones? Evidently the people of Georgia think so, since a movement was afoot not too long back to have these bones taken out of Colorado and reburied at his birthplace, Griffin, Georgia. To date, Doc's bones still remain in Colorado.

Even so, one way or another, Doc's emaciated ghost will continue to ride the desolate trails of the once Apache-infested mountains until western story-telling comes to an end.

His one and only friend, Wyatt Earp, passed away on

Sunday morning, January 13, 1929, at his home in Los Angeles, California.

BIBLIOGRAPHY

Arizona, a State Guide, Writers' Program, WPA, Hastings House, New York, 1940.

Arnold, Oren, Thunder in the Southwest, *University of Oklahoma Press, Norman, 1952.*

Beebe, Lucius & Clegg, Charles, Saga of Wells Fargo, *E. P. Dutton, New York, 1949.*

Botkin, B. A., Treasury of Western Folklore, *Crown Publishers, New York, 1951.*

Breakenridge, William M., Helldorado, *Houghton Mifflin Co., New York, 1928.*

Breihan, Carl W., Great Gunfighters of the West, *Naylor Co., San Antonio, Texas, 1952. Paperback, New American Library, New York, 1977.*

Breihan, Carl W., Great Lawmen of the West, *John Long, Ltd., London, 1961. Paperback, New American Library, New York, 1978.*

Brown, Dee & Schmitt, Martin, Trail Driving Days, *Charles Scribner's Sons, New York, 1952.*

Burns, Walter Noble, Tombstone, *Doubleday, Page Co., Garden City, New York, 1927.*

Chisholm, Joe, Brewery Gulch, *Naylor Co., San Antonio, Texas, 1949.*

Corle, Edwin, Desert Country, *Duell, Sloan & Pearce, New York, 1941.*

Cunningham, Eugene, Triggernometry, *Press of the Pioneers, Inc., San Antonio, New York, 1934.*

Foy, Eddie, Clowning Through Life, *E. P. Dutton Co., New York, 1928.*

Ganzhorn, Jack, I've Killed Men, *Robert Hale, London, 1940.*

Gard, Wayne, Frontier Justice, *University of Oklahoma Press, Norman, 1949.*

Hart, William S., My Life East and West, *Houghton Mifflin Co., New York, 1929.*

Hendricks, G. D., The Bad Man of the West, *Naylor Co., San Antonio, 1941.*

Hunter, J. Marvin & Rose, Noah H., Album of Gunfighters, *Bandera, Texas, 1951.*

King, Frank M., Mavericks, *Trail's End Publishers, Pasadena, 1947.*

Lewis, Alfred Henry, The Sunset Trail, *A. S. Barnes Co., New York, 1905.*

Lockwood, Francis C., Pioneer Days of Arizona, *Macmillan Co., New York, 1932.*

Ludlum, Stuart, Great Shooting Stories, *Doubleday & Co., New York, 1947.*

McClintock, James H., Arizona, *S. J. Clarke, Chicago, 1916.*

Martin, Douglas D., Tombstone's Epitaph, *University of New Mexico Press, Albuquerque, 1951.*

Myers, John Myers, The Last Chance, *E. P. Dutton & Co., New York, 1950.*

Parsons, George Whitwell, Private Journals of George Whitwell Parsons, *Arizona Records Project, 1939.*

Raine, William MacLeod, Guns of the Frontier, *Houghton Mifflin, Boston, 1940.*

Stanley, F., The Las Vegas Story, *World Press, Denver, Colorado, 1951.*

White, Owen Payne, Autobiography of a Durable Sinner, *G. P. Putnam's Sons, New York, 1942.*

Wilson, Rufus Rockwell, Out of the West, *Press of the Pioneers, New York, 1933.*

CHAPTER III

THE SAGA OF TOM HORN

I

Tom Horn first saw the light of day on November 21, 1860, in Scotland County, Missouri, near Memphis. Tom had three brothers and four sisters, and he lived the normal life of a frontier lad of the time, hating to attend school or church as most kids did then.

The lad loved to hunt the abundant deer, quail, rabbits, and other wild game, often spending weekends doing so, returning home late on Sunday to the whipping he knew he would get for skipping Sunday school.

"Son, this hurts me worse'n it does you," said Mrs.

Horn, as she whipped Tom until he cried.

On the other hand, Tom once told friends, his mother was first to call for his help and that of his dog, Shadrick, when some night prowler would kill some of her chickens.

"I remember as a boy," said Tom one day, "that Pa would take Shad to some auction or shooting match or something, and the dog would get into fights with other contending dogs, usually getting whupped bad. He would come back looking a mess and would never leave my side until his wounds had healed."

One day a neighbor boy named Sam Griggs and Tom went 'coon hunting, both boys bringing their dogs. Sam brought a mutt named Sandy; Tom brought Shad. Usually the hunt ended up in a fight between the boys and the dogs.

"I recall one amusing incident," laughed Tom. "One day we treed a 'coon so Sam Griggs shinnied up the tree, lost his hold and fell. Funny thing, his dog, Sandy, must have thought he was a 'coon since he bit Sam in the arm. My dog would have more sense than to think I was a 'coon."

On the rough frontier of Missouri most kids worked the farms in the summertime and went to school in the wintertime. So it was with Tom Horn, although he admitted he hated school, much preferring tracking or trapping the fur-bearing animals of the forest. Many days Tom would miss school, more intent on following the trail of some animal, whose tracks he had noted in the snow.

"I'll never forget my cousin Ken Markley," Tom remarked one day. "He was a sissified kid who came to live with us, and he didn't know the difference between a singletree or a hames. But he made an impression on my parents because he was refined and always combed his hair properly and kept his clothing and shoes neat. He was a great hit with the womenfolks.

"One day he hit Shad with a stick so I jumped him. He was 17 and I was 13, but I whupped him proper. This I did before the women were able to pull me of'n him. After that we kept some distance between us."

One day some folks moving west passed near the farm of Tom's dad. One of the young men walking behind the wagon stopped to talk with Tom. Tom noted the young man was carrying an old, single barrel shotgun."

"What do you do with that thing?" asked Tom.

"I shoot game with it, why?"

Tom, who was an expert marksman and always shot his squirrels through the eye, replied, "Well, anyone who shoots game with such a gun isn't much good."

"I can shoot as good as anyone," bragged the passerby.

"Wanny bet?" asked Tom.

"All right, get your rifle and we'll see."

"We'll use that little bird up there on that limb for a target," suggested Tom, returning with his rifle.

"You're crazy, kid; that's ninety yards away or more."

"All right, we'll call off the bet," said Tom, as he started to walk toward his home.

"Let's put it this way, farmer boy. You hit that target, and I'll give you a dollar. If not, you give me the rifle."

"Fair 'nuf," smiled Tom; "I'll just take that bet. He fired, and the bird fell to the ground.

"I'll bet also that I hit the bird in the head," said Tom.

"Hell with that."

Tom knew by the way the bird floated to the ground with wings outstretched that it had been hit in the head, and such proved to be the case.

The situation ended up with Tom and the stranger on the ground, hammering away at each other with clenched fists. Just then an older brother of the bet challenger sprang to assist his brother. It was a bad mistake. Old Shad snarled, grabbing him first by the arm and then biting him in the leg. Tom thought it was time to stop so he got up and walked over to see that Shad did no further damage to the boy.

"Damn that cur dog!" cried the older boy, grabbing his shotgun and blasting away at Shad. With that both strangers leaped up and raced ahead to catch up with their wagon.

Poor Tom! He carried Shad home, and that evening the dog died. Horn later stated that he felt it was the first and only real sorrow he had known throughout his eventful life.

Tom Horn was fourteen years old now. He wanted to go out on his own, but did not know just how to do it. The chance came shortly. Some minor disagreement caused Tom and his dad to come to blows one day. The boy, of course, came out second best.

"That's the last time you'll whup me. I'm leaving home for good!" said Tom, tears streaming down his cheeks, unable to rise from the pile of hay in the barn where he had fallen.

"Good, you'll be back when you get hungry."

The elder Horn had done his beating job well. Tom's mother and several of his brothers and sisters carried the boy into the house. There he lay for a week in his bed, unable to move. He asked his mother to sell his old rifle for him as he was going to leave.

"Well, mother, the time has come," said Tom several days later, "I'll miss you and the kids, but this had to be."

"Yes, son, I well know that. Here's $15.00 I got for the rifle, and some food to tide you a while on the trail."

The young lad kissed his mother and his sisters and brothers for the last time, paused a moment at Shad's grave, then without a glance backward Tom Horn headed for Kansas City.

II

Tom covered the seventy-five miles from his home to Kansas City in three days, often stopping off at the homes of friendly farmers along the way for food and drink. Some women even packed food for Tom to take along; others gave him clean clothing to wear.

At that time, 1874, Kansas City no longer was the boom-town of tent saloons, and gunfighting frontiersmen; it had lost some of its wildness in the transition from stage-stop to railroad terminus. Tom remained there several days and then went to Newton, Kansas, employed to work on the Santa Fe Railroad.

Railroad work did not appeal to the likes of Tom Horn, now nearly six feet tall, lanky, tough, and adaptable to any situation. Besides, the Indians contested every mile of the railroad, making life miserable and dangerous for the laborers.

So, after back-breaking work for about a month, Tom drew his pay of $30.00 and went with a man and his two teams toward Santa Fe. It was Christmas, 1874, when the frazzled lad entered the capital city of New Mexico.

Tom's next stop was Las Vegas, New Mexico. There he was to meet another young fellow, quite arrogant, and boasting of his prowess with the sixgun. He was Billy the Kid, about the same age as Tom Horn, but not as tall and lanky as Tom.

At the Main Plaza in Las Vegas, the two youngsters met and hit it off to a bad start. Horn tried to be friendly.

"Name's Horn, hail from Memphis, Missouri."

"Too bad, that's Jesse James country. Does that make you tough or something? You're pretty damned big, I'll say, but can you shoot?"

"Name your weapon," smiled Horn back at the leering buck-toothed Kid. Tom had done extensive hunting and trapping while just a mere punk, and was considered quite an expert with the rifle as well as with the revolver.

"Well now, ain't you a smart cuss, how'd you like to try some big gun, say a buffalo rifle or the like," grinned the Kid.

"Don't have no rifle with me; how about pistols?"

"That's all right with me, buster, but did I tell you I was William Bonney, otherwise, Billy the Kid?"

"Don't recall you did, friend, what difference does that make anyhow?"

If the Kid thought his name was going to impress Horn, he had another thought coming. Tom decided that he was going to play the game cool and level-headed; he could easily see the resentment and hatred glowing in the eyes of the Kid. Half the battle is won if you keep your wits about you, he'd been told by experts.

The two lads decided to use a card for a target, the trick being to split the card.

Tom Horn backed off the required distance, took aim and fired, cutting the card neatly in two. The Kid did not take his time. He whirled like a striking rattler and his pistol boomed. The card jumped from the ground.

"Good, quick shooting, friend, easy to hit a man that

way, but you did not cut the card," drawled the lanky Missourian.

"Damn you, Horn, you trying to make a fool of me?" demanded the Kid in a threatening manner.

"No such thing, Kid, let's try lighting matches, it will calm your nerves a bit." And so saying, Horn stuck six wooden matches into tracks in the Baca Corral fence.

"Ready whenever you are," grinned Horn.

One quick look at Billy the Kid told Horn that he was in immediate danger — he could see the killer glaze in the boy's eyes. Quick as a flash his fist shot out, and the Kid sprawled in the dust.

"We'll make it five shots — not six," Horn said.

"What the hell's the matter with you, farmer boy?"

"You know well enough. C'mon now, no tricks. We'll use five matches. I don't aim to have you around me and me with no bullet in my gun. This way I'll have one left after the match, and that'll be enough to send you where you belong if you get too fresh with your own gun."

The results of the shooting match showed that Tom Horn had lighted two matches; the Kid broke two and lighted only one.

"To hell with this, how about some cards?" snarled the resentful Kid, disgusted and possibly ashamed that someone had come along out of a clear blue sky and had outshot him.

Not many people in Las Vegas like the Kid, and that feeling also prevailed in the Martine saloon-gambling joint, where the two youngsters went to play cards. But the Kid got away with a lot of meanness because of his age.

It did not take long for a crowd to gather around the two boyish players; some of them rooting for the stranger, many neutral, some even who wished this plucky kid from Missouri would rid the place of the boastful killer.

Luck seemed to favor Horn, for he kept on winning, and with every winning hand, he watched more carefully. He knew he was up against a mighty poor loser, one who would kill him at the slightest opportunity.

The Kid tried every angle he knew to arouse Horn's anger but got nowhere. The calm, deliberate movements of the boy from the Show-Me State stood him in good stead now as they did in later years when he was a fighter in the Spanish-American War, a detective, a Pinkerton agent, and several other callings.

The climax came when the Kid deliberately dropped, face up, an Ace of Spades. The onlookers gasped. Surely something would happen now . . . it did.

Tom reached across the table, but instead of picking up the card, his steel-like fingers clamped down on the Kid's wrist. The Kid squirmed, yet the wrist which no handcuff could hold was seemingly a part of Horn's own hand.

"I've had enough of this penny-ante quibbling," he said slowly. "Someone take off this jasper's guns."

Several bearded men jumped to comply with the request, anxious to see what was going to happen next. When the Kid's guns were safely aside, he turned the boy loose. Then the vicious Billy experienced something that he probably never had before or ever would again. Tom Horn began to slap his face — loud and hard slaps — so they would be heard all over the place. The slapping kept on until the embarrassed and tear-blinding Kid rushed from the saloon. He had indeed met his match in Tom Horn.

III

Early in January Tom learned that the Overland Mail Route was hiring men for the route from Santa Fe to Prescott, Arizona. He sauntered into their office one day and spoke with the manager.

"Hear you all are hirin' men for stage work," he drawled in his Missouri brogue.

"Yes, $50.00 a month and we provide rifle and ammunition."

"Suits me."

"You'll take the route from here to Los Pinos instead of to Prescott, that is covered already," said John Murry, who, Tom later learned, was the manager.

Tom covered other routes as well. One day he was

instructed to return to his home base at Santa Fe, where he was instructed to accompany another stage employee to Beaver Head Station, in Arizona, on the Verde River, with some mules to replace animals there.

After completion of the Beaver Head Creek assignment Tom rode on to Camp Verde, a government post, where he went to work for a man named George Hansen, essentially hauling firewood to the post. Here Tom worked with more Mexicans than whites, so it was only natural that he became an expert in that language before quitting the logger job some three months after.

Although he was only sixteen years old, Tom's next job was that of boss of the quartermaster's horse herd. His job was to herd the animals until they were picked up by the various departments of the army which dotted Arizona at the time, all assigned to the Fifth Cavalry. Things happened fast for young Tom. He was out of a job just as soon as all the horses had been delivered, but he always managed to latch onto something else.

Colonel Al Sieber, Chief of Scouts, rode into Fort Whipple from the Tonto Basin area. At the fort he learned of Tom's prowess with weapons and his ability to speak Spanish fluently. One day the colonel called Tom Horn into his office.

"Young man, I am getting ready to head south again. How would you like to come along as an interpreter at $75.00 a month?"

Tom hesitated.

"You'll be with me all the time. I know the country and you'll like it."

So it was settled. Tom went with Al Sieber in midyear of 1876 to the San Carlos Indian Agency. Horn thought it was odd that he had been taken along since he never did anything. In later years he had this to say about it, "I think old Al wanted me along for company. I was young and could do his cooking and tend to his wants. Anyhow, it was fun and quite an experience, to say the least."

On the Apache reservation young Tom quickly learned their ways and their language, much to the delight of Al Sieber, who had a genuine liking for the Missouri youngster.

"He was one of the finest men I ever knew," Tom Horn later said of Sieber. "He'd die for a friend with no questions asked. He never got mad; only once did I see him really angry. This was once when he caught an Apache brave making whiskey, which was forbidden. The brave grabbed his rifle, but before he could use it, Al nearly slicked his head off with one swift sweep of his Bowie. It was awful. It made me sick for a spell. Al then took the body and threw it into the pot where the whiskey was being made. Sieber told the squaws to take the dead Indian to their village and to warn them against making more whiskey.

Tom later stated that things were uneasy in camp for the next two days; the men spoke little, and kept a constant vigil day and night, fearful that an Indian reprisal might occur on account of the death of the brave. However, no attack came.

It was in the area of their later camp on White River that Tom Horn met the Apache Chief Pedro, so named because he spoke Spanish. The chief was amazed and pleased to converse with Horn both in Apache and Spanish.

Horn and Sieber were discussing plans to visit with Chief Pedro for a while when twenty troppers of the Fifth Cavalry rode into their camp.

As Lieutenant Wheeler dismounted, he spun around on his heel, saluted Sieber, and said, "Colonel, we have news that the Indians are holding you and Horn captive here."

"As you can see, Lieutenant, we are safe and sound. You can tell the people of San Carlos not to worry about us; we are in good hands here," grinned the amused Sieber.

Shortly thereafter, the squad of soldiers left the camp and returned to San Carlos.

One day Sieber took Tom aside, telling him that Chief Pedro had taken a personal liking to him and wanted him to remain in the Indian camp when Sieber left.

"Tom, you are cut out for this type of life, I think. You can ride, shoot well, scout, speak Spanish and Apache fairly well . . . you're a natural for this, if you like it," Sieber told the young man.

"Well, I sure like to hunt and to loaf and do no work, all right. I may just try it. What about my pay and standing in the army?"

"You'll still get your monthly pay' besides, you'll be a special government representative in this Indian camp."

That especially appeared to Tom so the deal was closed under those conditions.

On a trip to San Carlos one day Tom met some Mexicans with a herd of horses to sell. Tom knew the animals had been stolen, nevertheless, he bought eight head of them, as well as several saddles and bridles. It was near Christmas of 1876 so Tom brought a Mexican blanket, which he gave to Chief Perdo as a present. He was very pleased with the gift since he liked Tom very much.

IV

In early 1877 Major Adna Chaffee was appointed the first military Indian agent of the San Carlos Reservation. Major Chaffee sent for Tom Horn and asked him to seek the help of Chief Pedro in bringing rebellious Indians onto the reservation.

At the council of talks Chief Pedro told Chaffee he should take his soldiers and kill off all the trouble-making braves so that peace could again come to the land.

Major Chaffee asked Horn to seek Pedro's advice as to whether Horn should be sent among the bad Indians to live with them and perhaps effect a friendly attitude as he had done with Chief Pedro's people.

In effect, Horn interpreted Pedro's message as follows:

"No white man can go among these Indians and come back alive. He would be tortured and killed and maybe worse. The chief refuses to send me there unless I have an escort of 200 braves."

At the end of the talks which lasted nearly two weeks, Major Chaffee agreed it would be foolhardy to send Horn into the treacherous Indian country of the Cibicu, so the Major, Horn, and his men returned to their White Mountains camps, remaining there until late in May.

Returning to San Carlos, Horn was informed by his

superiors that the Department of the Interior had failed to appropriate more money to pay for the services of the scouts and interpreters.

"Worse than that, Tom," Major Chaffee said, "you'll not be allowe to live on the reservation either since you are a white man."

Tom Horn returned to Chief Pedro's camp to wish him a sad farewell. As he left he took with him many handmade articles he had made while living with the Indians. These were quirts, bridles, and pouches made of hair or rawhide.

"Where will you go, my son?" asked Chief Pedro.

"Sieber and some of us plan to visit Tucson."

Accompanied by Al Sieber, Frank Leslie (later a famous gunfighter of Tombstone), and Ed Clark, Tom Horn and several others made their way to Tucson, where they remained for several months. There they met Ed Schieffelin, another scout, who had discovered silver in the mountains near Camp Huachuca, an army post in the Hualapai country of Arizona.

Some time before Schieffelin had told Sieber he had found a rich silver deposit in the mountains, and to which Sieber replied, "Ed, all you'll find in those mountains is your tombstone."

Schieffelin never forgot that statement. Ed had ridden into Tucson from the mountains on muleback to record his "Tombstone Mine" on August 25, 1877. Sieber and the rest of his group got a big laugh out of it.

"Al, you and your friends should come back with me and brother Al. There's enough silver in those mountains for the lot of us."

"Maybe so," said Sieber, "but the Dragoons are the stronghold of some of Cochise's relatives, to say nothing of Geronimo when he gets the notion to break from the reservation."

Al Sieber and Tom Horn staked a claim, later selling it for $3,000.00. Tom claimed it was not worth that much money. Tom was not a miner to begin with; he hated the work and confinement. He decided to supply the various mining camps with fresh meat from wild game, making a fairly good living at it for a while.

In October a detachment of soldiers visited Tombstone seeking Al Sieber and Tom Horn. It was about this same time that the two men had sold their mining interest to Charley Leach, so they were ready to listen to what the army had to say.

In a letter addressed to Al Sieber, General Wilcox requested that he and Horn report to Fort Whipple for a consultation about the Indian trouble that was brewing. The general told the two men that the Indians were again dispensing home-made whiskey to the braves and causing a heap of trouble by so doing. He asked that Sieber take up his old position of Chief of Scouts in an effort to supress an Indian uprising.

Early in 1878 Nana sent word that he and Geronimo, both living in Mexico, wanted to return and live on the reservation. They would talk with no one except Sieber, whom they instructed to some to the Terras Mountains, where some of the Apaches would direct him to the Indian camp.

"Tell Geronomi that we will meet him in the full of the May moon. Only three of us will come," Sieber told the courier.

From San Carlos, Sieber, Horn, and a Mexican raised by Nana's people, followed the San Bernadino Creek from its head to its junction with the Bavispe River in Mexico. As the three men were crossing the river they saw an Indian brave coming down a ridge on foot from the Terras Mountains.

"I know you two," muttered the Indian, pointing to Sieber and the Mexican, "but who is this man?"

Al Sieber explained to the brave who Tom Horn was and the explanation seemed to have the desired effect.

The Indian on foot proved to be the messenger sent by Nana and Geronimo to meet Sieber's group.

"What a handsome Indian," Horn remarked to Sieber.

"Maybe so, but mean as a rattler. He is a half brother to Natchez, and he is one of the worst hostiles in the whole lot."

The brave, whose name was Halzay, told Sieber and Horn that Nana and Geronimo were waiting at the top of the mountains for them, at the same time telling the Mexican to follow him to another place.

It was nearly noon when Sieber and Horn reached the

top of the mountain and saw stretched before them the main Indian camp. Camp fires glowed everywhere, indicating that there must have been well over a thousand Indians in camp. A young Indian lad directed them to a place where camp was made for them. There they also were fed and advised that the council talks were scheduled for sunup the following morning.

Mejijilda, the Mexican, who had been raised by these Apaches, asked Sieber if he might take Horn and show him around the camp. It was amazing how well Horn was received by the Indians; they appeared to think very well of him.

At sunup all the women and children left the camp, leaving the area exclusively for the council talks. It was at this point that Horn first saw Geronimo.

"He was a grand looking specimen of a man," Horn later said. "He was graceful, intelligent looking, and had eyes that pierced right through you."

Geronimo addressed Sieber and asked him what he had come to his camp for and who his interpreter was to be.

Pointing to young Horn, Al Sieber indicated that Tom would act in that capacity. Although Sieber was capable of acting as his own interpreter, he suggested Horn do so in order that there might be no misunderstanding in the contents of the upcoming conversations.

Geronimo began his talk with a tirade against many who had wronged him, and then said that he wanted to return to live on the reservation, but feared reprisals from the Indian agents and the soldiers. He talked for several hours, not being interrupted by Sieber or anyone else in all that time. The records indicate that Tom Horn related the following message to Geronimo as stated by Sieber.

"You have asked everything that I cannot give you, except to have these mountains moved up into the American country for you to live in, and I will give you until sundown to talk to your people and see if you don't want these mountains moved up there to live in. If you are entitled, by your former conduct, to what you have asked for, then you should have these mountains too." With that Sieber turned and left the meeting.

Geronimo rose and spoke, "We will meet here again at

sundown."

Tom Horn spent the day visiting various places in the Indian camp, making friends at every turn. His presents of beads and other trinkets endeared him to the hearts of the Indians as a whole. Sieber spent his day at their camp, working on what he would tell Geronomo that evening.

A fire of tremendous size marked the evening meeting place, and it was surrounded by hundreds of warriors dressed in various attire.

Al Sieber stepped into the center of the gathering, looked around carefully, then began his speech of record.

"This morning you asked for many things, and you knew I could not give you many of the things you asked for. I think that you asked for the most of them because you love to talk, and not because I could or would do as you asked me. Anything I promise, you know full well you will get; for you have ever found me as I said I would be. I am not the fluent orator that you are, neither do I put in my time asking for or trying to get that which I know I can never obtain.

"Now, this I do say to you: Go to the reservation, and do as you will be advised to do by the Government, and you will get all that the Government can give you, for you have lived there and drawn your rations, as many Indians are doing now. You will also be given a blanket for each of you and other things just as you have received before. I can promise you no more, for it is spoken by my Government that you will get no more.

"Geronimo, I have no idea you will do as I say, for you do not love peace. You are a man of war and battle, else you would not be war chief of the Chiricahua tribe. You could go to the reservation and stay maybe one season, and maybe only one moon. But within this camp may be some who do really want to come up and settle down to a peaceful life. Any and all such I will take back safely, and most of your people know what you will get. Twice already have I taken you there, and twice have you become uneasy and left. Never did a complaint come to the Government that you were not fed. Never did you complain of not having clothing and blankets enough. But there would be a row between this tribe and some of the other tribes, or someone would sell you a lot of whiskey and you would all, or a great many of you, get drunk and away you would go; and until now you have not complained of not getting what the Government promised you.

"This thing cannot last. The white men are as the leaves upon the trees. There are hundreds and hundreds of white men to every Apache. It is true many of the white men cannot protect themselves from such warriors as there are here, for it is my opinion in the world there are none better. Still, all the Chiricahua and Aqua Caliente in existence, or nearly all, are within hearing of the words I am saying now, and they cannot stay on the war path and not be exterminated. Slowly, of course, but one by one you will be killed or captured, and who will replace you?

"True, you can say the Americans cannot and will not be allowed to come armed and in force into this, a Mexican country, to fight you. Such have been the conditions so far, and I know that you have no fear of the Mexican soldiers, and many a time have I heard your women say they could whip the Mexican army, and that the Mexicans were poorer than the Apaches. To that I will say that within a short time, a year or two, or maybe three, a peace talk will be held by the Mexican and American Governments, and arrangements will be made to allow American soldiers and scouts to enter these mountains in force and in pursuit of you, and then you will be doomed to capture, or will be exterminated. As I said before, the American troops are without number. I have never spoken words of advice to you in council. Never have I told you one lie, and not a warrior here now will say he thinks I talk two ways.

"Consider well what I have said to you. I leave in four days for San Carlos."

Without further comment, Sieber turned and left the council.

When Sieber and Horn were set to leave for San Carlos, some sixty Indians were ready to accompany them, among them the chiefs Nana and Loco, the latter now more than eighty years old.

When the party was about to leave, Geronimo walked up

and addressed Sieber and Horn. "I am glad to see these old people and widows leave; they will be safer and more comfortable on the reservation." Then he turned to Horn and said, "You are a young man, and young Americans will always be at war with me and mine. If you have further word from the officials of your country, come to me with them. You will not be harmed."

The Indians from Geronimo's camp were brought back to San Carlos without incident, and camped near the fork of the San Carlos and Gila Rivers. Several days later word reached the reservation that other Indians were ready to return from Mexico. Sieber was laid up from an old wound so Tom Horn was instructed to go with some troops to escort them in.

There were about fifty Indians in the group, and they were herding about 500 head of horses and mules. Horn saw through their plan they wanted to bring the stolen Mexican animals into America where they could dispose of them at a high profit. It was a ticklish situation to say the least. For months Tom Horn went back and forth from San Carlos to the Mexican line, each time bringing back a number of Indians and a much greater number of stolen stock.

V

In June of 1879 the scouts and interpreters were again dismissed due to lack of funds provided by the Government. Again, Tom and his counterparts went back to Tucson.

Horn's next job was that of providing beef for the Indians at San Carlos at a salary of $150.00 a month. It was a difficult job for Tom in trying to handle some 5,000 head of cattle, horses, and mules, with no help from the army since Major Chaffee had been relieved of his command there. The agency was under control of an Indian Agent named Tiffany. Instead of much-needed soldiers to control the agency, there was only a small force of Indian policemen under Chief Albert Stirling. Although the chief was a fearless and brave man, he could not cope with thousands of Indians with a police force fo about fifteen men.

Besides, the agent was so busy selling Indian supplies to merchants, prospectors and the like, thus making a fortune for himself, that he cared little about the Indian affairs at San Carlos. In due time, however, he was arrested and charged with selling government property to private sources, but nothing ever came of the matter.

In the spring of 1880 renegade Indians from Mexico appeared in San Carlos, intent on taking Chief Loco and his braves back with them. On the morning of May 5th, Tom Horn heard a lot of firing in the direction of the Chiricahua camp. Word came shortly thereafter that the Indians were preparing to go on the war path. Chief Stirling heard the firing at the same time Horn did, and, mounting his horse, accompanied by one Indian policeman, he rode right into the Indian camp. Just as Stirling reached the bank of the San Carlos River he was shot and killed, but his companion managed to escape.

By that time most of the people of San Carlos, including Tom Horn, had taken refuge across the Gila River on high ground, well fortified with natural rock barriers, and just above where all the action was taking place. From that vantage point Tom saw a group of the Indian policemen follow the Indians for a short distance, stopping only to seek shelter after several of the officers had been killed.

After the large number of Chiricahua had passed Horn's place of shelter, the group left and returned to the agency. Everything was in an uproar. Those people who had remained behind were dishing out rifles and ammunition to anyone who asked, many of them Indian bucks. It was thought that a general uprising was taking place, but such was not the case.

Tom Horn, realizing that it was most important that the army be advised of events, saddled up a fast horse and started for Camp Thomas, some thirty miles distant. Crossing the swollen Gila River at San Carlos, Tom raced toward Camp Thomas, reaching it just as the two troops of cavalry there were getting ready. The commandant had learned from Indian signals that something was wrong at San Carlos, but exact details were lacking, since (contrary to common belief by the whites and shown in movies) such information cannot be given by signals.

Al Sieber was there, and he made arrangements for the soldiers to advance toward Ash Creek. There Al and Tom swam the river, proceeding to Ash Flats, about ten miles from Camp Thomas. Tom was stunned as he observed the long line of Indians marching toward the Mexican border.

"Great Scott! I've never seen so many hostiles in my life in one spot."

"You'll probably never again see such a sight," said Al.

"They're cagey, too," Al continued, "they'll break up into small groups and then regroup for the crossing into Mexico."

Just then Horn pointed toward six Indian bucks riding in their direction.

"They are side guards," muttered Sieber. "Just do nothing and they'll probably pass us by."

Apparently the braves wanted to use the high elevation as a lookout point, but on seeing the two white men, turned and rode back toward the main body of Indians. Al and Tom immediately high-tailed it to where the troops were, about 45 men, and informed the officer in charge, Lieut. Charles B. Gatewood, what conditions were.

"We'll attack them and give them a good fight," declared Gatewood. "We may not have numbers enough to do too much good, but we'll give them a good scare."

Al Sieber looked stunned . . . what a stupid decision to make. But the lieutenant was firm in his foolish decision. For his trouble six soldiers were killed the next morning when the little group of soldiers attacked a far superior force of hostiles. Gatewood himself was shot in the shoulder, but he refused to return to Camp Thomas with several other wounded soldiers.

"Gatewood," said Sieber, "These warriors can outfight your men any day of the week; it's suicide to try another dumb stunt like the last one."

Instead of further combat with the hostiles, Lieut. Gatewood and his men rounded up several hundred head of horses abandoned by the Indians, then striking out from Eagle Creek for Fort Thomas. Horn, Sieber, and another scout named Free, continued to trail the Indians as they realized more troops from Fort Bayard, Bliss, and other points, would hasten to the affected area.

The three scouts followed the Indians all day until they reached the Blue River. They switched their trail and headed for Clifton, where they learned that most of the settlers had come into the various towns to escape the Indians. Sieber also learned that soldiers were camped at Ash Springs, so Sieber ordered Horn to ride there and tell the soldiers to ride to Cottonwood and Indian Springs.

On reaching Ash Springs, Horn found the troops in a wornout condition. The following morning Horn noticed Indians approaching the spot where they were watering their mounts. No doubt the Indians wanted control of the waterhole for the time being. Horn heard the warriors as they deployed their braves, advising them to attack and wipe out the soldiers. He informed the office in charge, stating it would be suicide to remain there. The lieutenant did not know what to do, so Horn suggested they follow the Indians, hopefully they would run into Sieber with more soldiers.

Horn and the soldiers followed the Indians until they turned into the Stein Mountains, from which point it was clear sailing to the Mexican line. At that point they heard intense firing coming from the east side of the mountains. The besieged group turned out to be Al Sieber and several groups of soldiers who also had been on the trail of the Indians. On reaching the crest of a high mountain, Horn and his men could see the soldiers fighting other groups of Indians who had branched off from the main column.

At full speed they raced their mounts toward the besieged soldiers. It was sundown when they dashed into Sieber's camp. About midnight Sieber awoke Horn and told him he was ready to follow the Indians.

"What are you talking about, Al? We cannot do anything against that bunch, alone, or with this bunch of bedraggled soldiers we have on our hands."

"Dammit, I'm past fifty years old, half-crippled and heaven knows what else. You and Free comin' or not? If not, I'll go it alone."

It was no use . . . Al won his point. Horn, Free, and

Sieber rode all that night until reaching San Simon Valley, where they found they were only a few miles behind the Indians. The Indians went into camp on Turkey Creek, remaining there all day. At 11 AM the following morning the dust of the troops could be seen in the distance beyond San Simon Valley, at least thirty miles away.

Late that same evening the troops pulled in and made camp a few miles below that of the Indians. The hostiles were swarming the hills about the soldiers in such a manner as to make believe they were going to attack.

"Don't let that fool you," said Sieber. "That's just a diversion. They're breaking camp and pulling out at this very moment."

Sieber, Horn, Free, and the soldiers continued to follow the Indians, and daylight found them near Cloverdale, just south of the Mexican border. There the Indians also camped. There was nothing Sieber and his men could do but watch what was going on.

Late in the afternoon the Indians began to cross into Mexico. Some went through San Luis Pass; some through Aqua Blanco, all with one purpose in mind . . . heading straight for the Mexican Sierra Madre Mountains.

Disgusted, Al Sieber turned and led his men back to Cloverdale. There he met Major Tupper, an old Civil War veteran, with about fifty men. He was anxious to tangle with the fleeing Indians.

"By golly, old Tup ain't afraid to go right into Mexico after them varmints," declared one of the troopers.

Al Sieber raised an eyebrow. "That so, Major?"

Major Tupper pulled Sieber aside for a discussion. Some time later the major returned and cried, "Mount up, men, we're going to Mexico!"

It was early morning when Tom ventured a question at Al.

"Does Tupper think he can whip hundreds of Apaches with less than a hundred men, including our scouts?"

Sieber grinned. "Well, Tom, he's itching for the chance, so we should do all we can to help him scratch a little."

VI

Once in the rough high country of Mexico, Sieber seemed to be running the show. He cautioned his Apache scouts to make certain the soldiers were hidden all the time and noise kept at a minimum.

"If they surprise us, instead of us surprising them, we're all goners for certain," he warned.

Sieber borrowed an old telescope from Major Tupper, and, taking Horn with him, ascended a point in the mountain range, from which they could keep watch on a spring on the west side of the mountain.

"I calculate them redskins will head for there," said Al. "They don't think we'd dare to cross the Mexican line, so maybe we can surprise 'em and lick 'em."

About noon Tom Horn looked through the scope and said, "I'll be damned! There they are, peaceful and content, as if they had no worries at all."

Sieber gave instructions to have Major Tupper and his men report to the point where they now were with the telescope. This accomplished, Sieber told the major he was going to check the Indian camp, alone. On his return he stated he did not feel that the Indians would break camp that night so he planned the attack for daylight.

Sieber assigned nine troopers to Horn, and just at daylight five Indians came toward the waiting soldiers. The fight was on! These five braves were killed before they could gather their wits about them, so great was their surprise up on seeing the soldiers. Horn did not get into the fight to any extent, later stating that if more than the five Indians were killed, they never knew of it. One soldier had been slain. The bedlam caused by milling animals, barking dogs, yelling women and children, plus the firing of rifles and revolvers led the Indians to believe that a much larger force of soldiers was waiting in the wings to out flank them if they gave a frontal attack on Sieber's party. Lucky for the whites that they di think that . . . otherwise Sieber and his whole group would have been exterminated.

The next morning Sieber and his men were joined by the troops of Lt. Col. George A. Forsyth, who had found the Indians in Horse Shoe Canyon, only to have them escape across the Mexican border, joining forces with those Sieber had been trailing. With the compliment of Col. Forsyth's five troops, added to his own group, Sieber felt they now had a striking force that could cope with the Apaches.

As Fate would decree, another helping hand entered the picture. For many years the Apaches had laughed in the faces of the Mexicans. The redskins occupied the mountains of northern Mexico with no molestation whatever. But at this particular time, things proved to be different. Colonel Gorenzo Garcia, of the 6th Mexican Infantry, with nearly three hundred men, learned that the Chiricahuas under Chato and Nachite had crossed the Mexican border to raid in Arizona. His plans were to ambush the Indians after they had entered Mexican territory.

Late in April Garcia's scouts near the Janos Plain, informed him that a very large party of fast-traveling Apaches was coming up the Carretas Canon from the north. Garcia correctly assumed these were marauding Indians returning to Mexico.

Colonel Garcia laid an ambush which took the Indians completely by surprise. He felt that his group would be a match for the strength of the Indians. On came the Indians, women and children at the front, warriors to the rear, watching the dust clouds made by Forsyth, Sieber and their men.

Garcia gave the signal to fire, and the following roar of gunfire must have sounded like the Battle of Gettysburg to Col. Forsyth and company. The Mexican volley hit the Apache column full force, dropping Indian after Indian . . . women, children, old people, and some bucks. A thick cluster of bodies showed where the lethal bullets had done their deadly work.

When the smoke cleared, close to two hundred Indians had been killed, many of them non-combatants. The real killers, Loco, Chato, and Nachite, had escaped into the wilds of the Mexican underbrush, never to be heard from again. Colonel Garcia had lost 22 men dead; fifteen wounded. It had been a crushing blow to the Apaches.

Colonel Forsyth and his men, anxious to learn what had

happened, reached the spot in several hours. Colonel Garcia seemed puzzled at first up on seeing American troops on Mexican soil. Since Garcia could speak no English, Tom Horn acted as interpreter for him.

"I am Colonel Lorenzo, 6th Mexican Infantry. Who are you, and what are you doing in Mexico?"

After explanations were given, Garcia told Forsyth that he would have to accompany him to El Valle, the head of his district and remain there with his men until Mexico and the United States had settled the question of the "invasion of Mexico by United States Troops."

Colonel Forsyth's reply in the record read like this: "I know I am violating an international agreement and I knew what I was doing when I came in here, and I know what I am going to do now. I am going to mount my command and go back as I came down here, and that was without order or command. I will not submit to go anywhere with you and your command. I will now bid you good day."

The soldiers left Mexico without further incident, Sieber, Horn, and Free going to San Carlos.

Tom Horn never forgot his dead friend, Chief Pedro, whose advice was always good, and before going to Fort Apache with Sieber and Free, he paid his friend a long visit.

At Fort Apache Sieber was taken into the commandant's office, where he held a private conversation with that officer. He told Horn and Free later that he had been ordered to take them and a detachment of troopers to Canyon Creek to arrest five dissident braves who were causing all kinds of trouble.

"Tom, Dandy Jim and Dead Shot, scouts whom you know, will accompany us to point out the men we are to place in the guard house," Al Sieber told his companion.

"Free, you will have to keep an eye on Dead Shot and you, Tom, will have to watch Dandy Jim. Both men are mean and treacherous. I think we are walking into a well-baited trap because the Indians do not want us to interfere with their activities." Sieber continued, "You will have to be alert all the time since I will be with the soldiers most of the time."

Dead Shot had tried to convince the adjutant that several soldiers would be plenty as the five men they wanted were not really bad. Fortunately for the party, the officer insisted that fifty men accompany Sieber and his small group.

At Canyon Creek Captain E. C. Hentig, 6th Calalry, whom General E. A. Carr had placed in command of the expedition, found a number of Indians, but they caused no trouble. Sieber suggested they make camp on that spot for the night. During the night a young Indian girl, daughter of Suneriano, crawled into Horn's blanket and whispered that they were headed for a trap; that there were over sixty warriors waiting for them in the hills. The girl then slid away as quietly as she had come.

In the morning Horn imparted this information to Al Sieber, who immediately suggested to Captain Hentig that they return to the fort.

"If you and your men are afraid, leave now," said the captain, "we can handle this matter. I know where one of the troublemakers is, and I want him. He is Nok-e-da-klinne, the medicine man."

"We are not afraid, captain," said Al, "but we don't want to have to bury all your soldiers on the slope."

Dead Shot and Dandy Jim knew they would now be watched constantly by Horn and Sieber so they wanted the soldiers to go down the canyon, but Sieber swung up the side of the canyon, later arresting the medicine man at his hut.

The entire command marched about five miles back toward Fort Apache and camped. Suddenly scores of Apaches from Nok-e-da-klinne's camp appeared on the scene, ready to spring the trap. Then the firing began increasing, and to make matters worse, the Indian scouts turned against Captain Hentig. Captain Hentig and Privates Bird, Sullivan, Miller, Livingston, Amick, and Sondergrass were killed by the first volley.

Dead Shot and Dandy Jim made an effort to release the medicine man, but a soldier named Ahrens fired three shots into Nok-e-da-klinne's head. But he was not dead. Late that night Sergeant John A. Smith saw the old Indian, more dead than alive, crawling toward a place of safety. Not wanting to create alarm by firing a shot at Nok-e-da-klinne, the sergeant picked up an ax and cut off the Indian's head.

Later on March 3, 1882, Dead Shot and Dandy Jim were hanged at Camp Grant for their part in the mutiny of the army scouts. Two others were sent to Alcatraz Island.

The fanatic Apaches became so frustrated in not killing Sieber, Horn, Free, and more of the soldiers that they fired upon Fort Apache before Lieut. W. H. Carter, who succeeded Captain Hentig in command, was able to make his report to General Carr. This meant an all out Indian war, and messages telling of the event were sent to Forts Thomas, Grant, McDowell, and Verde.

As soon as the attacking Indians left the area of Fort Apache, Tom Horn was sent to Chief Pedro's camp for advice and aid. He returned with sixty well-armed fighting braves, the cream of the crop, so to speak.

"Tom Horn," said General Carr, "take your men and find these renegades; destroy them or send me word and I'll come with my men to assist you if the task is too great for your small force."

It was easy for Horn to determine that the sixty braves were headed toward Green Valley, so he sent word to Fort Apache for Carr to follow. In the wake of their path the Apaches left death and destruction. One night a large party of men were heard approaching the camp.

"It must be cavalry," said Tom. "I can tell by the sound of the horses' feet."

The group proved to be Major Chaffee, Al Sieber, and Pat Kehoe. Horn was glad to see them, and told Chaffee that he intended to strike the Indians the following day. Sieber agreed.

At 10:00 o'clock the next morning, July 17, 1882, the group reached the Meadows' Ranch. They found Meadows dead and two of his sons badly wounded. Several troopers were left to attend the Meadows family as Chaffee and his command raced toward Crook's Springs. There before them was a canyon known as Chevelon's Fork of the Canyon Diablo, which cut its way through the Mogollons, seven hundred yards wide at the top, dropping away fully a thousand feet deep, its steep sides actually overhung in places, with pine trees growing wherever they could gain a foothold.

There Nan-tia-tish prepared his ambush. Marksmen awaited along the side of the canyon in such a way that when the soldiers descended into it, as they would if they followed the trail left for that purpose by the Indians, they would be caught in a trap.

Al Sieber suggested that Chaffee send five men with Pat Kehoe to go below; Tom Horn among them. As the men came to the banks of the canyon the Indians were just starting up the other side. On the opposite side of the canyon, the trail would have to turn on a wide bench for some distance to find an opening in the bench to allow the Indians to pass through. The distance was about six hundred yards, a good distance for shooting.

It took the Indians an hour or more to reach this particular spot on the trail — it was the only way they could now get out of the canyon. Not one horse got over the trail, however, for the lead horse was shot and killed, blocking the narrow trail. The Indians tried frantically to remove the dead animal, but could not. At the same time a rifle duel was in progress between the troops and the Apaches across the gorge.

The Indians were so busy shooting at Captain George Converse's men across the gulch that they did not observe two flanking detachments easing in on them. Lieut. Frank West had discovered a steep pathway by which his men descended to the bottom of the canyon and then climb the other side. Captain Abbott, meanwhile, detoured around the rim of the canyon, engaging the surprised Apaches at the same time Lieut. West did.

About 4:00 o'clock that afternoon a violent hailstorm burst upon the scene, sending cold rain and hailstones enough to drive any man to shelter. After the storm all signs of the Indians had disappeared.

The following morning a wounded squaw came into camp and told Chaffee that there had been fifty-four warriors in the fighting force. Tom Horn and Al Sieber searched the battlefield and found twenty-one dead Indians, including the would-be chief Nan-ta-tish. One report stated that several wounded bucks lay in the brush and were disposed of by the scout named Free.

Nothing further was ever learned of the Indians who had escaped the fight at Chevelon's Fork. Major Chaffee returned to Fort Verde and Tom Horn went back to Fort Apache, where he disbanded his scouts. At the fort the commanding officer asked Horn to bring in the four Indians who had been wanted at the time of Hentig's death. Horn sent a message to Jon Dazen on Canyon Creek, telling him that if the four badmen were not surrendered to him, he would go to Chief Pedro for warriors to force him to give up the men.

Of course, Danzen did not want that so he brought the four men into Fort Apache for trial. This end had been arranged for by Chief Pedro, as Horn later learned.

Al Sieber retired to San Carlos for the winter, while Horn remained to look after matters on the reservation. During the winter Tom received a letter from General Wilcox, Department Commander, stating he was submitting Tom's name to have a medal presented to him for bravery on the field and for his strategy against the Indians. When asked about the medal later on, Tom grinned, "That was the last I ever heard of it. I don't believe I even got the letter anymore."

VII

Just before Christmas a delegation of Army officers came to see Al Sieber and Tom Horn in regard to their participation in the raid into Mexico. Several of the officers were identified as Mexicans, one being the famous Colonel Emilio Kosterlitsky, known as the Mexican Cossack, feared and revered throughout Mexico. Although many questions were posed to Sieber and Horn, nothing ever came of the investigation, and it was soon forgotten by all concerned.

Early the next year Horn received complaints from Indians around San Carlos that Mexicans were stealing their horses, and they wanted him to do something about it. Horn contacted the chiefs at the reservation, learning that Mexican rustlers were indeed stealing the best Indian ponies in the lot, heading them on all occasions toward Turkey Creek.

About the middle of February word came that the

Mexicans had struck again. Horn summoned several men and went in pursuit, concluding the outlaws would emerge from the canyon close to Turkey Creek. At the top of the mountains was a place called Turkey Springs, and the rustlers would have an easy trail from that point, if they made it. Horn and his men took a cutoff route and arrived at the springs before the Mexicans. There were four of them. When ordered to surrender, they chose to fight, and all were killed.

Horn's companions, all Indians, refused to bury the dead outlaws, stating their bodies would be a grim warning to all other Mexicans who had the idea of stealing Indian ponies. Tom shrugged. At the same time a group of cavalry soldiers, escorting an army vehicle, drove by on the government road. The occupant of the vehicle was General Wilcox, making his rounds of the government posts with the department inspector.

"Good morning, General Wilcox. I suppose you remember me, Scout Tom Horn?"

"Yes, yes, but what is the meaning of these dead men?"

Horn tried to explain the situation but to no avail. The general told him it was no wonder such actions occurred when they were apparently sponsored by such men as Horn himself.

One word led to another, until Tom was so mad that he told the general in no gentle words what he thought about the whole thing.

Taken back, General Wilcox sputtered, "I ought to arrest you and throw you in the guardhouse."

Anyway, it all worked out all right, for the general soon forgot about the matter, but Al Sieber got a real boot out of the whole affair.

"Dammit, Tom, you take the cake; they want to give you a medal one day; then throw you in the pokey the next."

Things were idle for Tom and Sieber for a time, until news came that some Apache bucks had made raids into Arizona from Mexico, killing several families and driving off a lot of horses. The two scouts were ordered to report at Fort Bowie as quickly as they could.

Orders came down from General George Crook that Al Sieber and Tom Horn were to remain at Fort Bowie, since his

Tom Horn as he appeared without a moustache.
Union Pacific Railroad Museum

Tom Horn.

Tom Horn's father.

Tom Horn's mother.

John C. Coble, a friend of Tom Horn's.

Gen. George Crook.

Sheriff Perry Owens under whom Tom Horn served as a deputy.
Arizona Historical Society

Famous council meeting between Geronimo and Gen. George Crook in Canyon de los Embudos, Sonora, March 27, 1886. Geronimo is seated with scarf on head to left. Gen. Crook is bearded man seated second from right with hat facing Geronimo.
War Department

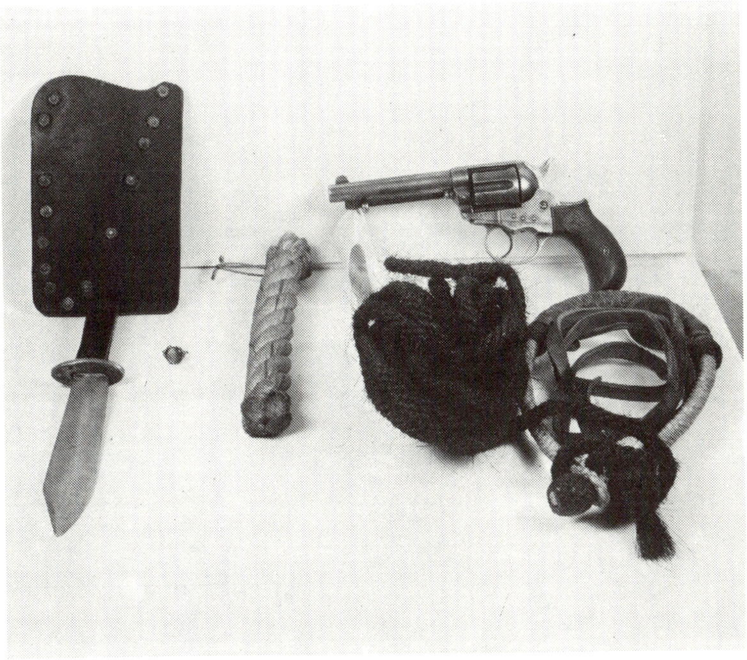

Tom Horn's quirt, rope, revolver and knife.
Union Pacific Railroad Museum

Tom Horn's grave marker in Columbia Cemetery, Boulder, Colorado.
Boulder Daily Camera Library

3rd Cavalry was coming into Arizona Territory and the 6th Cavalry was moving on to New Mexico. Nothing of any significance occurred during that winter, but early in spring a number of Indians crossed over into the United States at Dog Springs, raiding within a few miles of Deming, New Mexico.

Sieber and Horn again got into trouble when they crossed into Mexico, killed an Indian at Hot Springs, and captured a squaw whom they held prisoner. The scouts told the authorities they had captured the woman in the United States, but her story and the finding of the dead Indian at Hot Springs disproved that.

Horn and Sieber were ordered to report to Fort Bowie to be investigated. Al was madder than a wet hen; Horn just laughed about it. The adjutant of the post ordered the two scouts to be brought before him.

"Gentlemen," he said, "the officers who are making this investigation have found that you, Al Sieber, Chief of Scouts, and you, Tom Horn, scout and interpreter for the Department of War of these United States, did, as an armed body of men, cross this so-called international line between the United States and the Republic of Mexico, and that you did this without the order or sanction of the military commander of this district, of which Fort Bowie is headquarters. The order of the commission that made this investigation is, that you be censured for the violation. Now that this is over, let's have a drink."

After that, Sieber and Horn were ordered to report to San Carlos, where General Crook stated he was going to reorganize the entire department. When General Crook arrived he was followed by large crowds of Indians, all eager to hear his plans. Crook set out his plans patiently and skillfully, consulting with such leaders as Cha-lipun, Eskimo-tzin, Santos, Chiquito, Huan-klishe, and others of importance. After a week of long talks, General Crook returned to Fort Whipple, while Sieber and Horn were ordered to return to Fort Bowie.

The records indicate that on October 5, 1882, General Crook issued his general orders regarding his policy toward the Indians . . . it read as follows:

The commanding general, after making a thorough and

exhaustive examination among the Indians . . . regrets to say that he finds among them a general feeling of distrust and want of confidence in the whites, especially the soldiery; and also that much dissatisfaction, dangerous to the peace of the country, exists among them. Officers and soldiers . . . are reminded that one of the fundamental principles of the military character is justice to all . . . Indians as well as white men . . . and that a disregard of this principle is likely to bring about hostilities, and cause the deaths of the very persons they are here to protect. In all their dealings with the Indians, officers must be careful not only to observe the strictest fidelity, but to make no promises not in their power to carry out; all grievances arising in their jurisdiction should be redressed, so that an accumulation of them may not cause an outbreak.

He accomplished another important matter prior to this by encouraging cooperation of the American and Mexican Governments to work together for a common cause against the Indian marauders. So, on July 29, 1882, a treaty was signed between both countries, permitting soldiers of either to cross the borders of the other in pursuit of hostiles.

VIII

Early in 1883 a Chiricahua courier from Mexico came to San Carlos asking for a talk with General Crook. A wire was sent to Crook at Fort Whipple, and he, in turn, wired Al Sieber at Fort Bowie to report at San Carlos within the week. Tom Horn and Sieber later took this warrior to General Crook's camp for a pow-wow. In essence, this is what the Indian said, "My talk is from Geronimo alone . . . he wishes to return to the United States and to the reservation. He wants Crook and a big army to come to Mexico to escort him and his people back. He knows your soldiers now can come into Mexico."

General Crook wired Washington as to the nature of the developments, receiving an immediate reply to report at the capitol city at once. Pee-Chee, the Indian courier, was turned loose after being told he would be contracted again when

General Crook returned from Washington.

"Tell Geronimo I will give him my answer on my return," said Crook. "We'll have Tom Horn meet you in two moons at a place in Mexican San Luis Mountains."

On his return from Washington, General Crook summoned Al Sieber and Tom Horn to Fort Bowie. Horn was instructed to meet Pee-Chee and bring him to the conference table, and this was done.

"Go tell Geronomo that I will gather a large outfit to escort all the Indians from Mexico who want to come to the reservation. We will meet him at Rio Viejo in the Sierra Madres. I would like to talk with all the Chiricahuas."

Pee-Chee was again taken by Horn to the Mexican border, being advised to carry the general's message to Geronimo as quickly as possible.

General Crook supervised the proceedings at the fort as things were made ready for the trip into Mexico. Rations for two months were ordered, and the cavalry compliment consisted of three troops of seasoned men. Five pack trains and some fifty Apache scouts also accompanied the column.

General Crook and his men crossed the Sierra Madre to Yaqui River; then by way of Bavispe and Nacori, they crossed over to Rio Viejo. There they met Pee-Chee, as agreed, and he stated it would take another five days to reach the Indian camp.

In due time the camp of the hostiles was reached. There the soldiers camped in as beautiful a spot as one could ever see, Horn later stated. The talks were to commence the following day.

Geronomo did not like the idea that Mexicans named Antonio Dias and Jose Montoyo had been chosen to interpret the talks. Geronimo stated he wanted a man they could trust, not the two mentioned. The old chief was adamant in his stand, stating that Sieber had trained Tom Horn long and well, and that the Indians trusted him. He would listen to no other interpreter than Tom Horn. Thus it happened that the youthful Tom sat in as official interpreter for the talks between General Crook and Geronimo.

There were talks for days on end. The Americans

charged that the Apache had killed and robbed Americans and laid waste to the land; Geronimo counter-attacked by agreeing with the charges and arguing that the whites were driving the Indians to what they were doing. Finally, with some influence thrown in by Al Sieber and Tom Horn, Geronimo agreed to take his people to the reservation; at least, all those who wanted to go.

The surrendering Indians were camped at Fort Bowie for some time, causing no trouble, but in the fall Geronimo wanted his people moved to Turkey Creek, near Fort Apache, and the Government complied with his washes.

At this time, Sieber became ill as a result of his old wounds, and was placed in the army hospital. He sent for Horn, telling him that he had made arrangements for him to become Chief of Scouts. Al Sieber had gone on his last scouting trip.

Chief of Scouts Tom Horn had Christmas dinner with Captains Crawford and Gatewood at the Chiricahua camp, and it was about that time that Horn also inaugurated a system of counting the Indians each day so some of them could not slip away. Of course, Geronimo did not like this setup and told Horn so. However, the matter was settled.

Horn's next move was to check the Mexican border for crossing renegades. He rode into Mexico to see what he could find, leaving his scouts scattered in small units to do likewise on the Arizona side of the border. Horn learned through the Indian signals that they planned to cross over into Arizona in several days. He raced his mount and the next day rode into the yard of John Slaughter, on the San Bernardino River, where he obtained a fresh mount. Slaughter was later to become the famous sheriff of Cochise County.

At day light the next morning Horn met his scouts at Tex Spring, where he informed them of the impending trouble. About the same time Lieut. Wilder with twenty troopers rode into camp, sent by General Crook to assist Horn along the border.

The following morning Horn and his men, accompanied by the soldiers, started for the Chiricahua Mountains to pick a spot where they could command a view of the Mexican border for miles distant. Tom's group was later joined by several cowboys from the Slaughter ranch.

Tom and Lieut. Wilder figured all the next day as to which way the Indians would come.

"Well, I figure they'll come from the Pillares and then by way of the Wild Bull Hills; then they'll probably make for the southern point of the mountains," said Horn.

However, the Indians did neither that nor come by way of Dry Gulch, as some others had thought; they kept on the ground at the foot of the mountains in the open.

Horn deployed his men. Lieut. Wilder and his troops were to strike the Indians at the rear, while the cowboys, led by Free, would strike from the front. Horn kept his scouts with him. Struck from three sides, the renegades were demoralized. The fight lasted for about five minutes, and when it was over, not one of the renegade Indians was alive . . . twelve lay dead on the ground. The horses which had been with the Indians were turned over to Slaughter's men, to be used as best he saw fit.

Five days after the fight Horn and his scouts reached Fort Bowie. There he met Major John Burke, a member of General Crook's staff, who commended Tom for a job well done.

Several days later Horn visited Geronimo at his camp.

"Your people have been misbehaving and causing heaps of trouble," Tom told the Apache. "Are they not satisfied here? Are you satisfied, Geronimo?"

"No," replied the chief, "my people want to return to Mexico, as do I."

"If you do this General Crook will follow with a large army of soldiers and wipe out your entire people. I know you hate peace and never favored coming onto the reservation; why you did it is beyond me."

That ended the conversation. Tom went to San Carlos and told Sieber of his talk with Geronimo.

"I'm afraid that means a bitter war, Tom. That old wily Geronimo was only stalling for time by coming here. That gave his braves time enough to build up a reserve of horses and whatever else they need for an all-out attack on the whites. We'd best see Burke at Fort Bowie and discuss this matter."

Major Burke informed them that General Crook was in

Washington and would be delayed some time. About all that Horn and his scouts could do was to continue their search for hostiles until orders came through. He later learned that all the Indians were to meet near Sonora, Mexico, near a mountain called El Duranillo.

Horn immediately made tracks for Fort Bowie, where he notified Major Burke of the present conditions, and sent a wire to Colonel Louis E. Torres, the Mexican Governor at Sonora.

General Crook did not arrive for two months, but when he did, he was prepared for war. He ordered Horn and Sieber to San Carlos to enlist Apache scouts to go into Mexico. Over a hundred scouts were enlisted for a six months' tour of duty. After Crook had made all the necessary preparations, the group started out for Mexico . . . it was June.

It was decided to have the army headquarters at Nacori, with Tom Horn given the task of setting up a line of heliograph stations so that word could reach Fort Bowie in a short time as to what was taking place in Mexico. Most of the summer of 1885 was spent in preparing for the upcoming campaign against the Apaches. Camps and soldier outposts had to be established, the heliograph system completed, as well as posting guards at all water holes.

One day a message flashed to their camp that Horn was to report to Fort Bowie. This he did and met General Crook, who introduced him to Captain Emmett Crawford and Lieutenants Marion P. Maus and W. E. Shipp. These officers were in charge of a battalion of Apache scouts who were going into Mexico with them.

On November 11th the group left Fort Bowie, arriving a few days later at Fronteras, Mexico. Tom missed Al Sieber, who was unable to go along because of his illness.

To taunt the soldiers somewhat Ulzana slipped across the lines early in November, avoiding the water holes as he knew they were well guarded. With ten warriors he raced into Arizona, creating havoc wherever he went. On November 24th, he and his men killed William Waldo and William Harrison on Turkey Creek. On November 26th his little band surprised the friendly White Mountain Apache Village, killing fifteen of them and losing only one of his own braves.

Ulzana then decided to return to Mexico and took a route toward the Gila River, killing several more men near Solomnville on the way. This band is the same one which Horn had been notified to be on the alert for their return. The usual route back into Mexico was the valley which lay between the Dragoon and the Whetstone Mountains, and naturally Horn figured the renegades would use that route.

Ulzana laughed at the planned ambushes, swinging east and riding up the Gila Valley, entering New Mexico. He seemed not to fear the pursuit of the soldiers, stopping long enough to kill several more ranchers. Once again Ulzana escaped, his small following scattering like so many leaves in the wind, leaving no trace whatsoever. It was an amazing feat . . . in four weeks Ulzana and his ten braves traveled some twelve hundred miles or more through enemy country, killing at least thirty-persons, and capturing hundreds of horses.

Horn and his men had headed for Car-Cai, Mexico, in hopes of ambushing Ulzana there. Across the Haros River Horn struck more signs of Indians, but found nothing but a lot of cattle at a place where the Indians apparently had camped.

Horn and the troops camped all night, breaking the command into four groups in the morning. Horn would take the east side of the mountains and Lieut. Shipp the west side. Lieut. Maus was placed to cover the south side, while Captain Crawford patrolled the north side.

The still, dark canyon echoed to the rifle fire as the battle began, the Indians having been forewarned by their barking dogs. Geronimo was yelling for the women and children to run to the river. Lieut. Shipp lay in wait as the renegades raced toward the river, and when they were about fifteen feet from them, Shipp and his men opened fire, doing terrible slaughter to the astonished Indians.

The scouts killed women, children, and old people; instructions not to do so meant nothing to them. Above the bedlam Horn heard the yell of Geronimo: "Scatter, flee, and go as you can!"

One of the prisoners was old Nana, age ninety, once a famed war chief. All he did was laugh and mutter that the braves of the day ran like rabbits instead of fighting.

That night an Indian squaw came into Horn's camp, advising him that Geronimo and Nachite wanted a conference with him and Captain Crawford. But the talks were never to be held.

At daylight Horn saw a group of Mexican rurales under Major Corredor, coming toward them. "Looks like they mean to fight us for some reason or another," warned Horn, "so be on the alert."

"My God!" cried Crawford. "They must think we are renegade Indians."

The Mexican major yelled to his men to charge, and they came at a fast pace across the little basin, straight toward Horn and his entrenched men. The Mexicans fired, wounding three of Horn's detachment.

Tom Horn ran toward the advancing Mexicans shouting to stop the shooting. The Mexican major, also eager to prevent further bloodshed, yelled to his men to cease firing.

Meanwhile, Captain Emmett Crawford had leaped upon a high rock, yelling and waving a white handkerchief. At that moment a single shot rang out, and as the report echoed from the rocks, Captain Crawford fell, killed by a glancing shot. Horn yelled to his scouts to open fire. They did so with devastating effect. Major Corredor fell, shot through the heart, while Lieut. Juan de la Cruz was riddled by thirteen bullets. One can only guess how many actually were killed or wounded since the Mexicans scooped up their comrades and fled the field.

Tom Horn tried to rescue the body of Crawford from in front of a pile of boulders, but the Mexicans kept firing at him. Tom then realized that he, too, had been wounded . . . in the arm. Finally Tom was able to drag Crawford to the shelter of some rocks, not knowing that the brave captain was already dead. It was January 11, 1886.

Captain Lawton asked Horn if there was anything he could do. "Yes, I can go into Geronimo's camp and speak with him alone, and I'll have it no other way."

"But General Miles does not trust you," objected Lawton.

"I'll go alone or not at all."

About that time an old squaw came into view, telling Lawton that Geronimo wanted to speak to Tom Horn, and that he wanted the soldiers to stop chasing him until he saw Horn.

Captain Lawton refused to act until he heard from General Miles. The next day word came from the General that Horn and Gatewood should talk to the Apache chief.

"I still cannot go until I have some word to give to Geronimo," said Tom Horn.

"Tell him what you want," said Lawton. "Just get him to agree to meet with General Miles."

"No! I cannot tell him a lie for he'd kill me as soon as he learned of it. I will not go until Miles allows me to fix a date that he will meet Geronimo."

General Miles agreed.

Gatewood wanted to accompany Horn, and was given permission by Lawton, Horn also agreeing there would be no danger in it.

Geronimo met Horn and Gatewood on the Bavispe River, where a long talk was held. Arrangements were made for Geronimo to go to Skeleton Canyon, in the United States, and meet General Miles in twelve days. As Gatewood was the only other white man with Horn, he returned to Captain Lawton to tell him of the arrangements that had been made. Horn was to meet Lawton and his group at the mouth of the Caballon Creek, where Horn would be with the renegades.

When Lawton saw Horn he explained that he had sent General Miles a dispatch to meet them as agreed. Horn relayed the information to Geronimo, who few into a rage.

"Did he send you the message?"

"No, he sent it to Captain Lawton."

"Then we will not talk."

Tom Horn decided to send a dispatch personally to the general as things were now getting serious. Geronimo was ready to leave. The return reply read, "See Captain Lawton. He is in command in the field. I can't do any business with a civilian."

It was dark when Horn reached Geronimo's camp, where

he was told of the message. In less than five minutes, things changed.

"We are ready to go," said Geronimo, mounting his horse. He was followed by his people, about one hundred and fifty in number.

Horn rode back to Lawton's camp, several miles distant, and gave him the news, telling him that if General Miles ever agreed to handle the surrender through him, he would be available.

"Oh yes, I forgot to tell you; Geronimo and his people are gone."

Riding to John Slaughter's ranch, Horn stopped for a meal and a much-needed rest. Also camped at the ranch were a detachment of soldiers. About noon the officer in charge asked if Horn were around.

"Yes, he's asleep. He did not get here until daylight."

"Good heavens, man, wake him up' I've a message for him from General Miles.

The dispatch read, "Make any arrangements you want to for me to meet Geronimo. I will go where and when you say to meet him."

"By damn, read that, John," muttered Horn, handing the message to Slaughter. "And here I am, forty miles north and Geronimo riding south all night!"

Horn sent a message by way of the heliograph, stating that all troops should lie still; that he would track down the renegades as soon as he could do so. It took Horn over a week to catch up with Geronimo. He then sent word to General Miles to meet him in four days at Skeleton Canyon. The general was there on time!

Horn met Miles with Geronimo and Natchez. Miles had brought several interpreters with him, but Geronimo refused to do any business without Horn being the official interpreter.

"But he's not an official sworn interpreter," objected General Miles.

"That means nothing to me. To trust a man is more important. This boy and I speak the truth to each other, but you do not like him. I do not know why; you must have some reason. What is it? Sieber, the man of iron, taught him well.

My people have been fighting with Sieber for thirty years, yet he has never lied to us. You sent him word you would have nothing to do with him; I say I will not work with anyone but him."

So young Tom Horn again acted as official interpreter for the army. There is no doubt that he was highly instrumental in Geronimo's giving himself up. He could have roamed the wilds of Mexico until his dying day, but he chose to go with his people.

"I want to come in with my people. We are tired of war and running and killing; we are all tired out," said the old Chief.

Troops met the Indians at Fort Bowie, where they were placed under guard on the parade grounds. General Miles had wired for a special train of the Southern Pacific to come there as fast as possible.

There was no compassion or pity on the part of the army as the ragged Indians were loaded like cattle into the box cars. Foes and some friendly scouts alike shared the same fate. The train then pulled out, headed for an alien land to the Indian, two thousand miles away. Thus the dreaded Chiricahuas, the terror of Mexico and all the southwest, were gone, never to return to their native land.

General Miles did not keep his promise to Geronimo that all Indian families would remain together. After three years, public sentiment in favor of the Indians caused the Apaches to be removed from Florida to Alabama. Nearly seven hundred of them had gone to Florida; that number was greatly reduced by the time the transfer to Alabama occurred. Later, they were taken to Fort Sill, Oklahoma, where Geronimo died. In 1907, through the efforts of Dr. Henry Roe Cloud, a Winnebago Indian, the remaining two hundred and fifty Apaches were permitted to return to New Mexico, settling on the Mescalero reservation.

It had indeed been a vale of tears for the Indians!

X

Tom Horn returned to the reservation with his scouts,

discharged them and resigned from the service. He then returned to his mine, where he worked all winter.

In 1887 Tom Horn became involved in the "Tonto Basin War" which was a death struggle between Paul and William Daggs, sheepmen, the Graham family, the Tewksbury family, and the men of the giant Hash Knife Ranch. Tom was not a member of these factions but was a deputy sheriff under Buck O'Neill of Yavapai County, acting as the mediator for the warring factions. He also was a deputy sheriff under the famous Sheriff Commodore Perry Owens of Apache County, and later under Glenn Reynolds of Gila County, Arizona.

The Pleasant Valley War coming to an end, Tom Horn returned to his mining interests, but the work was slow and unappealing to the adventurous Horn. One night when leaving the spring which provided Tom with necessary water, he discovered a number of moccasin prints in the soft dirt. Quickly he dashed to his house, mounted another horse, and rode to the Indian Agency, some thirty miles distant.

At the agency Tom learned that the Indian police had mutinied; that a San Carlos Apache named Chief Toga had been killed by an Indian named Rip over some old disagreement of years before. The Apache Kid was the son of Toga, and he vowed revenge for the death of his father. Horn advised the young Indian against it.

Later, while Horn and Sieber were at Camp Apache, the Apache Kid, with five of his men, went to Rip's place and killed him. Captain Pierce, the agent at San Carlos, quickly returned to the agency with Sieber. Sieber told the Kid to come into the agency. This he did, accompanied by a number of his braves. In an ensuing fight to keep the Kid out of the guard house, the braves shot Sieber in the leg. They all escaped escept one, whom Sieber had killed.

When Tom Horn arrived at the agency he learned what had happened, and he was mad as a wet hen.

"Dammit, Al, that crazy Kid stole my horse to boot."

Lieutenant Johnson already was on the trail of the Apache Kid, following him up through the San Pedro country, then down the Sonoita River, where it was learned the Indians had killed several white men. In the Rincon Mountains the Apache Kid was trapped afoot, but gave a fight, in which several of his men were killed. After being captured, the Kid was carted by Lieut. Johnson back to the reservation. He was later tried for his crimes and given a long term in Leavenworth; but he was pardoned by President Cleveland after serving only a short time.

When the Apache Kid returned to the agency area he was arrested for the murder of a freighter who had been killed by the Kid and his men prior to his first arrest. For this crime he was arrested by the civil authorities of Gila County, Arizona. Among the arresting officers was Deputy Sheriff Tom Horn.

On July 4, 1888, Horn won the prize at Globe, Arizona, for tying down a steer, and there was a friendly rivalry among the cowboys of the Territory as to who was the best one at that trade. Charlie Meadows made a big brag that he could beat Tom at the tying contest to be held at the Territorial Fair in Phoenix. Tom's friends urged him to take the dare, even though Horn knew he would have to miss the trial of the Apache Kid, at which he was supposed to act as interpreter.

"I'll do it!" declared Horn. "They can get some other man to be interpreter."

The trial took place, with six Indians being convicted of the freighter's killing, and they were all sentenced to life imprisonment at the "Hell Hole" Territorial Prison at Yuma. Deputy Holmes and Sheriff Reynolds were to escort the prisoners to Yuma, together with a Mexican horse thief, who had also been sentenced to life. The Indians were coupled together in two groups of three each. The Mexican was handcuffed and placed in the stagecoach.

The stage road from Globe to Casa Grande crossed the Gila River at a steep grade, unable to be negotiated by the horses due to the number of occupants in the vehicle. The Mexican was left inside the stage, while Holmes and Reynolds alighted with the six Indians, each officer in charge of one group, who walked behind the coach.

PROCLAMATION OF REWARD

Office of the Governor
Executive Department

To all to whom these presents may come, Greetings:

It having come to my knowledge, that on the morning of November second, that Glenn Reynolds, Sheriff of Gila County, and W. A. Holmes, acting as deputy, or guard to said Sheriff, while enroute from Riverside to Florence, in Pinal County, and while traveling along the highway, and in the line of duty as such Sheriff and guard, having in their custody several prisoners, mostly Indians, whom they were conveying to the Territorial Prison at YHuma, were overpowered by these said Indian prisoners, and that said Indians thereupon fled, and made their escape, and are now at liberty.

Now Therefore, I, Lewis Wolfley, Governor of Arizona, by virtue of the power within me vested, do hereby offer and proclaim a reward in the sum of five hundred ($500) dollars, to be paid by the Territory of Arizona, upon the conviction of one, or more, of the above mentioned Indians of the aforesaid crime, or crimes, if captured and arrested alive, or upon evidence duly authenticated, of their having been unavoidably killed, by any officer or person, lawfully attempting such capture or arreast.

In testimony whereof, I have hereunto set my hand, and caused the Great Seal of the Territory to be affixed. Done at Phoenix the Capital, this Fifth day of November, A.D. 1889.

Lewis Wolfley
By the Governor.
Nathan O. Murphy,
Secretary of the Terr.

At a turn near the top of the grade the Indians whirled and attacked their guards, killing Holmes almost instantly, then tackling Reynolds, who was trying to use his rifle. However, as the Indians had his arms pinned down, he was ineffective. The other three rushed up, killed Reynolds, and removed the shackle keys from his vest pocket.

Gene Livingston, the stage driver, curious as to what caused the shooting, peered around the corner of the coach.

Immediately he was shot, the bullet creasing his head, stunning him. He lived to tell the story later on.

The Apache Kid remained an outlaw from then on, and it was reported that he had died a few years later from consumption, although his body never was recovered.

When Tom Horn learned of the news he was greatly disturbed.

"Had I been along, I don't think that would have happened. I won the prize at the fair, but the cost for so doing was too great."

Of course, Tom's notoriety had spread a great deal by that time, and he was greeted by most everyone in the local hotels and bars. One evening he was entertaining a beautiful girl when a Mexican officer came into the room. It happened at a local dance. The Mexican acused Horn of stealing his girl, going for his gun at the same time. Horn did not move a muscle. The Mexican fired one shot and missed . . . Tom did not miss. The man dropped dead where he stood, victim of his own jealousy. There were many witnesses present who stood up for Tom, telling the authorities that it had been a clear case of self defense.

"Even so, Tom," warned the sheriff, "this Mexican comes from a prominent family, here on official business. I would suggest you leave the Territory as fast as possible . . ." Tom said he would do so within a few days.

Horn returned to his old home place for the winter, working his mine as best he could. Early in 1890 Tom sold the mine to a bunch of New York investors. It is said that he was paid $10,000 for it.

Now thirty years old, tough and seasoned, one of the best men with a gun on the frontier, Tom decided to go to work for the Pinkerton Detective Agency at their Denver office. It was there that he met Sheriff C. W. Shores of Gunnison County, the man who helped Tom make up his mind that working for the Pinkertons would be a good way to earn a living. The sheriff also was on the payroll of that agency, working on special assignments for them.

James McParland, Superintendent of the Denver office of the Pinkertons, talked with Tom in his office.

"Horn, how would you like to investigate a train robbery which occurred on the Denver & Rio Grande Road, between Texas Creek and Cotopaxi?"

"That's fine, when do I start?"

"At once, and Sheriff Shores will meet you in Salem, Oregon, in a few days."

When Shores arrived in Oregon he was surprised to find Tom Horn in jail.

"Dammit, Shores, this is a hellova place to come to. There are so many lawmen after the robbers that everybody is arresting every else for one thing or another.

"What you here for, Tom?"

"They suspect me of robbing the Palace Saloon. It's just a matter of mistaken identity, but these guys won't believe a word I say."

Although Shores did his best in trying to convince the law that there had been a mistake, Tom was arraigned on April 11th. At the trial two victims of the Saloon robbery declared they thought Tom to be one of the two masked men who had robbed them. Tom's record book of his activities with the Pinkertons in checking railroad employees who were robbing the line blind did not set too well either with the jury.

In his own defense Horn explained his duties with Generals Crook and Miles; also reporting his sale of the mine, adding that he had more money than he'd ever need, and had no reason to stage a robbery.

Even so, the jury was split in its decision, so the trial was reset for September. After months of waiting in the jail, Tom was finally acquitted when a letter from General Miles arrived, attesting to Horn's character and to his honesty.

"Well, Shores, at least we can go after the train robbers now without being accused of being one of them. I see where all the posses and lawmen have been pulled off the case."

The two lawmen finally learned that the robbers had crossed the Sangre de Cristos range, passed near the Villa Grove iron mines, and backtracked to the east side of the Sange de Cristos Mosca Pass, then through the Huerfano Canyon and down to Trinidad. Tom and Shores kept on their trail. From Clayton, New Mexico, the train robbers went to

Ochiltree, Texas, headed for the Indian Territory, then went on to Canada.

At Washita Station they located one of the robbers at the home of a man named Wolfe. This man was Burt Curtis, whom Shores took to Denver, leaving Tom to wait for the return of the other robber. After several days of waiting, Tom was just about to depart, when the other outlaw came riding toward the house. He was Peg Leg Watson, wanted by nearly every law enforcement officer in Colorado. Tom met Watson at the door, gun in hand, and the surprised outlaw offered no resistance.

"Watson, who else was in on the robbery with you?" asked Tom of the prisoner. "We have reason to believe it was Joe McCoy. It appears he has left his home in Cotopaxi and no one knows where to."

But Peg Leg Watson refused to talk. Watson well knew that Joe McCoy had robbed the train to obtain money to assist in the defense of his father, who was held for murder in Fremont County, Colorado. Joe had also been arrested for this crime, but had managed to escape.

Horn delivered his prisoner to Denver, and was assigned to aid Sheriff Stewart of Fremont County, in an effort to capture Joe McCoy. From Rifle, Colorado, the sheriff and Horn went on to Meeker, where they learned that a man answering McCoy's description had left for Ashley, Utah, several days before. Many people were going there for the Christmas festivities.

Sheriff Stewart, Tom Horn, and Deputy Sheriff Sam Wear arrived at Ashley in the middle of the night, and could not locate their man. Next morning Horn learned where McCoy went for his meals so he walked into the eating room of the rooming-house and arrested McCoy with no trouble at all. Horn herded the man outside, disarmed him, and asked his companions if they were ready to return to Colorado.

The three lawmen took their prisoner by way of Fort Duchesne, Utah, and caught the D. & R. G. train at Price Station.

Peg Leg Watson and Burt Curtis were convicted of robbing the United States mails, and were sentenced to life imprisonment at the federal prison in Detroit. McCoy consented to plead guilty to involuntary manslaughter, and was sentenced to six years in the Colorado State Prison at Canon City.

XI

Records indicate that Tom Horn stated he worked for the Pinkertons until 1894, so it is possible that he participated in the Powder River Invasion of Wyoming in 1892 although no general agreement exists as to his participation. While some say Tom Horn had a prominent part in this invasion, others say that he was not involved at all. President Harrison was involved, however. He threatened martial law in Wyoming if things did not get better. Governor George Baxter was finally removed from office by Presidential order for his activities in the Johnson County War.

Evidently Frank Canton, former sheriff of Johnson County and a Deputy United States Marshal, was suspected to be the leader of the Wyoming raiders against the homesteaders. Everyone knew that Canton was associated with the powerful and ruthless Wyoming Stock Growers Association, a group which was suffering great losses of stock at the hands of rustlers. No doubt this suspicion caused his defeat at the polls to "Red" Angus when he again ran for sheriff. While no record exists to substantiate the idea, there is little doubt that Tom Horn recruited gunfighters for the invaders. His former experience against the Apaches would have made him a formidable foe in any field. He could have hit and run without anyone ever seeing him.

Tom Horn became known as the official assassin of the rustlers. Whenever a killing occurred his name was whispered. Every unsolved murder or the disappearance of known rustlers was laid at the doorstep of Tom Horn. And, oddly enough, Tom seem to enjoy basking in the limelight of his "reputation." His was now a life shrouded in mystery and legend. He fancied a speeding bullet from a .44 calibre rifle as his calling card.

At times he tried to respect the law by turning in rustlers whom he had caught red-handed. The last time he did this was with the Langshoff gang. He took them to the jail at Laramie, only to have the courts dispense short sentences or small fines on the violators. It was enough for Tom . . . he bothered no more.

John C. Coble, later of Bosler, Wyoming, and a close friend of Tom's, who also tried to aid Horn at his later trial, owned the Coble Iron Mountain Cattle Company. A nearby rancher named William Lewis, had the gall to boast that he had been openly stealing cattle from Coble. After a severe warning to desist, Lewis not only refused to do so, but boasted more about his thieving activities.

His body, riddled by three .44 calibre bullets, was found near Laramie in August of 1895. Of course, suspicion was at once centered on Tom Horn, Coble's friend, but nothing was ever done about it.

It is said that Horn received $300 each for his killings . . . not as much as Killing Jim Miller got for his assassinations . . . but enough to suit Tom, who seemed never to want for money. When asked for whom he worked, Tom would reply, "For the Swan Land and Cattle Company." It certainly would be interesting to learn who really paid Tom and who really gave him his murder assignments, if such were committed by Tom.

The last killing of record before Tom left Wyoming was the murder of Fred Powell, a squatter who lived a few miles from the Lewis place. He, too, had boasted of his exploits in stealing cattle from the Coble place, as well as others. He refused to obey an order for him to leave the country, an unsigned and mysterious message which he found one day attached to the front door of his home.

Shortly thereafter the spectre on the large horse appeared near the Powell camp. When he turned to leave the area, one shot had been fired, and Fred Powell was dead.

Tom Horn was next seen in Cheyenne, where he spoke openly of the Lewis and Powell killings. Whether he actually stated that he was the killer or not, is not known. At any rate, the authorities refused to arrest him, realizing there was no evidence to support their suspicions; besides, they considered a dead rustler a good rustler.

XI

When the Spanish-American War broke out Teddy Roosevelt went west and organized his Rough Riders. Many outlaws, including the Butch Cassidy bunch, wanted to join, if amnesty would be given them for their services to America. Their offer was refused since too many serious crimes had been committed by them.

Tom Horn enlisted as a scout, and found among the officers some of his old friends who had participated in the Indian campaigns with him. Dr. Leonard Wood now was a Colonel (Fort Wood in Missouri was later named after him), and friends Maus and Lawton now were generals. Also the tough and ready Adna Chaffee was now a general (an army camp was named for him later on as well).

But the kind of war to be fought in Cuba needed no scouts so Tom Horn was appointed packmaster for Shafter's army, with the rank and pay of colonel. Shortly thereafter, he was made master of transportation. When the train from St. Louis, Missouri, with its 520 mules and 133 packers arrived at Tampa, Florida, the port of embarkation for Cuba, it was quite a chore to load the animals onto the transport ships. Tom later said that he'd never take another ocean trip as it was a terrible experience, one that he never wanted to go through again.

Things were worse when the ships arrived at the Cuban harbor. It was discovered that the transports could get no closer than a mile to the shore, a situation which could cause grave consequences and one which worried Horn no end. He consulted the officers in charge of the transports, and then decided to speak to General Shafter about the problem. The general was personally known to Horn, so he quickly implored him to act in the matter since the Rough Riders would be in need of supplies.

"The ships cannot get to the harbor," sighed the general, "what can we do?"

"General, just give me the order to unload the animals."

"You have it, do what you must."

Disembarking the animals got under way quickly, in such a manner as only the resourceful Tom Horn would think of. Each animal was placed on the gangplank and simply pushed into the water. The 520 mules were thus unloaded, and by natural instinct they headed for the land, with only several of them being drowned.

Except for the energy and ingenuity of Tom Horn, there probably would have been no ammunition or supplies at the Battle of Kettle Hill. Several hours before the fight, Colonel Wood and Colonel Theo. Roosevelt met Horn as they trudged toward the front in the mud.

"Colonel Roosevelt, I'd like you to meet a great scout and a great fighter, also a good friend, Tom Horn," said Dr. Wood.

"Pleased to meet you, young man," smiled the colonel, his moustache dancing and his eyes twinkling behind his thick glasses. "Now what we'd like to have are two of those fine looking Missouri mules to ride."

In later days Tom described the San Juan Hill affair as a terrible fiasco, and asserted that the branding of the seventy-first New Yorkers as cowards was grossly unfair. He said they were not cowards, but were simply untrained and undisciplined. That was the only action Tom saw during the Cuban campaign. The Spaniards were less organized than the Americans, and casualties on the side of the Spaniards was much greater than those on the American side.

The victory of Admiral Dewey at Manila Bay was a lop-sided affair, to say the least. On May 1, 1898, Dewey's batteries destroyed the fleet of Admiral Montojo and silenced all the fortifications at a cost of seven wounded Americans. The Spaniards lost 634 killed and wounded. Rear-Admiral Sampson and Commodore W. S. Schley blockaded another Spanish fleet in the harbor at Santiago Bay, completely destroying it on July 3rd, killing 353 men of Cereva's command and wounding 151 more. Military forces under Maj.-General Shafter landed near Santiago, and took the city on July 16th, after a skirmish at Las Guasimas and a battle at San

Juan Hill, July 1st. Tom Horn later stated that 241 soldiers had been killed up to that time. The total United States casualties in the war, which lasted only from April, 1898 to December 10, 1898, were 279 soldiers killed and 1465 wounded; and 16 sailors killed and 68 wounded.

The real killer of the American soldiers was the fever. Close to 3,000 enlisted men and officers died of the malaria after the fighting had ended. Tom Horn also was stricken, but survived. When the troop ships landed in New York City, Tom was very effective as a male nurse in caring for the malaria-stricken men.

The congestion, noise, and constant rat-race of the big city failed to appeal to Tom, and as soon as he had drawn his accumulated pay from the army, he left for Wyoming, remaining there at the home of John C. Coble until he had fully recovered from the malaria. It is believed that the Coble ranch also served as a base for his operations during the next several years.

Next Tom's itching feet took him to the Brown's Hole region, the reputed hideout of the famous Butch Cassidy gang, as well as the Red Sash gang and others of like ilk. This area surrounds the point where Utah's eastern boundary and Colorado's western boundary join the southern boundry of Wyoming. The Green Valley River flows through this valley along the base of the Diamond Mountains, and it is as rough a terrain as God put on this earth. The treacherous trails and desolate hiding places made the area an ideal one for outlaws and wanted men of all types. It was a place indeed where lawmen and "angels feared to tread."

Brown's Hole consisted of but one street, and as Tom's horse plodded fetlock deep between the rows of ramshackle buildings, speculative eyes followed his progress.

These people did not know Tom Horn by sight, although most of them no doubt heard of his activities during the Johnson County War and other such affairs. All they saw that day was a tall man, riding straight in the saddle, the breeze tugging at his long mustache, his thinning hair struggling to find a place to land on his balding pate. Tom rode hatless much of the time, especially when not "on duty."

What the people did notice most, however, were Horn's weapons, worn, but well kept. The shiny-butted .45 Colts protruded from his holster, ready for instant use; the .44 calibre rifle nestled comfortably in the saddle scabbard.

"Another gunman," muttered several as Tom passed. It was not a new sight for these people, all of whom were on the outside of the law, to see new desperadoes and gunfighters enter "the hole" from time to time. The policy of the hole, as well as most of the west, of no questions asked of strangers, was strictly adhered to in that locality especially.

What the others did not know was that Tom Horn carried a list of names in his pocket . . . names of men who were to be officially exterminated by his hand. Two of these men, a black named Isam Dart and Matthew Rash, were at the top of the list, and they lived near Brown's Hole.

Ed and George Bassett, whose family lived in Brown's Hole, were slightly acquainted with Horn, but only knew him under the name of Tom Hicks, gunfighter. Tom quickly renewed his acquaintance with the Bassett family, knowing it would be a way by which to reach the men he wanted.

Soon Tom Horn was riding the range with Dart and Rash, rounding up cattle and discussing the local condition of rustling. No one suspected his real motive. Horn was staying with Rash for a time, and one day a note was found on Rash's door, telling him to leave the country and never come back. No doubt the note had been pinned there by the Bassett boys, whose sister, Josie, was supposed to marry Rash. Of course, the Bassett brothers did not cotton up to this idea for they had no use for Matthew Rash. Tom's plans now jelled perfectly.

"Rash," he said one day, "I appreciate your hospitality, but I must move on. I want to take a job at the Haley ranch not too far from here."

"Yes, I know the place. I'm going to Rock Springs myself for the rodeo and then on to my cabin on Cold Spring Mountain." It was the last place he ever went.

Several days later as Rash stood in his doorway, prepared to fetch a bucket of water from a nearby spring, Tom's carbine spat fire and lead, sending the unsuspecting victim crashing back into his cabin. Horn then calmly walked up to the doorway, looked in, and fired another shot into Rash to make sure his job was well done. He then calmly returned to the spot where he had tethered his mount, leaped into the saddle and rode off. To complete his alibi as to his "presence" at the Haley ranch at the time Rash was slain, Horn rode hard all day to reach the town of Baggs, near which the Haley ranch was situated.

Of course, no one around Brown's Hole suspected Tom Hicks as the slayer of Matthew Rash, although some comments were made to the effect that the killing appeared to be the handiwork of a hired assassin named Tom Horn from Wyoming.

Tom's next move was to take the two Bassett brothers with him to the home of Isam Dart, where they found that gentleman cutting logs at the rear of his home. Nearly 500 feet away from the house Horn stopped, alighted from his horse, took his .44 calibre rifle, aimed carefully, and shot Dart in the stomach, killing him almost instantly. The Bassett brothers fled the scene post haste, with a firm feeling they had best never mention the incident to anyone. It is a moot question as to why Horn, always a loner in his killings, permitted the two Bassetts to accompany him in the first place.

Later, "Mr. Hicks" was identified by people who had seen him near the Dart place the day of the shooting, as Tom Horn, from photos they had seen.

Horn again used the theory of speed to overcome first suspicions regarding his connection with the Dart killing. He raced all the way to Laramie in such good time that people said he could never have been at the Dart ranch at the time of the killing and be in Laramie also at such-and-such an hour. This same trick was used on occasion by the noted Missouri outlaw Jesse James.

Tom had the habit of stirring up trouble between the men he wanted out of the way. In this way, suspicion would be diverted to one of these men, rather than to himself. It also happened in the matter of James Miller and Kels Nickell. Both these men were at each other's throats most of the time, each claiming the other was infringing on his property line. They even took the matter to court several times, sometimes

Miller winning; sometimes Nickell.

This see-saw feud was to Tom's liking. At one time the two neighbors met, and it appeared that Nickell or Miller would be killed, but, as it turned out, only Miller received a slight flesh wound with a knife.

On the morning of July 19, 1901, Willie Nickell, the fourteen year-old son of Kels Nickell, was shot and killed near his home. James Miller was instantly suspected of the foul deed, but it was known that he always carried a shotgun and did not possess a high-calibre rifle with which the killing had been done. A search of the area revealed a spent cartridge about three hundred feet distance from the pasture gate, it was the famous .44 calibre, now a trademark on the frontier. Young Willie, wearing his father's coat and hat, had appaarently been mistaken for Kels Nickell, and killed because of that error.

At the coroner's inquest on July 22nd, strong evidence tended to show that Victor (James) Miller was the killer, but the evidence was not strong enough that a warrant was issued. He had witnesses who stated he was at home entertaining guests at the very time young Nickell had been killed, and they all swore under oath that Miller could not have been at the scene.

"I don't care what they say," Kels Nickel stated later, "I believe they will try to pin this on Tom Horn, Coble's friend, but I am sure it was Miller."

Sheriff Shafer of Laramie County made the best investigation he could, launching a severe search to see where Tom Horn had been on that fateful day. Tom had witnesses that he had been on a train enroute to Cheyenne when the killing took place, so the case was left hanging.

Later Deputy United States Marshal Joe LaFors entered the case at the request of Sheriff Shafer, who had taken ill. As the summer wore on, things began to slacken; all the sheep had left the area and there was little or no rustling going on. Therefore, Tom was thrown out of his job. Through the efforts of his friend Coble and Deputy Marshall LaFors, who claimed to be Tom's friend, it was arranged for Horn to take a job in Montana.

Borrowing a buckboard and a team of spirited horses, Tom left for his new job. At Laramie he stopped and got drunk, and when he reached Cheyenne to talk with LaFors further about the job, he was still drunk. In the marshall's office, with Deputy Sheriff Les Snow and Charley Ohnhaus, court stenographer, hiding in an adjoining room, with door slightly ajar, LaFors began to question Tom about various things.

Naturally, LaFors skillfully channeled the conversation to include the death of Willie Nickell. Tom's habit of placing himself in the midst of every and any conversation was one which proved fatal.

"You have had an interesting life, Tom, especially with the army, Al Sieber, and all; it is a shame that you wasted all that by turning professional killer. It was not a manly thing to do, that killing of young Willie Nickell."

Tom shifted in the captain's chair, apparently ill at ease.

"Things changed, LaFors, and I'm not so sure I can trust you, either. If I killed the Nickell kid it was a mistake. I never shot any kids in my life."

Unknowingly, Tom Horn had trapped himself. Much more conversation followed, with LaFors always pounding away at the Nickell murder. Before long, he had Tom thinking he had actually killed the boy and practically had him admitting it. That was enough.

On January 13, 1902, a warrant was issued for the arrest of Tom Horn, charging him with the willful murder of one William Nickell, and the warrant was served by Sheriff Ed Smalley, his chief deputy Dick Proctor, and Sandy McKneal, Chief of Police.

The evidence which the authorities held was not made public until the hearing was held on May 10th. It was then disclosed that in an interview with LaFors, with hidden witnesses, Tom Horn had confessed to the murder of Willie Nickell. It had been a case of mistaken identity; he had meant to kill Kels Nickell, the boy's father. Many thought the evidence was obtained under duress and fraud, yet the verdict was guilty, as charged.

The verdict was rendered on October 26th by a jury consisting mostly of small ranchers, men who had no use for the likes of a man such as Tom Horn. Many people knew that members of the jury were known cattle rustlers, men who had sworn to "get Horn" for his thinning of their ranks. Some put it this way, "Show me a cattleman who is against Tom Horn, and I'll show you a rustler."

Appeals were made to various courts and to the governor, to no avail. On the very day of his execution at Cheyenne on November 20, 1903, Tom wrote the following letter to his dear friend, John Coble.

Cheyenne, Wyo., November 20, 1903

John C. Coble, Esq.,
Cheyenne, Wyo.

As you have just requested, I will tell all my knowledge of everything I know in regard to the killing of the Nickell boy.

The day I laid over at Miller's ranch, he asked me to do so, so that I could meet Billy McDonald.

Billy McDonald came up and Miller and I met him up the creek, above Miller's house. Billy opened the conversation by saying that he and Miller were going to kill off the Nickell outfit and wanted me to go in on it. They said that Underwood and Jordon would pay me.

Miller and McDonald said they would do the work. I refused to have anything to do with them, as I was not interested in any way. McDonald said that the sheep were then on Coble's land, and I got my horse and went up to see, and they were not on Coble's land.

I promised to stay all night again at Miller's, as McDonald said he would come up again the next morning.

He came back the next morning and asked me if I still felt the same as I did the day before, and I told him I did.

"Well," he said, "we have made up our minds to wipe up the whole Nickell outfit."

I got my horse and left, and went on about my business. I went on as John Brae and Otto Plaga said I did, and on to the ranch, where I arrived on Saturday. I heard of the boy being killed. I felt I was well out of the mix up.

I was over in that part of the country six weeks or two months later and saw McDonald and Miller, and they were laughing and blowing to me about running and shooting the sheep of Nickell. I told them I did not want to hear of it at all, for I could see that McDonald wanted to tell me the whole scheme. They both gave me a laugh and said I was suspicioned of the whole thing.

I knew there was some suspicion against me, but did not pay the attention to it that I should.

That is all there is to it so far as I know.

Irwin, who swore I came into Laramie on the run on that Thursday, just simply lied.

All that supposed confession in the United States marshal's office was prearranged, and everything that was sworn by those fellows was a lie, made up before I came to Cheyenne. Of course, there was talk of the killing of the boy, but LaFors did all of it. I did not even make an admission, but allowed LaFors to make some insinuations.

Ohnhaus, LaFors, and Snow, and also Irwin, of Laramie, all swore to lies to fit the case.

Your name was not mentioned in the marshal's office.

This is the truth, as I am going to die in ten minutes.

Thanking you for your kindness and continued goodness to me, I am

Sincerely yours,
TOM HORN

After the hanging, Tom's body was taken to Boulder, Colorado, by an older brother, Charley Horn, where it was buried with a proper marker, with proper inscription.

Story Printed in the Wyoming State Tribune, 1927.

TOM HORN

November 20, 1927, marked the twenty-fourth anniversary of the hanging in Cheyenne of Tom Horn, notorious character, known as the "Wyoming Man Killer". Horn was the last man hanged in a Wyoming county seat.

Twenty-five years ago, the Tom Horn murder trial at Cheyenne, was attracting the attention of the West. Horn was placed on trial October 10, 1902, in district court at Cheyenne, and on October 24, the jury found him guilty of murder in the first degree. He was sentenced to be hanged.

Horn's career is especially historically interesting because he was one of the first paid assassins in Wyoming, performing killings as those now undertaken by hired gunmen in the big cities.

He first came into prominence when he came to Wyoming as a detective for the Stockgrowers' Association. Learning that it was difficult to secure the conviction of a cattle rustler or range cattle thief, Horn adopted the policy of acting as detective, prosecutor, judge, jury and executioner, applying the remedy of death by shooting.

Horn gained his name as the "Man Killer" while in Texas in a similar capacity, and his activities in this state substantiated the cognomen attached to him by Texans.

The scaffold on which Horn was hanged is now at the state penitentiary at Rawlins. It was designed in 1892 by James Julian, a

Cheyenne architect, and the trap was sprung by a water system. Thirty-one seconds were required before the water emptied at Horn's execution, and the trap was sprung. Horn was pronounced dead 14 minutes later.

In 1900, Isham Dart and Matt Rash, ranchmen in Brown's Park, Colo., were killed. Horn was known to have been in that vicinity at the time and was suspected as their assailant. He encountered a posse on his return to Wyoming, and in the altercation he killed one member of the posse but incurred knife wounds that came near ending his career.

Later Lewis and Powell, ranchmen in the Horse Creek country were killed, and Horn was suspected.

The climax of Horn's ruthless ventures was reached when on July 18, 1901, the body of Willie Nickell, 16-year-old son of Nels P. Nickell, an Iron Mountain country ranchman, was found with a stone placed under the head and a ghastly bullet wound, telling the manner of his death.

Horn always placed a stone under the head of his victims. He employed this method to inform his employers he had killed his victim, and that the $700 he charged for the killing was due.

Horn had intended to kill the boy's father. On the day of the slaying the youngster was wearing his father's hat and coat, and Horn believed the boy was Nickell.

About a week later the father was shot from Ambush while working in his garden. One shot took effect in the arm, and the other in the hip.

Joseph LeFors, a deputy United States marshall, after the Nickell slaying, devoted his time to bringing Horn to justice. He made Horn's acquaintance and later became an almost constant companion. On January 10, 1902, while LeFors and Horn were drinking together in a room, Less Snow, a deputy sheriff, and C. J. Oldham, a clerk in the United States court, were in an adjoining room, hearing all that was said, Oldham made a stenographic report of the conversation.

It was at this meeting that Horn made what was an "inspired" confession.

LeFors skillfully led Horn to boast of his deeds of crime, among which he listed the Nickell killings.

Two days later Sheriff E. J. Smalley of Laramie County, now a department of justice agent, arrested Horn at the bar of the Inter-Ocean hotel. R. A. Proctor, a deputy sheriff, standing a few feet away had instructions to shoot if Horn made a hostile move.

Horn made two attempts to escape, one of which was successful, on August 6, 1903. Horn and Jim McCloud of Thermopolis, another killer, overpowered R. A. Proctor, the deputy sheriff, Less Snow came into the jail, and, after witnessing the struggle, ran from the bastile and spread the alarm.

Horn and McCloud fled in opposite directions after getting out of the jail. Horn was captured about one block from the jail by a merry-go-round proprietor. Horn attempted to shoot him, but was in possession of Proctor's automatic pistol and did not know how to use it.

Horn made plans for another escape in which friends on the outside were to play an important role. His plans included a relay of horses for his use in his dash to the Laramie plains country. To carry out his plans, Horn was required to take into his confidence another prisoner. He selected a young boy who was serving a short sentence for a minor crime. He wrote notes to the boy on toilet paper, instructing him to take the notes to a rancher at Laramie.

After being released from jail, the boy deliberated on the wisdom of participating in Horn's pleas for freedom. He finally visited the office on the Cheyenne State Tribune, revealed the plot and upon the promises of the newspaper not to publish the story until he was out of Wyoming.

After the lad reached Ogden, Utah, the Tribune published the story, obtaining a big scoop in those days. After Horn's plan to escape had been exposed, a military guard was placed around the jail. The guard was maintained up to the time the scaffold trap was sprung.

BIBLIOGRAPHY

Baber, Daisy F., The Longest Rope, *Caxton Printers, Ltd., Cadwell, Idaho, 1940.*

Botkin, B. A., Treasury of Western Folklore, *Crown Publishers, New York, 1951.*

Burt, Maxwell Struthers, Power River, *Farrar, Rinehart, Inc., New York, 1938.*

Clay, John, Tragedy of Squaw Mountain, *Maders Printing Co., Chicago, Illinois, 1924.*

Coe, Charles H., Juggling a Rope, *Hamley & Co., Pendleton, Oregon, 1927.*

Fowler, Gene, Timber Line, *Covici, Friede, publishers, New York, 1933.*

Gann, Walter, Tread of the Longhorns, *Naylor Co., San Antonio, Texas, 1949.*

Garst, Doris Shannon, The Story of Wyoming, *Douglas Enterprise Publishing Co., Douglas, Wyoming, 1938.*

Horn, Tom, Life of Tom Horn, *Louthan Book Co., Denver, 1904.*

Kelly, Charles, The Outlaw Trail, *Charles Kelly, Publisher, Salt Lake City, Utah, 1938.*

Leckenby, Charles H., Tread of the Pioneers, *Pilot Press, Steamboat Springs, Colo., 1945.*

LeFors, Joe, Wyoming Peace Officer, *Laramie Printing Co., Laramie, Wyoming, 1953.*

Linford, Velma, Wyoming, Frontier State, *Old West Publishing Co., Denver, Colo., 1947.*

Mokler, Alfred James, History of Natrona County, Wyoming, *R. R. Donnelley & Co., Chicago, 1923.*

Monaghan, Jay, Legend of Tom Horn, *Bobbs-Merrill Publishers, New York, 1946.*

Oregon Trail, *Compilation of WPA Project, Hastings House Publishers, New York, 1939.*

Rollinson, John K., Wyoming Cattle Trails, *Caxton Printers, Caldwell, Idaho, 1948.*

Siringo, Charles A., A Cowboy Detective, *W. B. Conkey Co., Chicago, Illinois, 1912.*

Spring, Agnes Wright, William Deming, Wyoming Pioneer, *Arthur Clark Co., Glendale, Calif., 1944.*
Tittsworth, W. G., Outskirt Episodes, *Tittsworth Publishing, Avoca, Iowa, 1927.*
Trenholm, Virginia Cole, Footprints on the Frontier, *Douglas Enterprise Co., Douglas, Wyoming, 1945.*
Walker, Tacetta B., Stories of Early Wyoming, *Prairie Publishing Co., Casper, Wyoming, 1936.*
Wyoming, Guide to, *WPA Project, Oxford University Press, 1941.*

CHAPTER IV

JOHN KING FISHER GUNSLINGER DELUXE

Eagle Pass, Texas, blistered in a withering heat as the fiery evening sun set behind a jutted peak. The town's only street, a dusty thoroughfare, was deserted except for one cowboy who approached on horseback from the south. Calmly the stranger tied his mount to a rack some distance from the Ten High Saloon. He hummed tonelessly as he cast a glance at his claybank stallion; then shoving back his Stetson, he studied the bat-wing doors of the saloon. Then he sauntered toward the building. A tied-down holster belted to his lean waist held a pearl-handled Navy Colt. Piercing blue eyes watched the saloon entrance.

"Daugherty!" the man shouted. "I'm here! Aiming to

gun me down, or did my boys hear some yellow dog yapping?"

A man staggered through the bat-wing doors, then bounced to a halt as he noted the stranger. He stiffened visibly as he wiped his mouth. Anger flooded his swarthy face as he tugged a vicious looking .45 Peacemaker from its holster.

"Damn you, Fisher, you got a helluva nerve coming into town after what I said about you! Who you calling yellow?"

"Still trying to live up to your boast to kill me, Daugherty?"

Wrath suffused Bill Daugherty's face. His eyes bulged in their sockets. Trail-rough, lawless and proud, no man swallowed such an affront. The pistol in Daugherty's hand coughed and a slug tore at Fisher's sleeve.

Fisher fired twice. The slugs slammed Daugherty backward, blood gushing from shattered wrists. His Colt thudded to the splintery walk. Two more slugs from Fisher's pistol toppled the victim to the dusty street, dead.

Ten High patrons called it a fair fight; Daugherty had fired first. It didn't matter to the sheriff what they called it. After he reviewed Fisher's sadistic handiwork, he arrested him and a court hearing was hastily scheduled. But a few hours later the gunslinger was out on $2,000 bail bond.

Later, the tiny, stifling courtroom was jammed for what was expected to be a matter-of-form hearing. The surprise on most faces was genuine when the prosecutor, in summarizing the evidence, called it murder and demanded the jury find the prisoner guilty.

Naturally, King Fisher was prepared for this turn of events. Into the courtroom pushed twenty-five heavily armed men, all friends of the defendant, who, without a word, took stations along the walls of the room. The judge glowered, the sheriff swore hoarsely, and the startled jurors paled visibly.

Dead silence fell as the prisoner arose and spoke to the judge in a quiet drawl.

"Your honor, I request permission to address the court in my own behalf, and I don't need no damned attorney."

The judge was the calmest man in the room. He returned King's stare, unafraid.

"Very well, but watch how you address this court. I can

declare a mistrial and hold you without bail for another trial."

King Fisher laughed and turned to the jurors.

"Gentlemen of the jury, I am not inclined to leave this matter in your hands, without first stating that I would greatly appreciate hearing your foreman pronounce the words NOT GUILTY," he said, then calmly resumed his seat.

The startled jurors fixed their gase upon the gunmen blocking the only exit from the room, then went into a huddle without leaving the jury box. The foreman arose, wiped his brow and announced that a verdict had been reached.

"We find the defendant not guilty!"

King Fisher then rose and favored the court with a handsome bow. He thanked them for their indulgence, then took his majestic departure from the court, surrounded by his gunmen.

Such was John King Fisher. He is among those in the outlaw hall of fame where stands many stalwarts of the western frontier, men whose fame as handlers of the sixgun went down in history before they died. Fisher was one of those colorful characters who strode majestically across the stage of time, performed his act, and made his abrupt departure. He was a product of the border, a Texan, who as a boy was thrown upon his own amid surroundings which in no small measure were responsible for the life into which he drifted.

John King Fisher was born in Kentucky in October of 1855 when war clouds were gathering over the nation. John's father later fought well for the Confederacy under General Lee in the Army of Northern Virginia. After the war, father and son were more like strangers, and his mother, who was in ill health passed away shortly after the return of her husband.

The Civil War had dealt harshly with all those connected with the Lost Cause, and John King Fisher, Sr., found only desolation and carpetbaggers at home. He was so embittered by prevailing conditions that he took his son and left Kentucky. In 1873 Fisher and his son came to Fort Worth, Texas, where the father remarried and settled near Paint Rock.

Things around home were not too pleasant for the teenage John, for he and his step-mother did not get along very well. The young man left home to accept odd jobs from ranchers around Goliad until impatient feet got him on the move again.

Near Goliad he asked a rancher named "Uncle" Doc White for a job.

"What's your name, son?"

"John King Fisher," replied the boy. "And I'm alone in the world now."

White burst into a loud laugh.

"That name sure fits you, boy. Split halfways up like a colt, and you sure are a dead ringer for one of them kingfisher birds. But you'll name a good hand."

The name stuck with John. From that day until his death he was known only as King Fisher.

The boy did not mind work and soon adopted himself to this new home. Rancher White became Uncle White, and the missus became Aunt Lou. Second to the White's home King found the ranch of Charlie Vivian the most attractive. The boy had taken a great liking to Sarah Vivian, (also spelled Vivion) Charlie's pretty daughter, and always managed to spend some time there.

But the land-hungry Goliard ranchers, ever fearful of being hemmed in by advancing multitudes of people coming to Texas, learned of vast acreage that was just going to pot in the Nueces Strip, an area 100 miles wide and 300 miles long between the Nueces and Rio Grande Rivers. It had few inhabitants, men who were on the dodge; wanted by the law and desperate men to tackle. A wagon train, headed by Doc White, was made ready for a journey to the strip. The area remained a refuge for outlaws from 1865 until 1885, when it was placed under the jurisdiction of Maverick County. Few family men cared to risk settling in that territory.

In early spring a number of families, headed by Doc White and Bob Vivian and his brother Charlie, herded their cattle into one mass, and with loaded wagons started for Pendencia Creek, now a part of Dimmit County, Texas. King Fisher had requested permission to accompany the caravan, but Uncle Doc White turned him down.

"We're going into rough country, son, and we'll have enough trouble without looking after another young person.

I'm sorry."

"Might be later on you'll be needing me, Unk, and if you do just give me a yell, and I'll lend a hand."

White laughed. "Reckon I'll make out all right."

Yet the time was soon to come when White would welcome any and all assistance. To King, the refusal to accompany the caravan was a keen disappointment. He had fallen hard for Sarah Vivian, and vowed that he would find some other way into the Nueces Strip.

Homeless again, the gullible youth signed on with old Wes Burton and his sons, Wes and Bill. His naivete was short lived. The Burtons were well known cattle rustlers of the region, and under the guidance of the elder Burton, King Fisher soon became an expert gunman. A latent mean streak came to the surface and his dexterity with a Colt became uncanny. The combination soon made him the real leader of the outlaw gang.

Some historians rank him as a gunslinger equal to Burt Alvord, Wyatt Earp, and Doc Holliday. He certainly was fast. But where Burt Alvord was an ignorant, taciturn, treacherous coward, Fisher was the opposite. Where Earp talked down a fight, Fisher goaded others to draw. And where Doc was a cynical killer, Fisher used the deadly Peacemakers with obdurate sadism. Fisher was as deadly a shot with his left hand as with his right, and even today he is considered to have been one of the most remarkable pistoleers who ever lived.

King Fisher soon learned that Doc White was having problems at the new settlement at Pendencia Creek, where White had been elected Justice-of-the-Peace, the only order that prevailed in a lawless territory. Outlaws from across the Rio Grande, in Nacimiento and the Chohuila country, along with runaway slaves, were making off with most of the ranchers' stock, greatly reducing the herds of the Goliad ranchers.

An emissary to Goliad brought the sad tidings, and a request for assistance, but none of the Goliad settlers felt they cared to risk losing their stock.

Only John King Fisher lent a sympathetic ear. By now he was an expert gunslinger as well as a known rustler. But King would not desert his friends. Quickly drawing his forces together he raced for Pendencia.

The arrival of King Fisher and his men soon turned the tables on the men from below the border. Justice White quickly recognized the youth's ability to handle a rough situation, so he appointed King a deputy sheriff with orders to clean the range of Mexican marauders.

"That can be easily arranged," grinned King. "But you've got to let my men raid a bit so long they don't molest your cattle."

The arrangement set well with White and was carried out to the letter. The Pendencia settlers never lost a head. Soon Fisher was the "big wolf" of the district with a string of rustler camps through which he could pass on stolen stock until disposed of. King did not often take part in rustling cattle from the Mexican ranches, but would buy wet stock from Mexican rustlers who delivered the cattle to the King camps in Texas. Fisher was soon filling government contracts for beef at all the forts and in a short time he found himself a wealthy man. In less than a year he accomplished another dream . . . he married Sarah Vivian or Sallie, as she was often called.

As a married man and a deputy sheriff King Fisher set up headquarters on a ranch near Pendencia. Soon his broad range overflowed with rustled longhorns wearing his 7D brand. The majority of the brands had been working over with a running iron. Fisher was quite a striking figure as he pranced about, his badge glistening in the bright sunlight. One old timer put it this way: "King Fisher was the most perfect specimen of manhood and frontier dandy and desperado I ever had the pleasure of meeting. He was tall, beautifully proportioned and exceedingly handsome. He always wore the finest clothing obtainable, but all of it was the picturesque, dime novel kind."

Fisher always wore a broad-rimmed white Mexican somebrero, which was profusely ornamented with gold and silver lace and had a golden snake for a band. His fine buckskin Mexican short jacket was heavily embroidered with gold. Beneath it, a brilliant crimson silk sash was wound about his waist. His shirt was of the finest and thinnest linen, and was usually worn open at the throat, a silk handkerchief knotted loosely about the wide collar. At his hips swung two shining pistols, their pearl handles filled with notches, their plated silver barrels glistening. His boots were of top-grade leather, tooled with careful precision, their high heels cut perfectly. From the point of each silver spur dangled a silver bell.

This flashy eyeful was further set off by *chaperojos,* leather chaps to protect the trouser legs during a ride through brush or while herding cattle. Fisher's chaps had come from a special animal and had been especially made. King had spotted his future breeches one afternoon in northern Texas while he and some bawdy friends were attending a circus. The gang literally kidnapped the circus, holding the owners and spectators at gunpoint while Fisher killed the animal, strapped its carcass to a horse, and rode off. A few days later Fisher appeared in those famous chaps . . . made from the skin of a Royal Bengal tiger and decorated with gold and buckskin fringe.

John King Fisher was as fine a horseman as he was a pistol shot, and his favorite mount was a lemon-colored palomino stallion with a cream mane and tail. There were few Texans who did not know or were not at least familiar with the striking tiger-chapped gunman from Pendencia Creek, in Dimmit County. When he rode, or when he relaxed at his ranch, he was surrounded by forty or fifty plunderers, cattle rustlers, free-booters, gunslingers, and holdup men, all of them living off booty.

Dimmit County was unorganized, but was attached to Maverick County for judicial purposes. Yet no lawmen was ever known to invade the Fisher domain. King did his transactions in an open manner. All the settlers were his friends and his actions were unhampered for he never molested their stock. His rustler exchange camps never were bothered by anyone. King himself rarely worked, simply directing the business.

Oddly enough, as deputy sheriff, King Fisher faithfully performed his official duties as he saw them. But at the same time he openly headed a gang of desperadoes and rustlers. This paradoxical situation lasted until the Texas Legislature voted a special commission to Captain Leander H. McNelly, to organize a body of Texas Rangers and stamp out lawlessness then existing along the border. Soon after, Adjutant-General Steele issued his famous "Texas Bible," a pamphlet which listed over five thousand names and descriptions of men wanted in Texas. In this book, of course, was the name of John King Fisher, charged with being a rustler and slayer of seventeen men. To Captain McNelly the Beau Brummel killer was just another name on the wanted list.

Just how many men Fisher really killed will never be officially known, but the figure is high. In one instance King made a deal with a Mexican horse thief to deliver a herd of animals to his camp near Espantosa Lake. When it came to settling up, the rustler wanted more than the agreed price.

"Damn you! I'll take them at your price, but you'll not run a whiz on me again, remember that," snapped Fisher, his face darkly ominous. The Mexicans did not catch on. Not until sunset, when a fusillade from ambush caught them in a defile. Then it was too late. Fisher took his gold from the riddled corpse of the Mexican leader and had his men bury the dead. Again, no bodies, no proof of murder.

This had happened once before when a Mexican rustler had demanded more than he had agreed upon. This time, however, King ordered his men to fire on the spot, killing all the opposition. He did not bother to set up an ambush.

Some time later Fisher took a trip to Eagle Pass on deputy sheriff business. Two Rangers spotted him leaving the Ten High Saloon.

"Hold it, Fisher!" barked Sergeant Armstrong, yanking out his Colt. "There's a warrant out for your arrest. You touch your guns and you're dead!"

Too smart to buck certain odds, Fisher smiled wryly and submitted. They locked him up, telling the jailer they would bring back a warrant. A former Goliad man, Jailer Barrett's idea of justice did not include holding a friend that way. Before the Rangers returned, King Fisher was long gone.

The Ranger captain was furious and told his men to take Fisher directly to Laredo the next time he was arrested. He said he was sick of being tricked by Fisher's friends.

Captain McNelly was fast becoming the scourge of the

badmen. McNelly had been a former leader of Texas scouts and spies during the Civil War, and had served in Louisiana. He was well fitted for the job alloted him. Cash was scarce but the merchants and ranchers were eager to furnish him men with mounts, rifles, ammunition, and other items.

McNelly's company set about cleaning up the desperadoes along the border. Outlaws had migrated to Texas to such an extent that officers from other states, when unable to apprehend an outlaw, simply stamped their records "G.T.T" — Gone to Texas.

After McNelly and his men had cleaned up much of southern Texas, they worked their way north, and soon reached the Nueces Strip. The spring of 1876 found the daring young captain and his Rangers camped at Carrizo Springs, some twelve miles northwest of King Fisher's domain. McNelly contacted Levi English, the owner of a general store, who had suffered pillage at the hands of the rustlers. He was eager to supply the Ranger with a lot of information concerning Fisher and his operations.

At midnight the Rangers descended upon the sleeping ranch like a swarm of locusts. Before bleary-eyed cowhands knew it, the bunkhouse overflowed with grim-faced men with leveled carbines. Not a shot was fired.

At the ranchhouse they found King Fisher in his nightshirt, trying to light a lamp. His wife, covers pulled to her chin, trembled in the bed. On the bedpost hung King's brace of holstered Peacemakers.

Beneath his flowing mustache, teeth flashed in a wry smile.

"Well, captain, you're a *mucho* he-wolf; I ain't outfoxed often," he said with polite sarcasm.

The bunkhouse coughed up six other wanted outlaws, Bill Wainwright, Al Roberts, Bud Obenchain, Billy Templeton, and the Burton brothers. Daylight found them locked in cells in Encinal. McNelly had decided to round up some witnesses before continuing south with his prisoners.

"What charges you having me hold them on?" the sheriff wanted to know.

"Rustling, mainly. Fisher for murder, with no bail!"

The sheriff scratched his head.

"I don't know, cap'n. Fisher's a big man hereabouts. Less you prove murder, I'll lose a bunch of votes over this."

"By God! You know he's a killer!" exclaimed McNelly, who seldom swore. "Book them all for rustling, then. I'll be back some time tonight."

That evening the Rangers were nearing Encinal with two fightened witnesses when a knot of riders topped a knoll just ahead. One wore a huge white hat and Bengal tiger chaps.

"Cover them!" snapped McNelly, figuring they had broken jail. He scowled then, as they came on, ignoring the Ranger carbines. Kneeing his mount up to King Fisher he barked, "What's the big idea?"

"Why, captain, we posted bond," said King.

"Bond!" exclaimed the Ranger.

"Yep, seven thousand Yankee dollars worth."

McNelly'd bronzed face mirrored chagrin. He knew he had been taken; that he should have suspected the soft-talking sheriff and posted his own men around the jail.

Turning in his saddle, McNelly told his men to turn the witnesses loose. To arrest Fisher again would be folly. His lawyers would howl to the state house in Austin. Certain anti-Ranger politicians were just waiting to get something on them. The rustlers guffawed as McNelly booted his Winchester in disgust.

Following the Encinal affair, Fisher made it a point to stick close to Sarah and his deputy's job. Anything to convince McNelly — the only man he ever respected enough to fear — that he had abandoned the outlaw trail. When McNelly died later that year Fisher wired his widow condolences.

Ranger Commandant George Hall was furious at the turn of events. He ordered three of his best men into Eagle Pass and gave them explicit instructions.

"If you do get him this time, take him out of Eagle Pass, and we'll get him into a court where he doesn't have so many friends."

King Fisher stood in no fear of the law, and before long had again taken a jaunt into Eagle Pass and into the arms of the waiting Rangers. Upon orders from Ranger Allen, King was taken to the Ranger camp immediately.

"What the hell's the meaning of this?" demanded King.

"So you won't get off so easy this time, we're taking you to Laredo, *pronto.*"

The prisoner was not handcuffed, but his feet were securely lashed beneath the belly of a mule, and the beast with its human load was placed in the center of a string of pack animals. Fisher did not lose confidence in himself as they traveled on, but joked and grinned, all the time seeking a way to escape. As the packtrain wound its way along the Rio Grande bank on a narrow trail, the outlaw saw his chance, and he acted. Off came the wide-brimmed hat as Fisher shouted at the top of his voice and rushed his mule into those in front of him. He then jumped his own mount over the embankment, plunged into the murky waters of the Rio Grande and crossed into Mexico. The disgruntled Rangers and their pack animals continued on to Laredo, minus one mule and their prized prisoner.

Shortly after, trouble in east Texas took the Rangers out of the Nueces Strip. Again Dimmit County became an owlhoot paradise.

But the episode of his dunking in the Rio Grande made a profound impression on King Fisher. It convinced him to tread more softly, and shortly thereafter he became a "respectable" rancher.

Fisher moved into Maverick County and established his ranch. Where the county road entered his ranch he put a sign: THIS IS KING FISHER'S ROAD — TAKE THE OTHER.

And none disputed this.

To the north lay Uvalde County. Aware of King's ability in handling renegades and outlaws, the authorities there induced King to become a deputy sheriff. He wore this peace officer's badge honorably and dutifully until the day he died.

In March of 1884, a fence-cutting incident took King Fisher to Austin. There he met Ben Thompson, the noted Englishborn gunslinger. Ben was square-jawed, black-haired, thick-set and blue-eyed. He began working as a printer's apprentice, but wound up a professional gambler, peace officer, prisoner of war, and a gunman second to none.

Mutual respect had long since made the dude gunman and swaggering outlaw friends. Ben decided to accompany King as far as San Antonio, since the deputy sheriff had to return to Uvalde County. At first Ben did not want to go. He knew that San Antonio was enemy country for him for just over a year ago he had killed Jack Harris, the popular one-armed owner of the Vaudeville Variety Theatre (now a bank) on the Plaza. It had been a useless killing, all over the non-payment by Ben of a gambling loss to Harris.

"I'll accompany you as far as where the down and up trains meet, King, and that's only fifteen miles out. I don't think I should go on to San Antone."

"All right," agreed Fisher.

Engaged in one thing and another they did not reach the train until it was moving out. They jumped into a carriage and drove rapidly across the Colorado River, where the train slowed down. They boarded it and went forward. When the trains met, Thompson had been induced to continue his trip to San Antonio.

When they boarded the train for San Antonio they were swaying. Fisher could handle his whiskey, but Thompson snapped. "Who's gonna make me set down, huh?"

"I told you to sit down and behave yourself, Ben," Fisher drawled, "and by God I mean exactly that."

"And if I don't, then what?" Thompson persisted.

"In that case, I expect I'd be forced to kill you."

"By God!" Thompson replied, a bit awed. "Damned if I don't believe you'd sure do it."

That was the only time Ben Thompson was ever known to "back off" from a showdown.

The two intoxicated killers were friendly enough by the time they reached San Antonio. They arrived at their destination about 8:00 o'clock in the evening and at once began making their rounds.

The two gunmen took a cab to the Menger Hotel, washed and had supper, then attended the Turner Opera House to see *East Lynne.* When the play closed they seemed slightly undecided as to what to do next. This was about

John King Fisher, noted gunman and killer who later became a respected peace officer in Uvalde, Texas.

Ben Thompson, city marshall of Austin, Texas, and Thompson's famous revolver, Colt's .45 caliber, 1871, Frontier single action.

Carl Breihan, upper
K. D. Sacre, lower

Ben Thompson in his heyday.

Kansas Historical Society

John Wesley Hardin, noted Texas gunslinger.

Killing Jim Miller.

Grave of Joe Foster in San Antonio, Texas. Foster died as a result of the Fisher-Thompson ambush. Unmarked, in foreground is lot where Jack Harris is buried — Sec. G, Lot 23. Harris was killed by Ben Thompson.

S. W. Pease

W. H. "Billy" Simms, partner of Jack Harris. Simms took over the saloon that he and Harris operated in San Antonio, Texas, after Ben Thompson killed Harris.

University of Oklahoma Library

Jack Harris who was killed in 1882 by Ben Thompson. Harris owned the Jack Harris Saloon and Variety Theatre in San Antonio, Texas, at the corner of Soledad and W. Commerce streets.

University of Oklahoma Library

Lt. John B. Armstrong, Texas Rangers.

Major John B. Jones, Texas Rangers.
Texas State Library

eleven o'clock.

They talked a few minutes, and then, hailing a carriage, they drove to the Vaudeville Theatre, in spite of Fisher's efforts to dissuade Thompson it was foolish to do so.

"Damned if I don't think you're afraid to go in there with me," said Thompson.

"Damn your stinking hide," Fisher growled. "King Fisher ain't afraid to do anything. I just don't see any damn sense in lookin' for trouble, that's all."

Ben chuckled drunkenly.

"King, I'm gonna see Foster and ask him to bury the hatchet. Wanna go with me? If not, I'll go by myself."

"Bury the hatchet, hell, you're just looking for some trouble. But I'll side you. Lead the way."

From the moment Fisher and Thompson got off at the San Antonio depot, they were as good as dead. Even though Thompson had been acquitted of the murder of Harris, his two friends and new owners of the Vaudeville Theatre, Joe Foster and Billy Sims, had publicly vowed to "get Thompson" if he ever showed his face in town. Rumor had it that these two had planned the incident which led to the killing of the former owner, and wanted to get rid of Thompson as the last witness to their plot.

At any rate, the threats that Foster and Sims had made were public knowledge in the city. So was the fact that Thompson, despite his acquittal, was well hated by the city's lawmen and had been secretly warned not to show his face in town.

When King and Thompson arrived at the Vaudeville Variety Theatre at the northwest corner of West Commerce and Soledad Avenues, they entered and bought tickets for the dress circle.

Ben's appearance caused quite a stir among those connected with the house, and from all evidence plans were quickly made by Billy Sims and Joe Foster to take advantage of the situation.

Sims saw the two gunmen in the bar a few minutes later, but to the general surprise of all, he showed no hostility. Instead, he walked over to them, smiling, holding out his hand.

"Hello, Ben," he remarked. "Glad to see you."

"Hello yourself, but you're a damned liar. Do you know Mr. King Fisher?"

King and Billy Sims shook hands.

Sims called over special Policeman J. S. Coy, and again there were introductions.

Sims' oily smile spread; he seemed to be gloating.

"Ben, I'm sure glad you came. It's time to bury the past."

Thompson drained his glass again, now pretty well oiled with liquor.

"I wanna be friends, Billy. That's why I brought Mr. Fisher here, to have an understanding with you and Foster."

"Good enough, no use holding a grudge," Sims seemed to agree.

"Where is Foster?" asked Ben, peering through the smoky haze.

"Upstairs," replied Sims. "Go on up. I'll order some drinks."

The two were shown to seats in a balcony booth. A waitress served them drinks and joked a bit. She left when Sims and Coy entered.

"Where's Foster, Billy?" demanded Thompson, his eyes darting around at adjacent curtained booths. "Don't try any tricks on me. I ain't here for any trouble, but I'm sure ready for it."

"That's right, Sims," spoke up Fisher. "Me and Ben's fixing to whoop it up after you fellows make peace talk. Better fetch Foster."

Sims set down his glass.

"All right, I'll get him."

He went to another booth and Foster appeared. They walked back whispering.

"Well, Joe," said Fisher, "sure good to see you again. Never forgot the time you supplied me with tobacco when I was in the hoosegow here. Shake hands with Ben and let's all be friends."

Thompson offered his hand without rising. Foster ignored it.

"You damn thief, I won't shake hands with you!" Foster cried.

"God damn you, I'm glad you won't!" Thompson growled.

Coy stepped over and placed one hand on his arm, but Thompson shook it off.

"Get out of my way and let me settle this affair with Foster!" he bellowed.

He moved like a rattler, his face red with anger. Leaping across a table he slapped Foster in the face, then drew his pistol and rammed the barrel into Foster's mouth. Coy managed to pull the gun away, but it roared, the bullet whistling past Foster's ear, splitting the wall.

"God damn you!" Thompson yelled. "Turn my pistol loose!"

"I'm an officer, Ben, stop this brawling and now," said Coy.

"I said turn my gun loose!" Thompson again demanded.

"Turn it loose," Foster chimed in behind Coy.

Foster and Sims were trying to slip away when Coy pleaded, "Don't leave, I need your help."

Thompson and Fisher arose, with Coy still clinging to Ben's gun. Neither had pistols in shooting position, but both Sims and Foster evidently were expecting something else. They jumped to one side, and as they did so a salvo of shots rent the air. The volley came from above and to the left of the doomed men. Without a chance to fight for their lives, both Fisher and Thompson dropped, victims of assassin lead.

The diabolical scheme of the two arch conspirators, Sims and Foster, had worked with accuracy, and no proof of their hand in the plot to dispose of their hated enemy, Ben Thompson, was ever unearthed. That Fisher died also was accidental, and it was a wonder that Coy did not die with Ben and King. Anybody with Ben would have shared the same fate that night. But one cannot help wondering about it all.

Fisher and Thompson lay dead, side by side, Thompson's arm flung across his dead friend's chest. Thompson had taken five bullets through the body. Fisher had been shot thirteen times, one bullet tearing through his left eye and directly into the brain.

This assassination caused a greater degree of sensation than any murder that ever occurred in Texas. The daily papers were filled with dispatches, editorials written, and communications published. A few of these are included herewith, for the purpose of giving the reader what may be gathered from them concerning Thompson and the horrible manner of his "taking off." The various given versions of this incident should prove interesting to the reader.

From the *Austin Daily Statesman*, March 12, 1884:

San Antonio, March 11, Midnight. Ben Thompson was shot and killed tonight at the Vaudeville Theatre. King Fisher was also killed, and Joe Foster was shot in the leg. Ben Thompson and King Fisher entered the Vaudeville about 10:30 P.M. and purchased tickets for the gallery. Shortly after they had taken seats they became rather boisterous in language, and William Sims, manager of the theatre, and William Foster, an attache, requested them to desist. On approaching the couple, Foster held out his hand, saluting them, and Thompson cursed him. It is stated that Thompson tried to draw his pistol, and Fisher who was as game a man as ever stepped, followed suit. Thompson's pistol was grasped by Jacob Coy, a Special Officer attached to the Vaudeville, and then the ball opened. An eye witness states that Thompson went down first, and Fisher next, although on account of the frightened crowd, the screams of the women and men, the dense smoke, the struggling knot of figures, and the rapid succession of reports, it is impossible at this time to obtain a lucid and intelligent statement. When your reporter reached the scene the two bodies were weltering in blood, and were laid out side by side, their hair and faces carmined with the life fluid. The stairs leading up to the scene of the horror were slippery as ice, and the walls were stained and the floor was tracked with bloody footprints. The dissolute women, with blanched faces, crowded around with exclamations and broken sobs, exclaiming, "Which is Ben? Show me Ben!" Even in death, amid the garish surroundings, the grim reputation of the man stood forth as strong as ever. Thompson was shot twice through the brain, one ball entering squarely through the left eyebrow, and the other just above it. Both holes could have been covered with a half dollar. His face wore a stern expression, and the upper lip is drawn tight across the teeth. The brain is visible through the wound in the eyebrow.

Andreas Coy, the brother of the policeman who first grasped Ben's pistol says that he is persuaded that Ben never fired a shot.

Fisher is also shot through the brain. the ball entering the left eye and completely smashing the pupil. He was Deputy Sheriff of Uvalde County, was about twenty-seven years of age, had a wife and family, and was, by all odds, the most noted desperado on the Rio Grande frontier from New Mexico to the gulf. He lay with his arms across Ben's body, as though unwilling to desist, even in death, from his desperate defense of his friend. Fisher's is the hand which struck down Joe Foster. Joe is shot through the left leg, just below the knee. He has bled terribly and may die. The coroner's jury is now in session with closed doors. If the result is made known will wire tonight.

It is currently reported and believed that Wm. Sims and Coy, the special policeman, did the shooting. Whoever handled the pistols, it was fatally well done.

Stories circulated through the city that Thompson and Fisher had been lured to their deaths. Two eastern drummers in another booth told newspapers that afterward the conspirators drew their revolvers and fired into the corpses. But Coy denied this. His version had Thompson curse Foster and slap him as he drew his pistol to kill. A general scuffle ensued, in which the victims were accidentally slain. He swore there was no ambush; that no others were there.

On March 13th, the *Austin Daily Dispatch* reported:

The general verdict in our city is that Thompson was lured into a trap and brutally assassinated, and that the affair was a well-laid, coolly prepared plan to murder him. The verdict of the coroner's jury is simply prepared to suit the case, and is not sustained by the facts. The evidence given before the jury is unworthy of credance, and was given merely by those who desired Thompson's death. That Thompson came to his death by shots from the pistols of Foster and Coy is unworthy of belief. Neither Foster or Coy or both together shot him that often or at all. In an interview with Billy Thompson, the brother of Ben, he declares that Ben and Fisher were shot by parties in the boxes or behind the scenes, hired to do the shooting, and all the circumstances point to this being a fact.

The jury having viewed the bodies where they lay on the

previous night, reassembled at ten o'clock the next day in Justice Adam's court. On account of the crowd which assembled thereabouts, the justice was compelled to give orders that no one be admitted to the room except witnesses, officers of the court and representatives of the press. The testimony was then taken, two recesses occurring between ten o'clock and the time when the verdict was rendered.

The testimony followed. A. Casanovas being sworn, said:

"I am constable of precinct No. 4, Rexar County. I was sitting on the left hand side of the Vaudeville Theatre about 11 o'clock, P.M., March 11th, and Ben Thompson, King Fisher and another man, whom I did not know, were sitting about six feet west of the entrance to the dress circle, when the shooting occurred. After they had been there a few minutes, I sawBilly Sims going up to Ben and shake hands and take a seat on Thompson's left. Ben put his arm over Sims' shoulder. They drank together and remained there about five minutes, where the whole party started toward the stairs. When they reached the door leading downstairs, Ben Thompson turned right around, and I saw Sims go down to where Foster was sitting, about three rows of chairs off. Sims said something to Foster, and they both came back to where Thompson was and engaged in a conversation which I did not hear.

"Thompson had a silk handkerchief in his left hand, was moving both hands and seemed to be getting excited. Billy Sims, Joe Foster, Ben Thompson and King Fisher, as I remember, were all standing together close in front of the door. Foster and Thompson were facing each other, and stood there about three minutes, talking loudly, when after something that I did not hear was said by Coy, Thompson drew back. I did not see his hands. The shooting then commenced, but I did not know who had pistols. I ran from where I was along the theatre with my sixshooter in my hand, toward the crowd, and when I reached them I saw Thompson and Fisher fall. During the shooting the whole party was close together, and I could see the pistol flashes as I ran, but could not see who was doing the shooting. I saw Coy rising up with a pistol in his hands, and think he and the other two fell together.

After this I gave information to the coroner. I missed Foster during the shooting, and did not know what became of him until after it; saw no pistol before it occurred. I helped carry Foster downstairs; I don't know who fired the first shot. I stayed until Marshal Shardein came."

J. S. Coy, being sworn, said:

"I am a special policeman at the Vaudeville, and was there on duty on the night of the 11th, when King Fisher, Ben Thompson and a red-faced man came into the bar downstairs, about 10 o'clock. I was standing between the bar and the entrance to the theatre with Mr. Sims, who called my attention to Thompson and Fisher, and asked if I knew them. I replied that I did. He said he was afraid there would be trouble, and warned me to be careful. I replied that I would, and that I had already informed the chief marshal, and had asked for more protection. After taking drinks, they went upstairs. I went to Mr. Casanovas and told him to go upstairs. He did so, and I went to Assistant Marshals Karber and Hughes and told them that King Fisher was armed, and my instructions were to allow none but the city officers to go into the theatre with deadly weapons. They said King Fisher had a right to wear the pistol, as he was a deputy sheriff. I went upstairs, and sat on the right, close to King Fisher. Thompson sat on Fisher's left. Thompson called a waiter, and told him to tell Billy Sims to come to him. Sims came and shook hands, and took a seat on Thompson's left. As soon as Sims was seated, Fisher got up and sat in front of me. He offered to treat, and asked the party what they would take. The order for the treat was two cigars, a glass of beer and one whiskey and seltzer. After the drinks had been taken, the conversation commenced, and the topic was the killing of Jack Harris, but was in such low tones that I could not hear or understand all that was said. At the conclusion of the conversation, King Fisher rose to his feet and said, 'Mr. Thompson, you told me we were going to have some fun; never mind talking about past times.' Thompson replied, 'Be easy, we'll get it pretty soon.' Fisher said, 'Well, let's go downstairs; come, Mr. Coy and Mr. Sims.'

"Thompson and I started ahead with Sims and Fisher

behind us. We were about to go downstairs when Thompson turned and said, 'Billy, ain't that Joe Fisher? Joe, will you take a drink with us?' Foster replied, 'Ben, you know I wouldn't drink.' Ben Thompson said something about shaking hands. Foster asked Thompson to let him alone; that he had mistreated him. Thompson was at my right, Sims on my left, and Fisher on Thompson's right, while Foster was in front of Thompson. Thompson said to Foster, 'Yes, God damn you. I'm glad that you don't drink and shake hands with me.' I requested Thompson to behave, and he said, 'Get out of my way; let me settle this affair with Foster.' He pushed me to one side. I told him again not to raise a disturbance, and, if he wanted to have anything to do with Foster, to go elsewhere, for I would prevent it here. As I started toward him and walked up to him again, he pushed me to one side, then called Foster vile names, slapped Foster in the face with his left, while he drew his pistol with his right hand. As soon as he drew the pistol, I jumped and grabbed it by the cylinder, and it fired. He ordered me to turn it loose. I refused, telling him to keep quiet. He said, 'God damn you, turn it loose!' Fisher also said the same thing. I said to Foster and Sims, 'Don't run, assist me.'

"We scuffled together from the door toward the corner, when Thompson, Fisher and I fell. Thompson fell in the middle, and as he fell, he loosened his hold on his pistol, while I still held it. No parties were around except Sims, Foster, Thompson, Fisher and I but I saw Casanovas running toward the end of the theatre. I never drew my pistol. I think, there were some twelve or thirteen shots fired altogether. I turned over Thompson's pistol to Marshal Shardein. I am not sure what time Thompson and Fisher came in. The parties who were shooting were behind us. I do not know whether Fisher had his pistol out or not. Thompson kept shooting all the time. I held his pistol until he fell. I was holding his pistol with both hands, and he was twisting it around to fire. One of his shots passed right by my ear. I was wounded slightly in the leg, but did not discover it until the shooting was over."

Marshal Shardein testified that he had not seen either Fisher or Thompson prior to the shooting; he arrived afterward to see the bodies lying side by side on the booth floor. While many claimed Ben Thompson did not fire his pistol, the marshal stated that when Officer Coy turned Ben's revolver over to him, he discovered that five shots had been fired from it. J. M. Emerson and Officer Chadwell also testified before the coroner's jury, but their testimony cast no new light upon the subject.

William Sims, being duly sworn, testified:

"Ben Thompson came upstairs last night accompanied by King Fisher, and when he first came in he walked up to the bar and called for drinks, a little before eleven o'clock. He stood talking to the bartender several minutes and then walked up to the balcony of the show. After he had been up there five or six minutes I followed on upstairs, and walked over and took a seat at the further end of the hall. After I sat there a few minutes he sent one of the waiters over to me saying he wanted to see me. I went over to him, and when I got up to him he turned and faced me, saying, 'Sims, I want to talk to you and tell you I haven't anything against you, but you haven't treated me right.' He talked on in a rambling manner, and seemed by his pantomine to be half crazy. He said, 'I'm rich now; I can get out of any trouble. People might think I was taking chances coming here, but I'm surrounded by my friends. I've got a sixshooter on, and I won't need to pull it, and if you move you will be killed.' I told him that I didn't want to have any trouble with him; that I had heard so much that I anticipated trouble with him. He said he didn't intend to hurt me, but thought I hadn't treated him right. I said, 'I'm glad to hear that, and that he had not come to take any chances from me.' He said a great deal of how devoid of fear he was and how rich he was. He jumped up suddenly and started toward the door. Just as he faced the door he whirled around and clinched my arm and kind of squeezed it. He commenced talking about Jack Harris, and said old Jack Harris pushed himself in the way; that he did not want to kill him. He turned and said, 'Joe Foster is the son-of-a-bitch who ought to have been killed.' He turned around suddenly and asked, 'Ain't that Joe Foster? Tell him to come over, that I want to talk to him.' I walked over and told Foster that Thompson wanted to talk to him. Foster got up, turned around in front of Thompson, looked up at him, adjusting his eye-glasses with both hands. Thompson reached out as if to shake hands with him. Foster seemed not to take notice of his hand at all. Thompson asked, 'Do you refuse to shake hands with me?' Foster replied, 'I've said, Ben, I cannot shake with you, and all I ask is to be left alone.'"

"Then Thompson said, 'Don't treat me that way. You refuse to shake hands with me. I'll bet you money you'll be sorry for that. I will live long enough to make you leave this country. I expose you as a thief.' Joe answered the threats by saying, 'Maybe so, Ben; I don't doubt it. I have been here twenty-five years and haven't stolen anything yet.' As Ben kept talking, he kept getting more wild and boisterous. He and Fisher seemed to keep backing up toward the wall. It was in a narrow place, on a little elevation, and when he got to this elevation he suddenly jerked his sixshooter and stuck it sideways in Foster's mouth, and cocked it as he pulled it back from Foster's mouth. As the pistol clicked, the policeman Coy grabbed it. As Coy grabbed it he said, 'Ben, I'm an officer; don't do that.' After the first fire, another pistol was drawn, and just as this pistol was drawn Fisher said, 'Don't you draw that, you son-of-a-bitch.' The firing then commenced on both sides. When it ceased, Joe Foster grabbed me by the shoulder and said, 'I'm shot; help me downstairs.' Thompson and Fisher had fallen by this time, and the firing had ceased. I did not notice Fisher or Thompson particularly then as I was helping Foster downstairs. Thompson fired the first shot. I think he fired twice before the other pistol was fired. I am not sure if Foster got his pistol out or not, but he reached for it, when Thompson said he had a pistol on."

Regardless of the scorching accusation of the press, a coroner's jury returned the following verdict after a deliberation of only fifteen minutes.

That Ben Thompson and J. K. Fisher both came to their deaths on the eleventh of March, A.D., 1884, while at the Vaudeville Theatre in San Antonio, Texas, from the effects of pistol shot wounds from pistols held in and fired from the hands of J. C. Foster and Jacob C. Coy. And we further find that the said killings were justified, one in self-defense in the immediate danger of life.

The verdict is still public record and is signed by George Hilgres, H. L. Ansell, J. A. Bennett, B. J. Gaston, J. M. Martin, and R. W. Walace, who comprised the coroner's jury.

Austin newspapers continued to harrass the city and its jury for returning a verdict which was considered unjustified. The *Austin Daily Dispatch* the same day commented:

The facts in the case do not bear out the verdict. A reputable gentleman, not a resident of Texas but who was in San Antonio the night of the shooting, and who saw and conversed with Thompson half an hour before he was shot, says he was informed by a police officer that the police force had orders to kill Thompson on the slightest provocation.

Joe Foster never testified. He died of blood poisoning eleven days later, after an unsuccessful amputation. He died with his lips sealed and the perpetrators of the murder of John King Fisher and Ben Thompson went unpunished. Foster was buried in the San Antonio City Cemetery #1. The wound he had received in his leg was self-inflicted during the commotion of the shooting. Coy always denied he had fired any shot in the bloody affair.

At noon on March 12th William Thompson, the brother of Ben, came after the latter's body. He requested permission to take it to Austin for burial. The city marshal granted the request, and it was borne from town on the afternoon train. On March 13th Ben Thompson was buried in Austin, Texas, amid crowds of people who gathered for the ceremonies.

Probably what the famous Bat Masterson said of the English-born gunslinger Thompson would fit him properly:

It is doubtful if in his time there was another living man who equalled him with a pistol in a life-and-death struggle.

King Fisher's remains were taken to Uvalde by United

States Deputy Marshal Ferd Niggil on the Sunset Express which left San Antonio the evening of March 12th. There it was turned over to his wife, who had her loving husband buried from their home at 128 West Mesquite Street, at which point friends came from far and wide to view the mortal remains of John King Fisher as the body lay in the cast iron casket.

Fisher was first buried in the original Uvalde Cemetery, where it was later lost to posterity. In later years Mr. Reading Black found the grave when he decided to create a Pioneer Cemetery out of the part of the cemetery which held King's grave.

In 1959 direct descendants of King Fisher had his remains reburied in a new steel casket about a half block from the original grave in Pioneer Cemetery at Uvalde. The window top of the old casket showed the remains of Fisher to be in a remarkable state of preservation.

The first child born to Kind and Sallie (or Sarah) Fisher was born at Eagle Pass, Texas, and she was named Florence. Their second daughter, Ninnie, was also born at Eagle Pass, while King was operating a saloon there. After Sheriff Boatright had been elected sheriff of Uvalde County he persuaded King to become a deputy and to move to Uvalde. It was at the West Mesquite address that their third child, a daughter named Mittie, was born.

Florence Fisher later married Frank Kellogg of Carrizo Springs; Ninnie Fisher married into the McDonald Family, later moving to California, and Mittie Fisher married Edward Campbell of Carrizo Springs.

King's family and his descendants have remained faithful and affectionate to his memory. Mrs. Sallie Fisher died August 10, 1946, having remained a widow for more than sixty-two years.

BIBLIOGRAPHY

Breihan, Carl W., Badmen of the Frontier Days, *McBride Co., New York, 1957.*

Breihan Carl W., Outlaws of the Old West, *John Long, Ltd., London, 1959.*

Bushwick, Frank H., Glamarous Days, *Naylor Co., San Antonio, Texas, 1934.*

Castleman, Harvey N., The Texas Rangers, *Haldeman Publishing, Girard, Kansas, 1944.*

Cunningham, Eugene, Triggernometry, *Press of the Pioneers, New York, 1934.*

Dobie, J. Frank, Vaquero of the Brush Country, *Southwest Press, Dallas, Texas, 1929.*

Douglas, Claud Leroy, Gentlemen in White Hats, *Southwest Press, Dallas, Texas, 1934.*

Farber, James, Those Texans, *Naylor Co., San Antonio, Texas, 1945.*

Fenley, Florence, Grandad and I, *John Leakey, Publisher, Leakey, Texas, 1951.*

Greer, James Kimmins, Grand Prairie, *Tardy Publishing Co., Dallas, Texas, 1935.*

Holloway, Carroll Co., Texas Gun Lore, *Naylor Co., San Antonio, Texas, 1951.*

Hough, Emerson, Story of the Outlaw, *D. Appleton and Co., New York, 1897.*

Jennings, Napoleon Augustus, A Texas Ranger, *Charles Scribner's Sons, New York, 1899.*

Peyton, Green, San Antonio, City in the Sun, *McGraw-Hill Co., New York, 1946.*

Raymond, Dora, Captain Lee Hall of Texas, *University of Oklahoma Press, Norman, 1949.*

Siringo, Charles A., Riata and Spurs, *Houghton Mifflin Co., New York, 1927.*

Taylor, T. U., Bill Longley and His Wild Career, *Frontier Times, Bandera, Texas.*

Texas, A Guide to the Lone Star State, *WPA Project, Hastings House, New York, 1940.*

Walton, William M., *Life and Adventures of Ben Thompson,* Edwards & Church, Austin, Texas, 1884.
Webb, Walter Prescott, The Texas Rangers, *Houghton Mifflin Co., New York, 1935.*
White, Owen Payne, Lead and Likker, *Minton, Balch & Co., New York, 1932.*
Wilson, Rufus Rockwell, A Noble Company of Adventurers, *B. W. Dodge Co., New York, 1908.*

HENRY STARR

He knew not fear, or whence it came
with a steady hand he played the game —
He raced across the plains with glee;
Robbing bank after bank in the Territory.

He spent many years behind prison walls
When released he always heard the call —
Gambling halls and banks appealed to him;
It was just more than an occasional whim.

This man was Henry Starr we all do know
And he was always ready to put on a show —
This outlaw tried to reach his goal;
Yet never would he shoot a soul.

He was toppled over by a rifle ball in Arkansas
Brought to his end by a citizen, not the law —
Perhaps not so spectacular as Jesse James;
Henry's career was overshadowed by such names.

CHAPTER V

BEAR-CAT HENRY STARR

The young rider shaded his eyes from the blistering Oklahoma sun with his right hand, his attention cast upon a little cloud of dust to the front of him.

"What the hell, Hank?" said one of the other riders. "Why are you trailing the posse when they are supposed to be chasing us?"

"Well," explained the other, "this way I'll know all the time just where they are."

This sounded like Henry Starr, one of the most spectacular outlaws in the history of the southwest, Jesse James and the Dalton Boys not excepted. This might be stretching a point. But one thing is certain, if Hank wasn't the most spectacular, he was certainly the most incongruous and astounding bandit who ever scowled down the barrel of a .44.

Henry had one weakness. He just loved to stick up banks. He was addicted to bank robbery the way some men are addicted to narcotics. The mere sight of the four letters "BANK" set his wheels clicking and his nerves hopping. It was an obsession with him. He just couldn't pass up an opportunity to step up to the teller's window and sing out:

"Hands up and hands steady!"

Unfortunately for Henry, he wasn't very successful at his calling. He was wounded half a dozen times and was a resident at various state institutions for more than 17 of his 48 years. He was probably the last of his breed and as for all the money he stole, his only asset when he died was the money for his burial expenses, paid to a Tulsa, Oklahoma, undertaker during his heyday. Henry fully believed that he would die while committing a robbery of some kind, and he wanted a decent burial without working a hardship on those he left behind.

Most men would have been discouraged, but not Henry Starr. He kept right on trying until his rather dubious luck ran out completely in 1921 at Harrison, Arkansas, where he was killed attempting a bank robbery in the grand tradition of the west at a time when most people had traded in their one horse shay for a tin lizzie.

Starr looked at his seemingly endless failures with a somewhat fatalistic attitude. He referred to his larcenous excursions as "scouting trips" and once told a friend:

"I'd love to quit but I can't. I enjoy scouting too damned much!"

The truth of the statement was borne out later. In 1919 Starr was hired at a fat salary by a Hollywood studio to play himself in the filming of one of his more spectacular — and unsuccessful — bank jobs, one in which his leg was shattered by a bullet and for which he subsequently served several years in the state penitentiary. On week ends, when things were slow, Henry wandered off to the neighboring communities for a few quick bank jobs. He didn't need the money; he just needed the excitement.

Starr was also an incurable gambler. He couldn't pass up a deck of cards or a pair of dice. If anything, his luck was even worse at games of chance than it was at robbery. He lost incessantly but never stopped trying. He had a will of iron backed up by absolutely no luck. But Henry was smart in one way; he never used liquor, tobacco, coffee, or tea. Damon Runyon would probably have called him a determined sucker.

Once, while escaping from a bank stickup at Caney, Kansas, Starr and two other men stopped to rest in a barn. The dice were shortly in play. By dawn the happy dominoes were still rattling off the barn door. The sheriff finally blundered onto the scene. Henry passed the dice along enough to parlay with the law. He shook hands with the sheriff like they were old Yale classmates.

"My chums and I are coming out at three o'clock," he said. "There are three of us. If you don't want your men to get hurt you better clear out. When we start we're going through." Then he went back to the game. Starr's reputation as a crack shot was well known. When three o'clock rolled around and the trio left the barn there wasn't a lawman in sight.

Starr's peculiar sense of honor also showed through his gambling craze. During his long career he held up every conceiveable type of business enterprise: trains, banks, depots, grocery stories. But he never stuck up a gambling table. If he didn't win it; he didn't want it.

Henry was born at Fort Gibson, Indian Territory, December 2, 1873, the son of George (Hop) Starr, a halfbreed Cherokee Indian, and Mary Scott, a quarter-blood. He attended the Cherokee Indian Mission there and lived in Fort Gibson until his father died in 1886. He finally took a job punching cattle on a ranch in the Cherokee Nation. Starr never blamed anyone but himself for his tragic criminal career, but it apparently can be traced to an injustice.

Henry was five feet nine and one-half inches in height, had straight jet black hair, dark eyes, and a good-looking, beardless face. He later was named the "Bear-cat" on account of his cunning and fearlessness under any and all circumstances. He loved to read all types of books.

Henry Starr was first arrested by United States Deputy Marshal Wykoff in June of 1891 for supposedly running whiskey in the Indian Nation, a Federal offense, and one which he claimed was rigged against him through circumstances, even though he would not divulge to the authorities what those circumstances were. A grandson of Deputy Wykoff, Roy Wykoff of Davenport, Iowa, a close friend of the author, imparted important data concerning Henry Starr. In February of 1892 Henry was arrested for alleged horse stealing but was released. He spent several months in jail, however, before being released at the Commissioner's trail. The man who had arrested him was Jasper Exendine.

In August of the same year he was again arrested, charged with horse stealing. Henry was released on bond furnished by his cousin, Kale Starr, and Chief Harris of the Cherokee Nation. Starr failed to appear at the designated time so his bond was forfeited, and Kale Starr offered a reward for his arrest.

Henry Starr told a different story about the alleged horse stealing. He told his friends that he had spotted a riderless horse wandering in the pasture where he was working one day. Three days passed and when nobody claimed the animal he saddled it up and rode into town. The owner of the animal spotted it, and Starr was arrested as a horse thief. He never forgot that experience.

Later he said:

"When I got out I was bitter on the world. I was just a kid and I had been brought up by my mother and father to think it was an awful disgrace to be in jail. I remember they used to chain me in bed at night. That was a terrible thing to do to a kid. When I got out I had blood in my eye. But I make no excluse of my bank robbing but lay a lot of it on this mistreatment I got and to my craving for excitement and ready cash for gambling."

Starr was no relation to the infamous, over-rated Belle Starr, the woman bandit. Many writers have erroneously referred to him as her husband or son. Actually his career as a banditt did not begin until 1892, three years after Belle was shot to death from ambush by her neighbor named Watson; although some folks in the area thought her son had killed her. Actually no relationship existed at all, since Belle married Sam Starr, a cousin to Henry, unless you wanted to say cousin-in-law.

Starr seriously tried to go straight several times during his life but he just never could make it as an honest man. When he was pardoned by President Theodore Roosevelt, Henry swore he would never turn another dishonest dollar. But the lure of the open safe was too much and sooner or later Henry always found himself back in front of the familiar teller's cage brandishing a sixgun instead of a checkbook.

As a boy, he became a deadly shot. Unlike most noted western badmen whose marksmanship was more a matter of legend than reality, Starr was a crack shot with both hands. A newspaperman sent to interview him found Henry sprawled out on the bank of a pond watching the turtles sunning themselves. During the course of the talk the reporter questioned Henry's ability with a pistol. Without a word, Starr stood up, pulled both guns, fired twelve shots from the hip and blew the heads off twelve turtles. That was the end of the discussion.

Despite his deadly eye, Starr claimed to have killed only one man and then only after an amazing display of his almost unbelievable sense of fair play. In July of 1892 the express office of the Iron Mountain Railroad at Nowata, I. T., was robbed by a band of masked men. The street burst alive with gunfire as the bandits were riding out of town with their loot, a paltry $400.00. One of the bandits bolted into a barbed wire fence and was thrown from his horse. He leaped up with one of his companions and escaped, but the saddle on the fallen horse was identified as one Henry had borrowed from a friend several days earlier.

Several weeks after the affair at Nowata, Henry Starr learned that a railroad detective named Dickey, and a special United States Deputy Marshal named Floyd Wilson, were at the "X.U." ranch, property of Albert Dodge, former employer of Starr.

Henry was determined to see what plans they had so he rode out to the Dodge place to investigate. He was personally unknown to Dickey and Wilson, who were awaiting his arrival, and when he came close to the house his presence was announced to them by Albert Dodge. The two officers mounted their horses and scoured the countryside, continuing the search a greater portion of the night, to no avail. At one point, they invaded the home of Henry's sister and threatened her if she would not reveal the whereabouts of her brother.

At noon the next day Henry again rode by the Dodge ranch house. Floyd Wilson raced from the house, mounted his horse, and gave immediate pursuit, with Dickey trailing behind on a bucking horse. When Starr saw Wilson in pursuit he dismounted. No doubt he thought some confrontation would occur, this measure would enable him to steady his aim if need be.

Wilson, cradling a Winchester in his arm, had also dismounted and was trying to reason with Henry. Suddenly the officer fired a shot; it passed harmlessly over Henry's head. Was it an intentional miss to frighten Henry Starr? If so, it was a bad mistake on the part of the deputy. Henry returned the fire, sending two lethal slugs at Wilson. The officer fell dead to the prairie, a total of four bullets in his body. Henry then sent several wild shots at Detective Dickey who fell from his horse, feigning death. Henry knew better. He laughed as he rode from the scene on Wilson's horse, his own animal having bolted during the course of the shooting.

"He was a damn fool," Starr later said. "I did everything to stop him short of shooting myself. It might have been a different story if his rifle hadn't clogged; he was a poor shot with his pistol."

Years later during a holdup, Henry shot a man's shoelaces off, as well as two buttons from his coat. Some people called it luck. Said Henry:

"I never killed a man in a robbery and don't intend to. Kill a man and the law never forgets it. But if you just rob somebody, everybody forgets it sooner or later. I hit what I aim at. I was just trying to scare him."

Between January and June of 1893, Starr committed at least eight robberies, possibly more. One of them was his first bank robbery. On a single day in January, Starr and several buddies held up two stores and the railroad depot in the town of Choteau. He was the only man who ever successfully carried off three robberies in the same town in the same day. The escapade at Choteau netted the outlaws around $400.00. The Dalton gang tried this trick a year before at Coffeyville, Kansas, with dire results. They had all been either killed or captured. Starr pulled three in one day the first time he ever tried his hand at robbery.

Early in February of 1893 Starr and Frank Cheney, an outlaw posing as a farmer, robbed the general store and depot at Inola, I. T., of $220.00. Starr's friends had urged him to leave the Territory for good to avoid capture and possible death. To secure funds for such a move he and Cheney decided to rob the bank at Caney, Kansas, a town of several thousand inhabitants. On March 25, the two outlaws rode up to the Caney Valley National Banks then rode to a back street, where they hitched their horses.

As the bandits entered the bank building Frank stepped to the cashier's window and Henry Starr to the left of him. Henry Starr then stepped behind the cashier's cage, from which point he could command a view of the door and at the same time hold his pistols on the people inside the bank. Cheney took a grain sack from his belt and entered the vault. Having stuffed the money into the bag, the two bandits calmly walked from the bank. Those inside were too scared to take any action against the brazen robbers.

After outwitting a small posse, the two robbers stopped at the home of a friend, some ninety miles from Caney. The loot amounted to $4,900.00, a small amount, Henry thought, for the efforts of their first bank robbery. Their chagrin knew no bounds when they later read in the newspapers that the foxy cashier had outmaneuvered them when he tossed $16,000.00 in large bills behind some ledgers during the excitement of the entry of the bandits into the bank.

By April half the cutthroats in the Indian badlands were rallying around the frisky young bandit, anxious to share in the gravy.

Henry Starr set up his gang headquarters at the ranch of Frank Cheney, near Wagoner, Oklahoma, with the entire band consisting of seven members: Henry Starr, Frank Cheney, a man named Watt, Link Cumpelin, Happy Jack, Bud

Tyler, and Kid Wilson. Only Kid Wilson and Henry Starr remained together towards the last.

Starr's escapades were not without their romantic overtones. On March 5, 1893, his gang held up the Katy Passenger train at Pryor Creek, Oklahoma. They seized $6,000.00 and a consignment of uncut diamonds. During the robbery, a young girl named Mary Morrison, of Nowata, rushed past Starr and ran into the thicket. Half an hour later Starr and his men found her cowering in the weeds. The next morning Starr placed the frightened girl on a train headed for her home town.

Riding into Arkansas on June 6, 1893, Henry and his five companions raided the Bentonville bank. The plan had been a good one. Starr and Cheney rode through the thickly settled portion of the county in a buggy, with two saddled horses behind, in order to hide their rifles. Kid Wilson was to distribute the rifles from the buggy to the outlaws as they dismounted near the bank. All went well until the outlaws emerged into the street, a half dozen hostages in front of them. Rifle fire erupted from the square, sending everyone into flight. Link was wounded by shotgun fire but not to any great extent.

Henry Starr, carrying the loot of $11,500.00, was the last to make a mad dash out of the valley toward Indian Territory. Close ahead of him rode Frank Cheney and the Kid. Early the following afternoon the bandits arrived at the home of Cheney, crossing the Grand River at Wagoner. Although a determined posse had given swift pursuit from Bentonville, the lawmen soon tired of the chase and returned home.

Henry's next appointment was with Mary Morrison near Nowata, in the Osage Country. A friend of the family had gone there previously with a covered wagon. It was Henry's intention to travel by wagon to Emporia, Kansas, with Kid Wilson acting as a guard. From that point they were to travel to the west coast, where Henry and Mary were to be married. They were going to take a fast train to California and travel into Old Mexico. They decided to stop in Colorado to replenish their stock of wearing apparel.

The trio alighted from the train at Colorado Springs on

July 2, 1893. Henry Starr was recognized by a man named William Feuerstine, a resident of Fort Smith, Arkansas, who was in Colorado on business. He informed the local police and they learned that the three passengers had registered at the Spaulding House as John Wilson and Frank and Mary Jackson. On July 3, the trio had returned from a sight-seeing tour of Manitou Springs, and Henry went to a nearby hotel for something to eat. Mary Morrison had gone on to the Spaulding House for a rest. Wilson rode on to a bawdy house, where he was later arrested.

At the restaurant Henry Starr was arrested without a struggle by four plain-clothes detectives. They told him they had been watching the trio but did not want to risk arresting either man until they had been separated. Mary Morrison was also taken into custody, although no formal charge was placed against her. Under the pillow of her bed the police found $500.00 in gold coin and $1,460.00 in currency.

The prisoners were taken from Colorado Springs to Denver by United States Deputy Marshal William Smith. There, accompanied by another deputy marshal named Brown, the trio was taken to Fort Smith, Arkansas, via Kansas City and Springfield, Missouri, to await trial in "Hanging Judge" Parker's court.

Henry Starr was indicted for the killing of Deputy Marshal Wilson, as well as being jointly indicted with Kid Wilson for the holdup and robbery of the Bentonville, Arkansas, bank. Starr was convicted of murder and sentenced to be hanged, the usual sentence when appearing before Judge Parker. His attorney appealed to the United States Supreme Court and he was awarded a second trial. This happened twice. In March of 1898 he pleaded guilty to manslaughter and was sentenced to five years in the Columbus, Ohio, prison. Kid Wilson was sentenced to serve twenty-four years in the penitentiary at Brooklyn, New York. Alfred Cheney, suspected of being an accomplice to Henry Starr, was also arrested and convicted of train robbery. He served ten years of the twenty-four years sentence imposed on him. No doubt, the reward money was the chief reason for the arrest of Cheney. Another strike against him was that he was the brother of Frank Cheney, Starr gang member. His conviction hinged mainly on the testimony of the railroad engineer at the Pryor Creek robbery. He stated he thought he recognized Alf as one of the train robbers. Henry's luck had again stood him in good stead. He actually should have been sentenced to 13 years in prison: 5 years for two train robberies; 3 years for manslaughter; 4 years for the Pryor Creek affair, and 1 year for the Nowata robbery. Judge Rogers later did impose the 13 years incarceration for the offenses as listed.

But if luck sometimes looked the other way on Henry Starr, he did at times manufacture a little of his own. In a nearby cell at the Fort Smith jail, where Starr was waiting to be transported to Ohio, was Cherokee Bill Goldsby, a burly Indian-Mexican halfbreed who was scheduled to hang for the killing of thirteen men. Goldsby was a madman. While attempting a stickup in 1894 he shot a man who was sitting at the window of his home. Goldsby said the man's looks annoyed him. If Goldsby wasn't, he certainly should have been superstitious. It took Judge Parker 13 minutes to instruct the jury, there were 13 witnesses against him, his trial lasted 13 hours, and of course, the jury and bailiff numbered 13. If that didn't convince him, Bill was sentenced to die on April 13, and there were 13 steps to the gallows, and 13 knots in the hangman's noose.

Cherokee Bill went wild after one of his colleagues, supposed to have been one Ben Howell, on July 26, 1895, smuggled a revolver to Bill by tying it to a long pole and passing it through the jail window.

He killed Lawrence Keating, one of the guards, and then holed up his cell for the better part of an afternoon, exchanging shot for shot with half a dozen prison guards and leaping into the air and gobbling like a turkey every time he fired a shot. Starr finally volunteered to disarm the man. The guards all agreed it was a good idea. If Starr got blasted it was all right, he had already cheated the judge's hangman anyway. Henry walked down the prison runway and disappeared into Goldsby's cell. The cubicle buzzed with whispers. Then Henry came back up the runway and handed the guards Cherokee Bill's pistol. He never told anyone how he had calmed the loco Indian down, but it was known that both Starr and Goldsby took great pride in the fact that they both had Indian blood. It was rumored later that Henry simply told Cherokee Bill to stop acting like an ass and take his medicine. Goldsby did just that.

On March 17th, the following year, Goldsby kept his date with Judge Parker's hangman, George Maledon. He had been given another trial for the killing of Keating and again was sentenced to be hanged. When asked if he had anything to say before the hangman dropped the trap, Bill replied classically: "I come here to die, not to make a speech."

Henry served eight of his thirteen years before his role in disarming the deadly Goldsby was brought to the attention of President Teddy Roosevelt, who granted him a full pardon. Starr then moved to Tulsa and settled down in the real estate business. He did all right. On September 11, 1903, he married Ollie F. Griffin, a part Cherokee young woman.

Henry and his wife were among the notables at the inauguration of Oklahoma's first governor, Charles N. Haskell. But the minute the Territory was admitted to the Union, the State of Arkansas dug out its old indictment against Henry. They hadn't forgotten the Bentonville stickup. Henry didn't wait around to see if Oklahoma was going to honor the extradition request, he flew the coop. Joining his old pal, Kid Wilson, who had also been released from prison by that time, he went right back to his old stand in front of the teller's cage.

It all happened through a misunderstanding. A friend had called Governor Haskell's office to see what his decision was relative to the Arkansas extradition request. The governor's secretary had said, "He hasn't granted it," but Henry's friend thought the report was "He's granted it."

Besides the spare build and features of his ancestors, Henry had also the inherent cunning and woodsmanship of the Indian. He used it to his advantage more than once. In the spring of 1908, Henry and the Kid held up the Tyro, Kansas, bank and set off a countrywide manhunt. One newspaper account at the time read:

> *. . . natives all along the way are out with corn knives and*

shotguns and it would be dangerous for a stranger to pass along the highway after the sun has set. Behind every fence post and every clump of weeds lingers one man or a dozen, ready to shoot down a bank robber or a peaceable citizen without the least provocation.

The reporter who wrote the story was apparently a frustrated fiction writer. Nobody even got shot at, including Henry, who rode right out of the county and dropped from sight.

In June, 1908, Henry and Kid Wilson popped up in Amity (now Holly), Colorado, long enough to dip into the assets of the Amity Bank. Friends who rode out to warn him that the sheriff and a posse were hot on his trail, finally found Starr trailing the posse.

Starr never strayed more than ten miles from Amity, but he wasn't caught. It was also about this time that Kid Wilson and Henry Starr parted company. Wilson never was heard or seen again. Many believed that Starr had done away with him but nothing was ever verified. Henry made one cryptic remark later about the matter: "The Kid was going nutty, and we parted; Wilson won't ever bother anyone else again."

Henry was always ready to try any new idea or scheme to outwit the law. He even tried camouflage once, painting his horse black and pasting white spots on it; then later washing the animal clean at a river. He resorted to fake mustaches, shaggy brows and beards but rarely ever wore a mask.

From Colorado and New Mexico Starr and his wife and young son, Roosevelt Starr (named after the President) went to Arizona to settle down in a small town named Bouse, sixty miles from the Mexican border. He wrote a friend in Tulsa, asking him to please dispose of some property Starr owned and send the money to him. The friend was a Judas. He told the authorities that Starr was in hiding in Arizona. He was arrested and returned to Colorado for the Amity Bank robbery. Sheriff Simpson had Starr removed from Lamar to Pueblo, Colorado, for fear he might escape. There he remained in jail from June 8 to November 24, 1909, for he was unable to raise the amount of his bond set at an exorbitant figure.

On the advice of his counsel, Granby Hillyer of Lamar, Henry Starr pleaded guilty to the charge of bank robbery and was sentenced to serve twenty-five years in the state prison at Canon City.

Henry served four years and then his glib tongue and charming personality worked for him again and he was released. One of the terms of the parole was that he would never agains et foot in Oklahoma. But Hank liked Oklahoma, regardless of what it thought of him.

Within two months he was living in a little white frame house at 1534 East Second Street, Tulsa, Oklhoma. Jim Wooley, the sheriff of Tulsa County, lived two doors away. They shared the same sidewalk and their children went to school together, and Wooley didn't know the real identity of his neighbor for two years. All the time they were rubbing elbows, quiet, respectable Henry was engineering robberies all over the state. He even dabbled in politics. His alias, R. L. Williams, was a name he had stolen from one of the candidates for Governor of Oklahoma at that time. One of his old classmates from the Oklahoma State Prison, the postage-stamp bandit Al Jennings, was also running in the race so Henry announced his candidacy. His name was added to the ballot, and the two ex-cons hoped they could confuse the voters. With two R. L. Williamses maybe they wouldn't know which one to vote for. Luckily the State of Oklahoma, the real Williams won the election.

On March 13, 1915, Starr broke away from the quiet little cottage on Second Street, and on the 27th he led a band of outlaws in a dual attack on the town banks at Stroud, Lincoln County, Oklahoma. As usual, Starr said he was just trying to get a stake so he could go away and settle down for good.

"I wanted to make a stake for my son," he said. "Make a big haul, fix the boy up and go off somewhere and be forgotten."

He was anything but forgotten. The robbers rode into Stroud, tethered their mounts at the stockyards and left one man in charge of them. Then they struck at both the town banks simultaneously. With $5,000.00 in loot, they started out of town. Starr's luck faltered as usual. A 17-year-old boy, Paul Curry, heard all the excitement and saw the bandits riding up the street. He jumped into a butcher shop, saw a sawed-off rifle used for slaughtering cattle leaning against the wall, grabbed it up and fired a shot as the bandits dashed by. The bullet tore into Starr's leg. Horse and rider went tumbling into the street.

"Throw away your gun, or I'll shoot you again!" the boy yelled from the doorway. Henry tossed his gun aside.

"I'm a bank robber and I've been caught," he told the sheriff. "That's all there is to say."

Another bandit named Louis Estes was also captured, but the others escaped.

The court said a little more . . . 25 years, which was getting to be the standard sentence where Henry was concerned. He almost did not make it from the Stroud jail. Veteran peace officer Bill Tilghman intervened and saved Henry from a lynch mob as it was about to break down the jailhouse door. Henry's popularity was definitely on the wan.

It has been the author's pleasure to have had contact with Lorene Hughes, the young girl who witnessed the robbery of the Stroud, Oklahoma, bank by outlaw Henry Starr, while his men robbed the second bank. Following is her eyewitness acocount of this event, and hers is probably the only such incident ever recorded by a child who walked into a bank while it was being robbed by a renowned bandit.

"It had been my habit to drop in and see Miss Nellie Neil, cashier at the bank, so on this Saturday morning I went in after mother had come to work at my dad's store next to the bank. When I walked in I hesitated at the door, seeing several strange men there.

"'Who is that?" one of them asked. It was the leader, Henry Starr.

"'Get out little girl,' the man said after I told them I was from next door.

"'Better let her stay,' Mr. Patrick said. 'She might say something and cause trouble.' He was an officer of the bank.

"'O.K. kid. Stick around for the big show.'

"The men continued sweeping money in bags. And Henry no longer pointed a gun at Mr. Patrick, whom he had threatened to shoot if he didn't open the time deposit vault. They said he wouldn't shed blood before a child as he had one of his own, a little boy.

"When they had finished with the money, he told the others it was time to go. 'We're robbing the other bank, too; we're meeting the others down there.' He told the bank employees he was going to march them down the alley. He put me on a stool and poured some pennies in my lap, and told me to wait and he would be back and we would get some ice cream. Later my mother came in, hearing the bank had been robbed, found me white as a sheet, sitting there and hanging my head.

"In the meantime word had gotten around that both banks were being robbed, and citizens had gotten whatever guns they could, and there had been a fight with the robbers as they backed toward their horses at the railroad yard.

"A seventeen-year-old boy, Paul Curry, had gotten a hog gun at his father's store, slipped up the alley and had wounded Henry Starr. His men had let him lie when he signalled them to go on. He was carried upstairs to a doctor's office over the bank. After his wounds were dressed he was removed to the county jail and sentenced to prison later on.

"He was later paroled when he was supposed to have reformed. He went back to Stroud with a film company to make a picture of the double bank robbery. Another girl of my age at the time, five years old, took my place in the film. Someone pointed me out in the crowd watching, and Henry Starr came over and handed me a dollar, telling me to get that ice cream he had promised me years back and to take some friends along."

After his escape from the lynch mob Henry was sent to the Oklahoma State prison, and his popularity blossomed back in full glory. He was his old, charming self again. Within four years, he had not only convinced the warden of the penitentiary, but the attorney who prosecuted him, the judge who convened at his trial and all the jurors, and the governor of the state that it was all a big mistake. He was really going to flip over the proverbial leaf this time. In 1919 he was paroled.

"I'm going into the motion picture business," said Henry. "After all, there's a lot more money in that than in bank robbing."

Henry was right. His first picture, a re-enactment of the Stroud robbery in which he played himself, was a great success. Paul Curry, the youngster who shot Starr and later distinguished himself for valor in France, even had a role. After this movie was completed there were other roles for Starr. He was making plenty of money.

In February of 1921, George Davis, a Tulsa motion picture executive, offered Henry a chance to go to Hollywood as a technical director for several westerns. The venerable Indian said he would think about it. Nobody had noticed that during the productions of the films, Henry frequently went off for the weekend. Invariably, wherever he went, the local bank would wind up "getting the business.: It happened in Chandler, and it happened in Davenport; Henry's weekends and bank holdups just seemed to coincide. But even with his scurilous record, nobody ever suspected that a successful movie actor would possibly be indulging in bank robbery. He didn;t need the money and bank robbery certainly was no popular hobby.

On the morning of February 18, 1921, while he was still mulling over the Hollywood offer, Henry and three friends drifted over to Harrison, Arkansas. It was a crisp winter morning and cars drifted by with their foghorns honking in the brittle wind. This was something new for Henry; he was used to riding a horse when robbing a bank, not a touring car automobile. Henry and company strolled into the Peoples National Bank at 10:00 A. M.

Suddenly the silence was shattered:

"Hands up and hands steady!"

Old Henry was back in the "saddlen again. Everybody in the bank raised his hands high but the bank president, W. J. Myers. Myers was a shrewd banker. His bank had never been robbed, even during a virtual epidemic of stickups a few months earlier. But Myers was a suspicious gentleman. He hadn't overlooked the possibility and twelve years before that

February morning he had put a back door in the vault opening into his office. While his customers were busy being scared to death and the outlaws were busy rounding up all the loose cash in the place, Myers slipped into the vault. As an added protection, he had placed a loaded .38 caliber, 1873 Winchester rifle inside the vault. He crept to the front of the vault and slowly pushed the door open.

Henry was busy stuffing money into a canvas bag. The first blast from Myer's rifle ripped through his spine. Starr fell to the floor, writing in agony. The rest of his crew went beserk. They could not figure out where the shot had come from. One of them leveled down on the bank cashier, Cleve Coffman, just in case.

"Don't shoot him!" screamed Starr. "Just get out of here." The boys took to the hills, leaving the ever unlucky Henry Starr behind.

"I don't blame you at all," Starr told Myers. "I would have done the same thing if I were in your place. You are at one end of the game and I am at the other and you won. You have a cool hand."

There was no one to notify about Starr's condition. His wife had divorced him the year before, claiming desertion and non-support. He was removed to a nearby building, where Cleve Coffman remained with him nearly all the time; when the end came for Henry he was also there.

"You saved my life," the young man told Starr.

"Yes, I know, and before I die, I want to give you my pistol as a souvenir. Use it wisely, son; I have never killed a man during the course of a robbery. I always tried to conduct my affairs, no matter what they were, in the whitest manner possible.:

The weapon Henry presented to Coffman was a .45 calibre Colt's, Army model revolver.

On February 22, 1921, the amazing career of outlaw Henry Starr came to an end. On the 25th he was buried at Dewey, Oklahoma, unmourned and penniless. Near his grave is that of his child.

PART II

LIFE OF OUTLAW HENRY STARR AS TOLD BY HIMSELF WHILE IN PRISON

HENRY STARR — HIS BOOK.

I was born near Fort Gibson, I. T., on December 2, 1873, and am of Scotch-Irish-Indian ancestry. My father, George Starr, was a half-blood Cherokee Indian; my mother, Mary Scott, is one-quarter Cherokee. There were three children by their union — Elizabeth, the eldest, Addie, the second, and myself, Henry George Starr, the youngest. I might mention that I was born in a cabin, the inevitable log-cabin, close to Fort Gibson, one of the oldest Forts in the West. It was here Sam Houston came when he fled from his beautiful wife and the governorship of Tennessee, and later married the fair Indian maiden, Talihina. Sam Houston was also famous for his ability to put much "fire-water" under his belt, and his accomplishments along that line were the envy of every Indian and soldier in that region.

Washington Irving also visited Fort Gibson, and it was while ruminating along the banks of the beautiful Grand River, that he wrote "The Bee-Hunt" and other stories.

James G. Blaine, he of the "plumed-knight" fame, after being so ingloriously unhorsed by fisherman Cleveland, sought to forget the sting of defeat by visiting the frontier, and stayed a long time at Fort Gibson as the guest of an army officer.

I spent my boyhood like thousands of other American boys. At the age of eight, I started to school, a distance of four miles, and I always made the trips to and from school on horseback. My teacher was a Scotchman from Canada — a highly educated and polished gentleman, but possessed of a most violent temper. All of the pupils were Indians and four-fifths of them of mixed blood. I went to school to this bullet-headed Highlander for two and a half years, and am proud to say that I held my own with all comers in class work. At the age of eleven I was in what I should judge would be the sixth grade; that ended my schooling. My father's ill-health made it necessary for me to stay at home and I can honestly say that it was with regret that I gave up my books to help win our daily bread. It was decided that I should try my hand at farming, so I hitched two horses to a ten-inch plow and literally dug into our farm. Critical neighbors said I couldn't plow; my sisters said I was too small to plow. This comment got under my skin and I made up my mind that I would not only prove to them that I could plow, but that I could also raise a crop of corn. My furrows were neither straight nor regular, but, barring whacks in my ribs and stomach, received from the plow-handles, I got my field plowed O.K. and with only a few days' help from a neighbor at critical periods, I really raised a splendid crop of corn.

This strenous work taught me patience and self-reliance, and a stick-to-itiveness that has been of great value to me all my life.

The Cherokee Nation, up to the year of 1904, elected a Chief, second Chief, Senate, Council, Judges, Clerks and Sheriffs by popular vote every four years. There was a penitentiary at Tahlequah, the capital. The convicts wore stripes, and as a child, the sight of them filled me with terror. There was also an Orphans' Home and a public school in all neighborhoods where there were ten or more children. In the early days there was no provision made for the education of white children in the Indian Territory. The tolerant Indian school directors allowed the white children to attend free. Since statehood, hundreds of full-blood Indians have quit attending school because they are taunted and insulted about their nationality. The teachers were afraid to take the part of the little red children lest the white parents become miffed. The scandal became so widespread that the Federal government took cognizance of conditions. White men could not vote or hold office, or be arraigned in court for any offense whatever against the life or property of an Indian citizen.

In 1886, my father died, and few months later my mother married a man named C. N. Walker of Arkansas and Texas, a sallow, malarial, green-eyed reprobate who rented an adjoining farm. He was a greedy rascal who saw a fine chance for exploitation of rich lands, with free range and no taxes. There may be a few good step-parents (I have seen a few myself) but I hold it does not pay to examine a snake's tail to see if it has rattlers. I had always looked upon the Indian as supreme, and the white renters as poor white trash who moved from year to year in covered wagons with many dogs and tow-headed kids peeping out from behind every wagon-bow, and who, at the very best, made only a starving crop. In the days of my childhood the Indian landowner was looked up to by his white renters, and always treated with courtesy and respect; but the years have brought about a great change; the white man holds power, and the same hypocritical renter has grown arrogant and insulting; whenever the Indian is spoken to at all, it is with a sneer. The Indian, and especially the fullblood in Oklahoma, is an outcast in his own country, and it is with a feeling of sadness and apprehension that I think of his future. Broken treaties, misplaced confidence and insult have made him lose interest in life. I have more white blood than Indian, and with my knowledge of both races, I fervently wish that every drop in my veins was RED. I admit that the white race is the superior, but oh, the price he pays for his superiority!

From the first I seemed to be able to read my stepfather like an open book, and we were secret, if not avowed enemies. He lost no opportunity to slip one over on me by exaggerating to my mother my most trivial misdemeanors, and was forever complaining of my utter worthlessness and meanness. I confess I was sullen and inclined to "talk back," and if he asked me to do any work I complied with poor grace. Why should I work for this scheming renegade, when I KNEW he would take eveything away from my mother, which he later did? It had always been the custom at home to allow the children to claim horses and cattle. I owned a saddle pony and saddle, independent of anyone, having earned the money to buy them. He and I got along without an open rupture for about six months, but one morning he told my mother a deliberate lie about some trivial thing I should have done, and I very promptly said it was a lie. Such a thing was less majesty, in the opinion of my mother, and a look from C. N. was a sufficient cue. She ordered me from the table, saying she proposed to give me a licking that I should remember. I replied that I intended to finish my breakfast; then if she and C. N. wished to try to whip me, they could. I had always stood for her switching as a matter of fact, but I did not intend that anyone should lick me over a lying stepfather. So when she came to begin operations I firmly pushed her aside. She called C. N. and the hired man to hold me, and by this time I was so angry that I told them I would certainly kill them if they laid hands on me. Of course, they could have easily over-powered me, but if they had, the stepfather question would have been settled for all time. Of course, this incident made things harder for me at home, and a few days later I ran away from home on a pretense of going hunting. I first went to a dance a few miles south, then to my father's sister's, where my sister and her husband also lived. They were glad to give me a home, and so I went to work for them. About a month later my mother came after me, and I told her I didn't intend to go back; she was very angry at my refusal and tried to whip me. My sister and her husband told her that I was getting too big to be whipped, and as I was satisfied with my work, why not let me stay with them. They knew my home life had become unbearable since the advent of C. N., and shared my dislake for him. So mother took my horse and saddle and went home. A few weeks later my uncle by marriage came to see me, and urged me to go back. Knowing that this uncle was my father's best friend, I listened to him. I still think his advice was bad, and can also see the fine Italian hand of my stepfather-the craven was afraid of criticism if I stayed away, and had begged my uncle to persuade me to come home. I returned with the understanding that no one would ever try to flog me. In January, 1888, we moved from the old home to the northern part of Indian Territory, and about twenty miles south of

Coffeyville, Kansas. Before leaving, my stepfather showed his petty, grasping nature by selling my pony and saddle. The new country filled me with high hopes-miles and miles of prairie, where one could rise unhampered by high fences and timber. I aspired to own cattle and horses to graze on this fine range, and in the spring I began planting corn at 50 centers per day.

My stepfather had two grown brothers and a couple of sisters living near, and I must say that these two boys were as fine and honorable fellows as I ever met, and they both knew what sort of a fellow my stepfather was. Each of them had numerous chances to betray me in after years, when large rewards were offered for me, dead or alive, but they weren't that kind. And at this writing I hold the friendliest feelings for the entire family, excepting C. N. I cannot perceive how brothers could be so different. Through Jeff, the oldest of the two boys, I got a job on the half-circle-box ranch in the fall of '81. My boss was James S. Todd, an old Texas cowman, and one of the finest I ever worked for. He was well educated and possessed of plenty of common sense, and I believe, even now, he will testify that I was always on the job. His present home is in Fort Worth, Texas.

Guess I would be working for him yet and all the things of the past averted if it hadn't been for the following incident: One morning before breakfast, just as I returned from wrangling horses, I happened to be riding the favorite horse of the man we were boarding with. I met Todd as I rode into the yard, and he said that a large number of cattle were about to cross the backwater of a creek, and for me to hurry as fast as I could and throw them back, as about a hundred had already swam over. Now, I had always been anxious to serve Mr. Todd to the best of my ability, so I forgot that I was on the favorite horse of another man, and rode him at a clip to make the sweat and lather come in profusion; about an hour later his owner arrived, and when he saw his pet all but out, he was wild with rage. I told him of the boss' order to throw the cattle back without delay, and that I intended to do it if it killed every horse on the ranch. We had some words, and when I got back to the ranch I informed Mr. Todd that I intended to quit, and why. He told me I could work on if I wished; that the other fellow and his horse were working for him and for wages, just the same as I. But the bee was in my bonnet and I quit. You don't find many as square as James S. Todd.

I was idle only a few days. I got a job close by, herding some fine beef steers, and after shipping I visited my kinfolks back at the old home, going a distance of a hundred miles on horseback. This was in the fall of '90, and I had blossomed into a man, weighed 144 pounds and was very proud of the fact. This same fall I began work for the Open A people, a small Nester outfit with a ranch near Mr. Todd's. They bought cattle wherever they could, and from one head up. This work lasted until the first of the year '91. Then I secured work with a Mr. Roberts, who had a small outfit in the same locality. I had not been fired by the Open A people; their cattle had all been shipped and there was nothing to do. I rode for them again the following year.

While working for the Roberts boys, two strange horses drifted into a pocket formed by two farms and a pasture joining them. As there was no water in this pocket, it was plain that they were runaways. The boys said for the first one who rode that way to let them into the gate to water, as no doubt some one would be on the hunt for them soon. I let them in and, noticing that one of them bore saddle marks, I rode him several times. I also informed other ranchers that he was a stray. In something like a month, Charles Eaton, his owner, came after him, and seemed pleased to find him in such good condition, even offering to pay me for my trouble. This was in october, '91, and in December, same year, while I was in Nowata, a small railroad town near the ranch, a vicious-looking fellow, who said he was a Deputy United States Marshal, read a writ charging me with the larceny of Eaton's horse. I was too badly scared to be indignant over such a fake charge, as I knew nothing about laws, courts or justice. The warrant had been sworn out by Charles Eaton, the same fellow that had been so profuse in his thanks for the care I took of his horse, and that simply stunned me, nor do I know to this day what made him prefer the charge, as he swore the truth later. I asked to send word to my friends, but was refused. I was taken to a hotel and handcuffed and placed in a room, the loathsome deputy acting as guard. For supper they gave me a hunk of sausage and some crackers, and that night I was chained to the bed as though I were the foulest murderer. Even now, murder gets in my blood when I recall the cold chains on my innocent limbs. My faith in the majesty of the law and in my fellow man weakened, and during those long hours on my way to Fort Smith I was still handcuffed. The marshal told me that a certain attorney there might be able to get me out of this trouble, and as I was inexperienced, I took the bait. Hence, on our arrival I was conducted to the office of this legal vulture and gave him $22.00, all the money I had, and a bill of sale for my horse and saddle. Shame upon the fair name of our government for being a party to such a condition of affairs; instead of giving that protection pledged in sacred treaty to the Cherokee Indians, here was a commissioned officer of our government conspiring with a contemptible lawyer to cheat an innocent Indian boy out of a few hard-earned dollars. I shall not honor this lawyer by giving his name; he is only one of many of that stripe who disgraced that bloody and corrupt Federal Court at Fort Smith, Arkansas.

From the attorney's to the jail I was not accused of being faint-hearted, but the sight of that old structure and the rough attitude of the officials chilled my heart. I could also hear the yells and the curses of the 200 prisoners, who were allowed to scream as loud and as long as they desired. I was put on the second floor, the location for horse thieves and highwaymen, and no sooner was I thrust through the door than a bleached-out prisoner let out a series of yells and cries at me of "Fresh Fish!" whereupon the rest began to taunt me and laugh. I was hustled down to the "Kangaroo Court" by this sheriff and a deputy, the sheriff all the time bawling, "Oh, yes, the Honorable Kangaroo Court is now in session," This business was all Greek to me. The judge fined me fifty cents for breaking into jail without consent of the inmates. Of course, I didn't have a cent, and the sheriff knew it. The bleached-out heavy one noticed a light gold ring on my finger, and made a grab at it, saying that the "Court" would keep it for security. The ring had been loaned to me by my sweetheart, and to have that foul old jailbird even touch it was a desecration. I forgot that I was in jail or court, and smashed him on the nose and the sheriff on the chin, and we went at it for keeps. It was soon evident to his friends that he was overmatched, and they started to help him. At that minute a big, full-blooded Creek Indian came up and kept everybody off while I put the finishing touches to my man, and I certainly made him let out the big squeak. I was not tired nor hurt, and expressed my willingness to accommodate any of his friends, but they didn't seem at all anxious. Of course, this incident didn't make me at all popular with the sheriff.

The odor of a large, poorly-kept jail is worse than the odor in the animal section of a circus, and this particular jail was the worst ever. I was assigned to a cell, the bedclothes reeking with filth and covered with lice. I sat all night on a small box as far from the bed as I could get, and one never placed in a like position has no right to speculate on my thoughts. I, who had never possessed a cent dishonestly, and who had been taught to respect and revere the law from infancy — that a thief was a low, vicious person, and a jailbird one to be shunned — was put in amongst such men on a charge that I was perfectly innocent of, and was degraded and disgraced forever. In the twenty-three years since, I have passed through some pretty tough tests, but during the lonely vigils of that night my soul passed through its supreme baptism of fire. I am not ashamed to confess that I wept hot tears — not of fear, but of outraged young manhood. Aside from the trouble I had had with my step-father, my life had been cleaner than that of the average boy, and I felt that the future could never hold any good thing for me again. My cousin, Charlie Starr, a prominent cattleman, had heard of my arrest, and had me arrained the next morning, going on my temporary bond. The lying deputy asked the commissioner for the time to get some more witnesses. Of course, this request was a fake, pure and simple, but it was granted, and I was taken back to that vile cell. During the week that passed most the good went out of me, and I became a soured, sullen man, brooding over this great wrong that was being done me. As no witnesses appeared, I was brought up for a preliminary heating. My cousin, Charle Starr, had seen the commissioner and explained my case. The scoundrel, Eaton, who had sworn out the warrant, knew my cousin would not stand for a crooked swearing, and when he was put on the stand he swore to the truth, namely that he had offered me pay for taking up his horse and caring for him and was forced to admit that there was a doubt in his mind that I had attempted to steal his property. Mr. Eaton was the only witness on his side, and I was promptly discharged. The commissioner gave Mr. Eaton and the deputy a severe reprimand in open court, but I can see now that this was only horseplay to appease the just wrath of my uncle. He should have had Eaton arrested for perjury and taken the deputy's commission away from him. I should have been given a hearing before being put in jail, and the reason I wasn't was because the deputy got $125.00 for committing me to jail; he also got something like $40.00 for mileage, 50 cents for the sausage and 50 cents each for the breakfasts I was supposed to get, but didn't. Eaton received over $20.00 for mileage and $1.50 per day while waiting for the trial, making a total of between $95.00 and $100.00 that the government was out. (Every word can be corroborated by records at Fort Smith.) A good investment for the making of outlaws. This ended my first introduction to Fort Smith's famous and infamous court. Later I shall have more to say about it, as I have only scratched the surface in the telling of the foregoing.

I returned to Nowata with a sad heart. I was lowered and cheapened in my own estimation; to have been arrested for horsestealing was something dreadful, and I was not able to appreciate that being discharged removed the reflection from my character. I was ashamed to visit my sweetheart, but the sly miss came to where I was staying, and with true woman's intuition, brought up the subject. She told me that everybody who knew me knew I was innocent, and invited me over to see her the following Sunday.

Am I a child of misfortune, or is it just plain "damn bad luck"? Privately, I don't believe completely in anything that has or ever will happen; only in the inexorable law of total obliteration and nothingness.

I again began to work on the Open A ranch. On my way to the Delaware Indian payment a few miles distance, I passed through Nowata. A man I had known for four or five years asked me to take his grip over to the payment grounds. He had come over horseback and I was in a buggy, and pleased to be of any slight service to him, so I put the grip in and started for the grounds. About two miles out two deputy United States marshals overtook me and commanded me with drawn guns that I get down out of the buggy and allow them to search it. I readily complied, and to my surprise and consternation, the grip contained two pints of whiskey. I told them that I had no knowledge of the grip's contents, also that I did not drink. "So," said one of them, "then you must have intended to sell it, and what makes the charge against you more serious."

It was a penetentiary offense at that time to sell liquor in the Indian Territory. I did not inform on the owner of the grip, for I was satisfied that it would not help me. I knew that those scheming officers were stuck to make fees out of my bad luck. My previous experience with the law had taught me the instability of justice. A United STates court covering whiskey and misdemeanors had been established in Muskogee, Indian Territory the year before, and they took me there. That night, for the second time in a few months, I, an innocent man, felt the murder-breeding leg-irons and chains.

The men I was working for immediately signed my bond and took me back to work for them. They knew I was innocent, but advised me to plead guilty, pay a fine and have it over with, instead of fighting a long-drawn-out trial, with no witnesses to help me. When my case was called to trial about two months later, I made a plea of "guilty." One of the deputy United States marshals, on being questioned by the judge, was man enough to say that he didn't think I was a whiskey peddler, and aside from the former charge of hose-stealing, which had been disproved, my reputation was an excellent one; he didn't believe that I knew anything about the whiskey being in the grip. The judge fined me $100.00, a stiff fine for that offense. I paid the amount and went back to the ranch in debt, and worked hard and faithfully until cattle shipping time.

I was disheartened and disgusted. My respect for the law had taken an awful tumble. I began to think that so long as I had the name of being a "bad one" I might as well have the game. I went to Nowata, a town of 300 people. Everybody there knew me, and beside, I was the champion local footracer. I went over to the depot to see the train come in, and noticed a fat roll of bills in the safe. I became possessed with a desire to make good my bad reputation by robbing that safe. Before the two arrests, had I found $100.00, or even $10,000.00, I would have returned it to its owner, but now the spirit of retaliation was strong within me, and I was filled with a spirit of injury that made the contemplation of such a deed seem a pleasure. I at once went into the country and told a young man I knew, who was inclined to be tough, that I could show him how to make some money. I had never associated with a fellow that was crooked before, and had a bare speaking acquaintance with this one. He was ready for any old thing, so I told him how easy it would be to hold up the agent at night, as he kept open until 10 P.M., and was always there alone.

Three days later we met by appointment. This was in July of the year '92. As soon as night came we rode out from hiding and like a streak to Nowata — had less than an hour to make ten miles. We hitched in the stockyards and put on our masks, which we had made out of handkerchiefs. Held up the agent and two officials and three loungers with Winchesters and .45 Colts. It was child's play, and as we came out, I fired a few shots, more to let off nervous tension than anything else. We got $400.00.

The night was dark. I was riding a bad horse, and a few miles out of town my horse bucked into and literally astride a wire fence. I slipped from the saddle and the horse escaped in the darkness. The other fellow had furnished the horse, but the saddle I had borrowed from a party in Nowata, and I knew I would have to find him before morning and get the borrowed saddle, or I would be accused of the robbery. I came back to the location early in the morning and found that the horse had gone to a nearby house, and was cut beyond recovery. The farmer had taken the saddle with him to Nowata and turned it over to the authorities. Of course, the railroad detectives and deputy marshalls soon had me under arrest, and off we went again to Fort Smith. This time I did not care, for I was guilty, but I pleaded "not guilty," and my bond was fixed at $2,000.00. It was signed by E. E. Starr, a relative, who was at that time treasurer of the Cherokee Nation, Chief Harris and Mr. Ridge Paschal, Cherokee attorney and politician. I admit I hadn't the least intention of going back to stand trial.

This was in September, and my case was slated for November. I went to stay with my aunt near Fort Gibson, presumably to wait trial. About November 5th, or a few days before trial, I went to Nowata. Milo Creekmore, a fellow who had been staying at my aunt's, went with me. My lack of interest in my coming trial caused my friends and relatives to suspect that I intended to scoot to the brush, and they all begged me not to skip my bond. Of course, I said I wasn't going to, but I don't think I convinced them that I was telling the truth. We went to Nowata by train and had only a small sum of money and an old white-handled .45 between us. The weather was cool and crisp and we had no horses or saddles.

A certain old-timer, well known around Nowata, said when I was arrested the first time that all Indians were natural-born thieves, and I MIGHT be guilty of the charge. We were near his house this night, and to keep his opinion of the Indian free from falling flat, I took two of his best horses and the only saddle he had. A few miles further on I took another saddle. I had turned my back on established authority and resolved from that time on to go the limit. We rode several miles and hid our trail and stayed all night at a friend's house. He told me that he had put $300.00 in a store at Lenapah, a small railroad town nearby, and we decided that this was about our size, as we had only one .45 and three cartridges. The next night we rode to Lenapah and took the farmer's hog money. He did not lose it, however, as the store made good his loss. Then we rode about sixty miles into the Osage country and got a friend to buy us each a .38-.56 Winchester and new revolvers and plenty of ammunition. I also bought a new Cheyenne saddle from a cowboy. We turned the stolen horses loose and bought others.

The day my case was called at Fort Smith we were in a deep canon far into the Osage country, chuckling at the absurdity of anyone trying to arrest me. A few days later, we robbed Carter's country store of $180.00 and drifted south to Fort Gibson. On our way, and a few miles from Wagoner, we stopped at the home of Frank Cheney. It was a cold, sleety night, and we were glad to get shelter. I had never seen Cheney before. He was with me afterward in some pretty snaky places.

The next day near Fort Gibson, Creekmore bought a couple of quarts of whiskey and proceeded to get tanked. I objected and we had some words, and he got on his horse and rode away. The drink business didn't go with me; I had determined to always keep a clear head, so if shooting occurred I could give a good account of myself. I had already settled in my mind that I was not afraid of anybody.

Well, I went back to the vicinity of Nowata, and in less than a month had a fight with Floyd Wilson, a railroad detective, and a former United States marshal. I killed him and made his companion hug the ground so close that he played "'possum." There were six eyewitnesses to this affair, Mr. Arthur Dodge of Granada, Colorado, being one, as it happened on the prairie right in front of his ranch, the "X U," eight miles from Nowata.

The railroad had secured the services of Floyd Wilson, an ex-soldier, and an ex-deputy marshal of Fort Smith, Ark., to hunt me, and they had openly boasted of what they would do to me on sight. The night before the shooting, these fellows had called at my sister's house to see if I was there, had broken down her door and acted in a manner unbecoming to officers and gentlemen. The insults to my sister made me nearly crazy, and their threats to shoot me on sight brought about the killing.

I was riding by the "X U" Ranch when they came out and opened fire on me. Every eye-witness to the affair swore that they fired first. Wilson took five shots at me, hitting my clothes twice. I took four at him and every shot went into his body. He died instantly. I took two shots at the detective and he played dead. I got off my horse to shoot, as I did not want to take chances of his spoiling my aim. My horse ran away, so I mounted Wilson's and leisurely rode away.

I had promised myself never to shoot unless it was to save

my own life, and have never had any qualms of conscience over that occurrence. It was simply a case of their lives or mine. They started the fireworks, and besides, it developed at the trial that the warrant they held was bogus. They were working for the reward offered by the railroad.

On my way into the Osage county I realized that I had done the one thing I had hoped never to do, and that there was now no turning back. I resolved, that being the case, to shoot as long as I could see gun sights. I scouted through the country, say, in a radius of 60 by 160 miles from the scene of the shooting, and nine-tenths of the people were my friends. They knew I had jumped my bond, was a highwayman and had killed my man, but they also knew of my two previous arrests when innocent, and that I had to kill or get killed in the engagement with Wilson and the other fellow. (Note: Who was the other fellow?) There was a reward of $1,200.00 offered for me, dead or alive, and yet I had scores of friends who would shield me and stand guard over me while I slept; and these men were honest, hard-working citizens, who could easily have shot me while I was asleep and claimed the reward. The majority of these men were white, and I of an alien race. I regard their loyalty as typical of the Anglo-Saxon's sense for fair play, and if I must have white blood in my veins, let it be of that kind. Having known them has made me a better and truer man.

Sometime in January, '93, while stopping at Frank Cheney's, seven miles north of Wagoner, he and I rounded the little town of Choteau on the M. K. & T. Railway. We took everything, including the two general stores and the depot; cleaned up over $400.00. A few days later we paid Inola a visit; cleaned out the general store and depot, securing about $220.00.

Frank Cheney was, of course, still posing as a farmer and I never allowed anyone to see me at his place. I was scarcely going around with a chip on my shoulder, but there are still lots of people in Oklahoma who will tell you I wasn't playing the coyote, either.

The two marshals who had arrested me when innocent, took to the tall and uncut. They found out that I was a dead shot, and having "got my man," might remember to their undoing, the large part they had played in making my life a wreck.

During the winter I came near having several encounters with different marshals, two of whom were known as brave men and who had got their men. But whenever danger was close, some good friend was at hand to put me wise to the fact.

They came one day to a house where I was staying; my horse and saddle, which they knew by sight, were in the stable. They stayed a long time. I was waiting for them in the hall at the head of the stairs with my rifle drawn, and could have killed them as easy as shooting two rabbits had I so desired. They went to the stable, where my horse and saddle was evidence to my nearness, but soon mounted their horses and rode away without once looking back. Many years later one of them told me that they both knew I was in the house, but at the time each assured the other that I was not any place around. There are five people living who were at the house that day. I was in no hurry about leaving, for I could tell by their actions that they did not want me very bad. A few days later I was at a friend's home when a marshal rode by, but he went away without learning of my presence.

In February I was going through Verdigris Bottom when I saw two officers coming toward me in a buggy. I slipped off my horse and covered them. They called to me not to shoot, that they were not looking for me. I kept them covered, and they lost no time in getting over the road. The same month I came back from the Creek Country to the Cherokee Nation. It was a winter night, though warm, and there was a dim moon in the west. I had ridden perhaps forty miles and it was about 2:30 in the morning, when I passed through a thick settlement. Every blasted dog in the country seemed to wake and bark. I knew that the barking of the dogs would reveal my course if anyone was out looking, and while I hardly expected to find officers out after me, I proceeded with some care. I had friends in the settlement, too, but hadn't been in those parts for several weeks, and knew they would not be looking for me. I came to a point where the road led north through the high hills with timber growing down to the road; there was a farm to the east and open prairie to the west. I dismounted and walked, my Winchester cocked and held in the direction of that timber. The faint moon was casting weird shadows and while not on the watch my thoughts were on higher things. If I had been an imaginative person I could have seen all sorts of hobgoblins and booger-men in the shadows. The spell of the night and the solitude was over me, and I was feeling from the depths of my soul what the peets so weakly express.

I knew there was a lane running east a short way ahead, and I approached it with extreme caution. I hope it will not be boasting on my part if I say that for keen sight and hearing I am there with the goods. I had spent most of my life with Indians who were raised in the open, but have failed to find one who could beat me in this respect.

About 100 yards from the lane I led my horse under the shadow of some trees and went forward to reconnoiter. I sensed the approach of someone, and when within about thirty feet of the lane, I saw two mounted men coming from the east. I felt certain they had not seen me, so stepped up to within ten feet of the corner and covered them, at the same time telling them in language more forceful than polite that I would mow them down if they did not ride straight ahead and not look back. They were scared to death, and as they rode away like two statues into the night, I taunted them with the fact I was Henry Starr, bandit and dead-shot, and why not come back and get me and the $1,200.00 reward on my head. Had the situation been reversed, they would have sent me to the boneyard. I rode about a half-mile to the east, and as I came to a creek-bed without any timber, I noticed three men riding out of a gully not sixty yards away. I was off in a jiffy and fell flat on the ground; they, too, dismounted and stood behind their horses. I saw their Winchesters glisten in the moonlight, and why they didn't shoot, or why I didn't, can be answered by the savants. I suppose they, as well as I, dreaded the consequence at such close range. After a few minutes had passed, and no word spoken, I knew I had the Indian sign on them. I told them that I was Henry Starr and was ready to fight them to the death; that I had just disarmed their two friends at the head of the lane, and if they didn't back off, I proposed to blow them off the prairie. That there is magic in a name is proved by the fact that they mounted and rode on without having spoken one word. I immediately cut a wire fence and galloped through a wheat field to a friend's house nearby, where I stayed for a few days.

The gossip among the country folk was of great benefit to me. Someone told that I wore a steel breast plate; another that I had shown him the breast plate and where bullets had hit it. This talk, together with my phenomenal accuracy and swiftness with firearms, made me a truly bogey-man to the best of them. As a matter of fact, I was but an average shot, considering I had handled firearms since I was ten years old. I did make a few scratch shots, however, as the following will show: In January, '93, while at the home of a friend and in the presence of several men, I shot a rabbit dead at 150 yards on the run. The following week I was buying a horse, and three or four neighbors, all friendly to me, were there. I galloped the horse a few yards, saying I proposed to shoot the two top wires on a fence about thirty yards distant. As I wheeled sidewise, I brought my gun up and fired two quick shots; the top and second wires were cut clean about half-way between the posts. I could do the trick about once in three times. I also killed a coyote at 685 measured yards — not flunk — but it was a lucky shot and witnessed by several friends. Of course, all of this reached the officers' ears with exaggeration common to such stories. One time a party said: "How brave you are!" but I quickly checked him up by saying that an outlaw could not get that high on the scale of courage. The word "brave" should only be applied to those who risk their lives in an honorable calling, such as fighting for their country. Give a man moral courage, and he's got the other fellow whipped; that is, if he believes sincerely in his own cause and holds a clear conscience. A lot of cynical people will smile at the thought of an outlaw having a conscience, but that very thing has given me a brand of courage that has made me entirely free from fear of anything, here or hereafter. You may have heard people say, "He has a brave heart.: To my thinking there is no such thing. The proper expression would be: "He has a brave head," — the heart has nothing to do with it, because you first see the

Henry Starr

Lorene Hughes, the young girl who saw Henry Starr rob a Stroud, Oklahoma, bank.

Lorene Hughes

Bill Tilghman, deputy United States Marshal who saved Henry Starr from being lynched after the Stroud, Oklahoma, robberies.

Henry Starr's Colt double action .45, Army model.

The Colt .38 caliber revolver owned by Henry Starr.

Lee Pollock, a deputy sheriff who once arrested Henry Starr.

J. Warren Reed, frontier lawyer who defied Judge Parker in court.

I. C. Parker who was known as the "Hanging Judge".

"Hanging" Judge I. C. Parker's courtroom in Fort Smith, Arkansas.

Outlaw Bill Cook who was arrested Jan. 11, 1895 in New Mexico and jailed.

Al Jennings, the train robber who ran for governor when Henry Starr did.

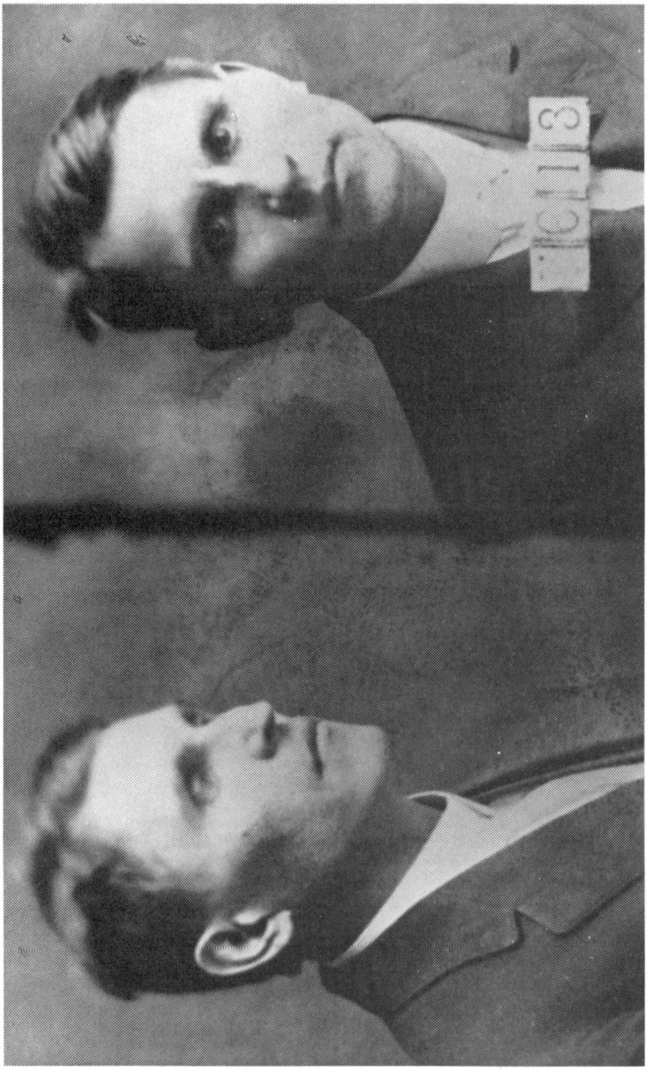

Henry Starr's prison photo.

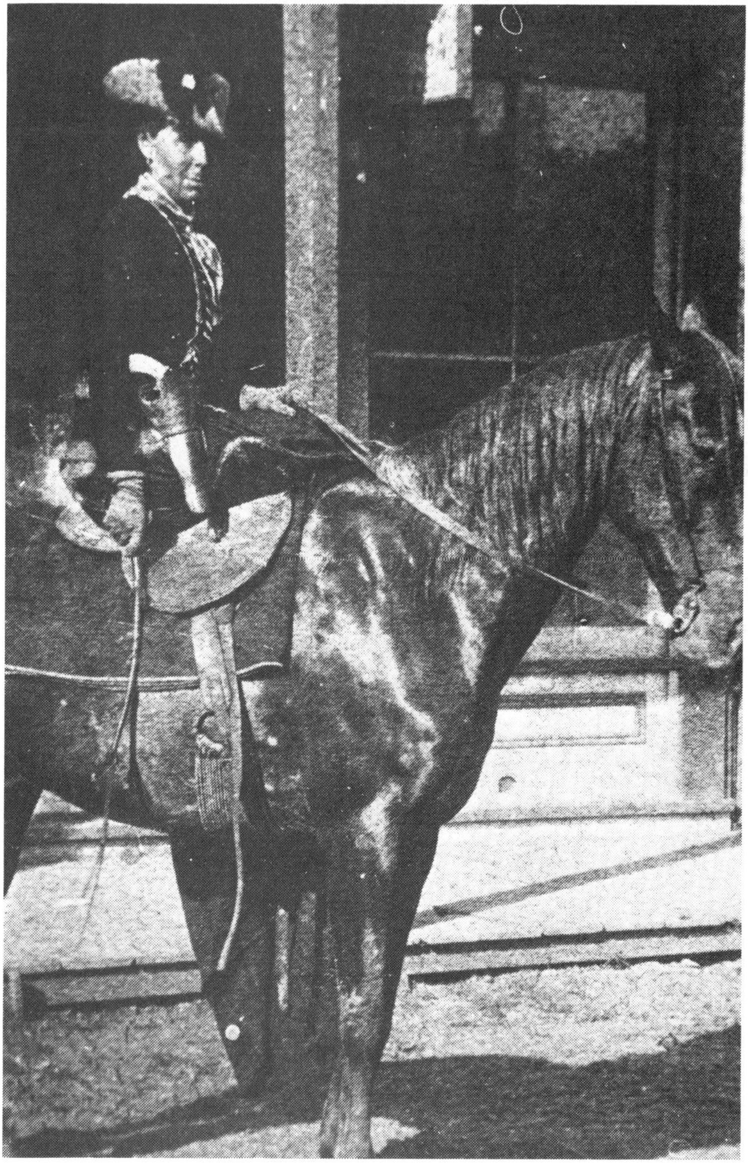

Bell Starr who was born in Carthage, Missouri, Feb. 5, 1848, and killed from ambush Feb. 3, 1899.

object to be feared, and the eye telegraphs the impression to the brain. The brain flashes it to the nervous system, and if the brain gives a false or exaggerated report, cowardice results.

Pardon this digression and I will go back to my story. During that winter I went to a number of country dances. People for miles around had known me since I was a mere child, and I was given a hearty welcome; and while I danced a couple of volunteers would stand guard outside to warn me of any danger. I was like all young men — flattered by the attention shown me by the pretty girls, and never missed a chance to be in their company. For two or three years I had had a Miss Mary Morrison as a sweetheart, who had grown into a young lady believing the good in me and rejecting the bad. Her parents made no objection to my calling on her still, and the country around, including the marshals, knew I was courting her. Despite the close watch kept for me, I managed to call every week or two. I make mention of her because she played a very important part in my career, as you will see later. She was my first love — I shall not rave over her beauty, as we are always daffy over our first sweetheart, but it might not be amiss to say that she was a beauty, was of Irish-Welch descent, and had auburn hair that curled naturally, large hazel eyes, and a fair complexion. I might add that she was as good as she was beautiful.

My friends urged me to leave the Indian Territory, and I decided to get a good sum of money and beat it. So, in March, '93, I broached the subject of robbing a bank to Frank Cheney and found he was willing. I selected Caney, Kansas, a town of two or three thousand, about two miles over the line, as our field of operation, and we started at once. Frank was riding a fine race mare and I a well-bred horse of speed and some endurance. When we reached the country around Nowata we stopped for a few days' rest and bought two extra horses (common cow ponies) to make our first run on. We left our good horses about twenty miles from Caney and the day before our venture we rode to a friend's house near Caney and spent the night. Of course, we did not tell him of our plans. There were two ladies in the family and we invited a couple of families in to dance. This lasted until 3 A.M. and after a few hours' sleep and a late breakfast, we saddled and started to Caney. (This was on the 25th of March, '93). Our idea was to ride slow and arrive in town about 3 P.M. We each carried two Winchesters and two revolvers, more than our accustomed amount of arms; but we thought that in such a big venture, the extra ones might come in handy. We planned to conceal our rifles about two miles from town and take a chance on doing the work with our two trusty .45 Colts. We felt that we would be able to do the bank and get to the street before the alarm was given; then a few more seconds would bring us to our horses; and if there was any shooting we could give a pretty fair showing with our pistols. Just as we were hiding our rifles, a light shower fell, making the ground a little slippery. I knew the town well and hitched about fifty yards from the bank on a back street. I looked at Frank to see if he showed any signs of "cold feet," but his jaw was set and his blue eyes were glowing with determination.

We separated and reached the front of the Caney Valley National Bank at the same time; as we entered Frank stepped to the cashier's window and I to the left. We both drew at the same time. There were several people behind the wicket, and two customers. The cashier ducked into the vault and another official ran toward the back part of the building, I after him; he bolted through a door into the back room, and as he started to close it I thrust the muzzle of my pistol between the door and the sash, and pushed it open. He had his hand on a big Winchester, but I shoved both pistols full-cocked into his face, and he dropped his before I could command him to do so. I brought him and his gun to the front of the bank and stood him in line with the customers. In the meantime Frank had taken a common two-bushel sack from his belt and as he entered the vault he said: "I have kept this sack on my farm for seven years for this purpose, so here goes."

While he was in the vault I took some gold off the counter, and the paper out of the cashier's drawer. Three customers came in separately. I was watching them and as each entered I put my hat on the counter and as they turned around to shut the door, I poked my gun through the cashier's window and commanded them to come around behind with the others. In a few minutes Frank came out of the vault with his sack two-thirds full of greenbacks; didn't even bother to take the silver. We were confident that there had been no alarm given, but knew that these ten or eleven men would certainly do some yelling as soon as we let them go, so we put them all into a high stockade of enclosure of boards about ten feet high in the rear of the bank that we noticed before we came in. There was no opening into the alley and the back door of the bank led into it. After turning the key on them, we made our way to the front. As I stepped out into the street I leveled the confiscated Winchester at a crowd on the other side; had no idea of shooting, as most everyone ran to cover. Seeing they were too scared to try to stop me, I walked down the street to our horses; Frank preceded me and had both horses untied. We lost no time in mounting and rode out of town at half speed. When we reached the outskirts we rode faster and were soon to where our Winchesters were hidden. As we had two apiece, we threw away the one we had brought from the bank, first bending the barrel over a fence. We were only a few miles out of town when several horsemen appeared a short distance behind us. Ahead of us was a hill with some scrub oaks on it and as we went over the hill south we turned due east. Our pursuers thought we had made for the Osage hills a few miles southwest and went that way. We got to our relay mounts long before night, ate our supper and started southeast, freshly saddled. Just as the dawn appeared, we unsaddled at a friend's house ninety miles from Caney. I was not very tired, so we counted our haul before breakfast. Although the bills made a roll big enough to choke seventeen hippotamuses, to our surprise and chagrin, it counted to only $4,900. The fox cashier had outmanaged us; we learned afterward that he had thrown all the bills of large denomination (amounting to $16,000.00) behind a pile of ledgers while we were taming the crowd. The bulk had looked so big when Frank brought it out of the safe that I never suspected that we had been shortchanged by the wily cashier who had tried to run away. Thus ended my first bank robbery.

This bank robbery I was never arrested for, but it is common knowledge that I did it, thought I was never indicted; for when arrested, the charge of murder came first. I was afterwards convicted on all charges I have referred to.

My reputation as a sure shot and perfectly abstentious man caused a lot of bad men to want to join me, and as the excitement of the game had completely enthralled me by this time, I conceived the idea of recruiting a band of men so desperate that everybody would stand in fear of us. By the last of April I was the recognized leader of as desperate a band of outlaws as ever infested the Indian Territory, and that is saying a great deal, as the Indian Territory has harbored some bad men.

We made our headquarters at Frank Chenney's home, near Wagoner. The gang consisted of seven men, including Frank and myself; we were all spoiling for a fight, and as Frank and I had shown what we could do, the others were anxious for an opportunity to do the same.

I don't think it would be amiss to give a brief description of these men. The names I will give are fictitious:

Frank Cheney, a Texan by birth, but most of his life spent in Colorado, New Mexico and the Territory. About thirty-five years old, fair hair and blue eyes. Daring to the verge of recklessness and a good shot. Possessed a fair education and somewhat of a wit.

Watt, about thirty-five, shallow complexion, blue eyes, dark hair, well educated, a dead shot and the gamest man I ever knew.

Link Cumpelin, age thirty, well educated, fair hair and eyes; a game man, but somewhat chicken-hearted.

Happy Jack, about twenty-seven years of age, dark hair and eyes; a square fellow and full of sand.

Bud Tyler, thirty years old, very dark and fierce-looking, but a little gun shy.

Kid Wilson, age nineteen; dark complexioned; willing to take a chance, but too hot-headed.

Their finish: Cheney was assassinated in the Indian Territory in 1894. Happy Jack was shot from ambush in the Territory in 1893. Watt was killed in a battle with officers in the Territory in 1895. Link died in Alaska in the same year; cause of death uncertain, but it was "natural." Tyler died a natural death in 1908, and Kid Wilson is still supposed to be a fugitive from justice. These statistics go to prove that a lawbreaker has all the odds against him. Few die a natural death or escape the long arm of the law.

To show our contempt for the dinky deputy marshals, we fitted out a chuck and ammunition wagon, and as Tyler was the weakest man at arms, we made him teamster. After leaving Cheney's we camped several days at Pryor Creek. On the 5th or 6th of May, '93, six of us went into Pryor Creek to rob the train. (Look up Kansas City and St. Louis newspaper files). We were afterwards convicted of this charge. It took us some time to get the crowd at the depot corralled, but we did and looted everything in sight. We kept the train in siege for an hour. There were two deputy marshals on the train, but the spineless creatures ditched their hardware along with the rest of them. We realized $6,000.00 and a consignment of unset diamonds and no one got hurt, although we did a lot of firing as a means of intimidation.

After the robbery we rode some twenty miles and established a camp; the country was thickly settled and we did not try to hide. On the second day we were in the vicinity of Nowata and made our way leisurely; we had crossed the Missouri Pacific and Frisco Railroads several times. We knew that our doings had been telegraphed all over the country, and for sheer hellishness, we decided to give our farmer friends a free daylight exhibition of nerve. We were all superbly mounted on well-bred horses and cowboy saddles. We wore spurs and each man carried a Winchester of large caliber, model eight-six, and two Colts in fine wide leather belts.

Instead of forming in line like cavalry, we formed fanshape; each man on the outside was to begin shooting always at the extreme right or left, and the center to center; this was done to keep two or more from firing at the same target. Well, we went through our maneuvers and frightened the whole neighborhood out of their wits.

I don't believe an outlaw camp was ever conducted along the same line as ours. We were shooting at least a hundred bullets a day each to keep in trim, and our expenses per day, not including our ammunition and clothes, was $30.00, or

$10.00 for each meal. We had every delicacy to be obtained in those days, and always the best obtainable. The railroad offered $1,200.00 for me, dead or alive, and the Pryor Creek trainmen $1,000.00, making $2,200.00 for this trick alone. We made no effort to conceal our names; rather, we boasted everywhere we stopped that we could whip all the deputies on the force. These same deputies were willing to arrest innocent and harmless boys and drag them off to jail, and with the fees thus gained drink Fort Smith whiskey and pose as heroes before the demimonde; but they wouldn't risk their whiskey-soaked and immoral hides in an attempt to arrest real violators of the law, though some of them were regarded as man-killers. I can't recall an instance where a deputy killed an outlaw in fair combat.

While out reconnoitering with two others of the gang about two weeks after the Pryor Creek affair, my horse went lame. I stopped at a nearby house to get another, but the man there was newly-married and talked me out of taking one of his. I went a couple fo miles further on and asked a red-headed man standing in the yard if he would sell me one of a number that were standing in a pasture a hundred yards away. He said that he didn't have any horses to sell to the likes of me, so as we rode by I made my choice of the herd and promptly dropped my rope on him. The man with the red hair did not try to stop me, but walked swiftly toward the house. (Note: This man still lived in the same place two years ago.)

I warned the boys to ride up, as the fellow meant mischief. There was a wire gate leading out of the pasture about 350 yards from the house, and just as we reached it, we saw the womenfolk run out of the house to the cellar, and knew the fireworks were about to commence. I jumped from the horse and passed the reins to one of the boys, telling him to keep the horse out of range while I entertained Mr. Redhead. I ran about thirty yards to the right and he sent in a first shot; it passed me a little to the right and high. I took aim at the spot where I saw the smoke coming from. I was lying on the ground and with an elbow rest, and we exchanged perhaps a dozen shots. His as a rule were well lined, but too high, and he had the best chance to hit, as the two windows and doors gave him a chance to alternate, while mine were all guesswork. Seeing that the horse was out of range, I decided to run for it in a southeasterly course; now a person not familiar with a bullet's flight will ask why I should run southeast. The wind was blowing from the south, which would have a tendency to blow the bullets north and behind me. Another reason is that unless he made allowance for my speed and the distance the bullet had to travel, he couldn't hit me in a year. The standard rifle sends a bullet at a rate of about 2,000 feet per second; a fellow running at a slow time of 100 yards in fifteen seconds travels at a rate of 25 feet per second, or about ten feet while a bullet is traveling nine hundred or a thousand feet. Hence if a man was running southeast at the rate of fifteen seconds to the 100 yards, and one was to fire a bullet point blank at him the bullet would pass about five feet behind him. My red-headed friend took about six shots at me, but all passed several feet behind me.

On our return to the Cherokee Country we agreed that train robbery was too tame and decided to rob a bank in approved style and shoot up the town while taking the money. This is the old charge that put me on the run this last time. These people found an indictment against me immediately after being taken to Fort Smith, but Uncle Sam had a murder charge and eight or ten cases of highway robbery against me and the state of Arkansas had to wait. Arkansas had the indictment renewed from time to time.

We selected Bentonville, Arkansas, as our town, it being the county seat and a rich town. It is about twenty miles beyond the state line. I don't think there can be any harm in telling of this affair, for if those Arkansas hill-billies ever get me back they will send me to a convict farm for life. We could get within fifteen miles of town and stay hid, but from there it was an open valley thickly settled. We hired a buggy in Bentonville the night before the robbery to transport our rifles across those farming districts without attracting attention.

The date was June 5th, '93. At 11:30 A.M., we started, aiming to make the sixteen miles into Bentonville in three hours. Frank and I rode in the buggy and led the horses. The other four rode two and two about a mile apart. As we neared town we closed up and all got to a back street at the same time. We had arranged that Kid Wilson and I were to lift our rifles from the buggy as soon as we dismounted and the other three were to see to the hitching and one stay with the team while the other two covered the ground between the bank and the horses. There were lots of people in town that needed watching.

I led the way at a stiff dogtrot, and as the bank door was open, I jumped far into the room from the street, Frank and the Kid at my heels. We gave the usual salutation and proceeded to get the cash. We had not been in the bank but a few seconds when the shooting commenced across the square; two men from under cover were trying to pepper us with rifles and we returned the fire with vigor, but no results. While Frank was in the vault, poor Link, who was walking back and forth just below the bank, was getting it from all sides. Four or five men were shooting at him — and hitting, too — with shotguns, the shot varying from buckshot to birdshot, and if he came too far up the fellows on the square opened on him. We were in the bank about five minutes and when we came out we brought everybody, the six people who were in the bank with us, but the shooting was so hot that they scattered in spite of our threats. We had one guy carrying a sack of silver, but he got away. (See files of Kansas City and Arkansas papers of June 6th, '93.)

We backed to our horses in good order, leaving three citizens down and dangerously wounded. Link, a mass of shots, one of them in his eyes, was suffering terribly and had to be assisted in mounting. I had our bottle (sic.), amounting to $11,500.00, on my arm, and Cheney and I were the last ones to ride out of the valley. We were riding at a mad pace toward the Territory. The sheriff, with a large posse, was soon after us, but as there were no telegraph or telephones on our route, he didn't have much of a chance to hurt us.

We had ridden perhaps fifteen miles with the sheriff and his posse at our heels — not within range, but just dogging our heels — when we passed through a small settlement and told some men to tell the sheriff we were going to ambush them and kill a few of them, and if he escaped and followed us we would get him sure. True to our word, about a mile further on, Frank, Kid and I doubled back on his flank and killed seven of their horses. The sheriff gave up the chase and went back to Bentonville. We rode part of the night and the next day about 3 P.M., got to Cheney's home. We made no pretense at concealment and rode down main roads, crossed the Grand River near Wagoner at Ferry, and as Frank's place was on the open prairie, everybody could see us ride up. Link was pretty badly shot, but stuck to his horse like a Spartan; his eye was gone and he could not use his rifle, as he had been shot in the arm. Frank and I decided to take him about seventy-five miles northwest to friends for rest and treatment. We passed within a few miles of Pryor Creek, the place we had trimmed a month before, and a certain party we had stopped over with hastened to Pryor Creek and told that three of us had just left his place and one was badly wounded, and so he could not fight.

This was at once telegraphed by citizens to the chief marshal at Fort Smith. He had to make a bluff of some sort, so he ordered out a number of deputies from various points near Pryor Creek to take up our trail and follow us until we were either captured or killed. The people in general regarded this as a joke. We rode only twenty-five miles that evening and stopped at a friend's home on the Verdigris River for a couple of days' rest; didn't stay at the house, but selected a camp near a deep ravine where three large oak trees grew — a fine place to put up a defense. The next day at 2 o'clock we saw sixteen horsemen a couple of miles away, who were apparently following our trail; we had plenty of time to have made a good getaway, as our horses had rested fourteen hours and theirs were bound to be jaded, but we had the deep ravine, the three big oak trees and were well-rested, while the officers had to approach us from the open. We thought the two of us under these conditions would be a match for the whole sixteen, which proves that at least we were not much afraid.

They dismounted at our friend's house, got a drink and inquired if he had seen us; our friend told them that he had seen three men riding north early that morning. The marshals knew he was lying, as they had trailed our shod horses in the soft ground to the very door, and also knew we were in the river bottom only a half-mile east; they rode north. Frank and I had each spread a blanket on the ground with about a hundred loose cartridges on them, so that we could grab them quick in case of attack. It would have been no battle — but slaughter. From our vantage point we could have mowed them down without exposure. In about an hour we heard fifty or sixty shots up the river, but stayed in our location until night. Link accidentally shot himself in the foot about June 20, so we left him at the home of a friend near Lenepah, Indian Territory, and never saw him again, but he got safely away from the authorities.

This brings to mind the last time that I saw Frank Cheney. He was riding in a flat some distance away. The day was partly cloudy. Just as he reached the edge of some timber, the sun came out bright and his white shirt and the flax mane and tail of his thoroughbred horse flashed in the sunlight. He wheeled to me and waved a greeting and disappeared. I was for a moment overcome with a feeling of inexpressible sadness, as it was understood ever since our return from Bentonville that I was to quit the country for good, and that noon we saddled horses — I to go west to the Osage Country, and he south to the Creek Country. We had been close friends and both felt the parting, but neither mentioned that we never expected to see each other again. Our friendship was too genuine for any theatricals or any affectation, so we shook hands quickly. Frank sprang on his horse and headed south and I west. I reached the top of the hill previously described, and Frank turned and waved his last adieu. May his brave soul rest in peace and the traitors that caused his death in eternal damnation.

I went at once to the Osage Country, where I met my friend, Miss Mary Morrison, who lived near Nowata. We had met by appointment and in a covered wagon, with a friend as driver and Kid Wilson as bodyguard, we started for Emporia, Kansas, to take a train for the west, aiming to be married when we reached the coast. In deference to the virtue and memory of Miss Morrison, and to put to route a coterie of gossipers concerning her, the reason why I didn't marry her while back in Indian Territory is evident to anyone. I did intend to and would have married her as soon as I was effectually out of the territory. I was betrayed by a party that is now dead. He received $500.00 for information that would lead to my apprehension, dead or alive. We were, no doubt, shadowed from the time we boarded the train at Emporia, Kansas. Our intention was to catch a fast train to California and go from there to Old Mexico. However, we stopped at Colorado Springs to replenish the lady's wardrobe on July 2nd. On Sunday, the 3rd, we were out sight-seeing and did not return until late. I left Miss Morrison in her hotel and went to a nearby hotel to get something to eat, when four plain clothes men jumped on me from behind and other policemen in civilian dress appeared. They did not use any guns, but simply mobbed me — what they term a "roughin."

I learned afterwards that they had been looking for a chance to get me all day, but were afraid to tackle me so long as Wilson and I were together. I was placed in the "holdover," handcuffed. Through treachery of the landlady of a house of ill fame, Wilson was arrested shortly afterwards. I admit that this time I was completely whipped without getting in a scratch. If you touch a man's vanity you are sure to touch a tender spot, and, of course, I had made up my mind to fight to the end, irrespective of time, location or odds. I had pledged myself that I would not be caught until I had fired my last shot, whether it was on the open prairies of the Indian Territory or the crowded streets of a big city. I, who had made the gun-fighting marshals of the Territories stand back — I, the "Bear-Cat" of a bunch of sure-bad hombres, had been arrested without a shot being fired, by four or five pot-bellied policemen! I felt utterly crushed and degraded.

I was placed ex-communicado and not allowed to consult an attorney. I hadn't committed any crime in Colorado; no one there could swear that I was really Henry Starr. Had I been able to see an attorney not with the gang, I could have gotton out on a writ long before officers arrived from Arkansas. For two days I was not allowed to buy meals with my own money, but a kind-hearted deputy sheriff at the county jail looked after me and brought in a big drink of brandy and a fine meal and allowed me to go to his office to eat. I didn't drink at all, but gave the deputy the brandy as a bracer to keep his mind off of the fact that he was entertaining so dangerous a man as Henry Starr.

I don't recall my old friend's name, but I remember the kindhearted deputy as a man of perhaps sixty, with a pleasing smile, long whiskers and a low voice.

As a petty police graft, I mention the following: I was not permitted to spend any money taken from me, but was allowed to pawn a diamond worth $300.00 for $50.00 and when I went back after the diamond later, learned that the ticket given me was a fake. As soon as officers arrived from Fort Smith, Wilson and I were taken to Denver and a few days later to Fort Smith, Arkansas, via Kansas City and Springfield. We were heavily manacled and accompanied by an officer from Fort Smith and Deputy United States Marshal Brown, from Denver, a fine officer and gentleman.

The sensational newspaper correspondents worked overtime. Mine and Wilson's pictures were on the front pages of all the big dailies, but the prize lie of the aggregation ran thus: That the young lady with me was the daughter of a wealthy Eastern family, and that while robbing a train I had been struck with her beauty, and taken her by force to an outlaw retreat, while she in turn had fallen in love with me. As I have already said the lady with me was my "kid" sweetheart then seventeen years old. *The St. Louis Republic* in particular, printed trash unreadable about her on the front page and the gapings of the crowd all along the line sure made me sore. At Monette, Mo., we were met by Chief Marshal George Crump, a strong force of deputies, and also the sheriff from Benton County, Arkansas, where we had visited with telling results a month before. This wizened-faced sheriff made himself obnoxious by asking foolish questions and I finally told him that a man of my reputation and dignity could not afford to hold conversation with a sheriff of a backwoods county in Arkansas. Of course this was horse play to get rid of him but it created a laugh.

An immense crowd was at the Fort Smith depot to see us come in. Photographers all along the line and reporters galore were at every vantage point. My attorneys had wired me to make no statements regarding the charges against me. It was July 13 — unlucky date — when we got to Fort Smith. The newspapers and local sentiment were very strong against me. This is not strange as Floyd Wilson, the man I killed at Nowata, had lived in Fort Smith for years, where he had been a policeman and later a deputy marshal, and his widow still lived there. I had about as much show for justice as a lone sheep in the midst of a pack of gray wolves.

I employed as council, the Hon. W. H. H. Clayton, Col. William M. Cravens, and Judge Thomas Barnes, all noted criminal lawyers. Messrs. Clayton and Barnes had each served as district attorney for the government at Fort Smith. Despite a hostile feeling and a prejudiced court these men, true to their professional honor, fought with a zeal and skill remarkable even in that famous criminal court. The more I learn of the world's hypocrisy and double-crossing the more I appreciate the gallant fight these men made for me.

In about forty or fifty days I was brought into court and fourteen indictments were read to me. One for murder and thirteen for highway robbery, as also were Kid Wilson and Alf Chenney, a brother to Frank. We were all convicted. Alf Cheney's conviction is a fair instance of the brand of justice dealt out at Fort Smith in those days. Alf was at the depot at Wagoner, Indian Territory, forty miles south of Pryor Creek when the train that had been robbed arrived at Wagoner, and proved that fact by a score of reputable witnesses and neighbors who had known him for years. It was also proved by four neighbors that lived in the same yard with him that he had not left the house all the day of the robbery, but in spite of this he was convicted. The only man that swore anything against him was the engineer, who testified that a man who might have been Alf Cheney came by the engine but he really did not see him clearly. The district attorney argued that Alf could have assisted in the beginning of the robbery and then got a freight train into Wagoner ahead of the passenger train. A very weak and absurd contention and in an ordinary court of justice the jury would have acquitted him from the box.

That the world may know, I will say that what convicted Alf Cheney was the $1500.00 reward offered by the railroad and the express companies for the arrest and conviction of the Pryor Creek robbers. The money was "cut" three ways — Assistant Prosecutor McDonough receiving $500.00; Byers, Cheney's attorney, $500.00, and Heck Bruner, the marshal who made the arrest, $500.00. A fat chance a man had with such a bunch when one gets double-crossed by his own attorney — a government official would conspire for $500.00 to send an innocent man to the penitentiary. The deputy marshal, with his average low order of intelligence and lack of moral courage, was hardly to be blamed.

Alf Cheney's lawyer should have moved for a trial for him separate from Kid Wilson and me, whose reputations were of the worst. As the case proceeded I could see a conspiracy to convict Cheney for the reward, and knowing that I would be convicted, and to save an innocent man, I told his attorney that I would go to the stand and acquit Cheney but my offer was rejected. The cowardly pettifoger was in the scheme to fix poor Cheney and he was given twenty-five years in the pen, ten of which he served. What that poor fellow must have suffered those ten long years is not pleasant to ponder.

If a man or a set of men do wrong, but with honest convictions, they may be censured but still respected, while on the other hand, when a Federal judge and district attorney conspire to deprive an innocent man of his freedom, through the domination of a supine and ignorant jury, then I say down with the law and society, and allow man in his primitive savagery to strike down the man that robs him of his freedom.

I was soon put on trial for the murder of Floyd Wilson. A man is supposed to be tried by a jury of his peers. The proceedings would have been a joke were not a human life at stake. What chance had I, a noted outlaw, of a different race, before a jury in the town where Wilcon had lived for years. The evidence was all in my favor and my attorneys felt sure that a verdict of manslaughter would be the severest verdict. The district attorney's argument was based chiefly on my reputation.

Former Representative Judge Isaac Parker's instructions to the jury lasted two hours and forty minutes, and for legal pomposity and hazy insinuations, it would rank high. Once he did descend on earth and said that a man like me charged with highway robbery, and one who had also jumped his bond, could not claim the right of self defense. This was a bad break for his high honor, as this was one of the nine errors the case was reversed on by the United States Supreme court.

The jury was out long enough to look respectable and returned a verdict of "Guilty of murder in the first degree," which meant the rope. The judge, to show his appreciation, ordered that the jury be given supper at the government's expense. I had been convicted of the Pryor Creek train robbery before this murder case came up, so was then put on trial for the looting of the depot safe at Nowata. Note the overwhelming testimony of one cheap detective, who swore that I told him I did it — a lie all the way through. Of course I was guilty but the methods these people chose and the ease with which they would convict was something beyond belief. In a few days I was convicted on the two cases of robbing. The traitor Creekmore turned state's evidence. If ever a poor devil was a fall guy, it was I about that time. If I was going to hang, why spend time and expense convicting me on these highway cases? Of course this exposed the prosecutor's weakness. Kid Wilson and Alf Cheney were given 24 years at Brooklyn, New York. I was not sentenced on the highway charges but was brought in pretty soon and sentenced to the rope. The judge, with his usual ornate vanity, gave me a twenty-minute lecture, but he failed in his object. That fellow never could scare me. He sentenced me twice to the hemp, but I never batted an eye. I was young and foolish in the head in those days. My attorneys promptly took out a writ and this stopped all hanging for me until the United States Supreme Court passed on the case. In about 15 or 16 months my case was reversed and I was remanded for a new trial.

The justice that handed down the decision took occasion to remark that the charge could not be greater than manslaughter. This was a victory for my attorneys and a great rebuke for the prosecution.

Isaac Parker, the Nero of America, was appointed by President Grant shortly after the close of the Civil War, and had jurisdiction over the Western District of Arkansas and all of Indian Territory for a number of years.

During Parker's regime as judge, if a poor devil happened to be sentenced to hang by him and was so bereft of friends and money to take an appeal to the Supreme Court he was hanged within thirty to sixty days after his trial before Parker. Eight-eight men were hanged by Parker's orders, and he sentened a hundred and thirty odd to the same fate and boasted that he wanted to have the "glory" of having had 100 men put to death by his orders.

My case was on docket for the autumn term in the year 1895. On July 26, 1895, an attempt was made to break jail by Cherokee Bill, a noted outlaw, under sentence of death. One guard was instantly killed and others were in immediate danger. I pledged myself to get Bill's gun if the guard would give me his word of honor that he would not shoot him when disarmed, which he did.

I went at once to Bill's cell and told him that he could not possibly get out — that he might be able to kill a few more guards, but that would avail nothing, and to take my advice and give his gun to me, which he did, loaded all round. I walked to the end of the corridor and handed the gun to the guards. This is a true account of that affair, and can be corroborated by a number of people still living.

A special jury was called, and as a culmination of high-handedness and injustice, I was handcuffed and arraigned with Cherokee Bill for the jail murder. The guards and officials at the jail were furious and indignant, and promised that I should get the best of it. That such a dastardly act was bound to have a reaction. The low cunning of the assistant prosecuting attorney was again shown; no doubt he and the judge had their heads together and smarting under the sting of the Supreme Court's rebuke, decided to play their trump card against me, by having me arraigned with Cherokee Bill, charged with the murder of a jail guard while attempting to escape, and all in the presence of the petit jury that was to try me for the murder of Wilson.

The second trial on the Wilson murder charge was practically the same in regard to evidence as the first. As an illustration of how sure the prosecutor was of his jury, I will cite this incident: When the argument of a case is closed it is customary to remand a prisoner to jail; but I was permitted to sit while another case was called. I remarked to my attorney that such proceedings looked bad. In one-half hour the jury returned a verdict of murder in the first degree. The indictment for accessory to killing the guard was nolled [dropped].

Arkansas is noted for ignorance and Hill-Billyism, and fifty percent of the jurymen were drawn from backwoods counties and were completely dominated by the powerful personality of Judge Parker, who was no doubt an able man, and of extensive legal learning. But he had fought evil-doers so long that it was claimed by even his most intimate friends that his mind was warped on that particular subject, and those closest to him admitted that he was a monomaniac on the subject of crime. I can scarcely take so charitible a view of the judge because he conspired to convict Alf Cheney when the densest mind in the court room could see that he was wholly innocent. And I have personal knowledge of two other cases where rewards were offered for conviction. I do not charge that he got any part of the rewards; on the contrary, I don't think he would have taken money under any condition, but he knew where the money went.

I was again sentenced in the fall of '95 and again took the case to the Supreme Court, and granted a hearing about sixteen months later. However, in the meantime, Judge Parker had a newspaper controvery with Judge White of the Supreme Court. Justice White flayed his honor of Fort Smith for flagrant abuse of power, and Parker replied, charging Justice White with a lack of knowledge of the law. Right then Judge Parker got in bad, and for him to say that a Justice of the Supreme Court of the United States knew nothing of the law is a striking example of this man's bigotry and exaggerated ego. I don't pretend to be on the inside, but I have a sneaking suspicion that friends of the offended Judge White got the ear of Congress and that body promptly and effectively stripped the Honorable Isaac Parker of his kingly power by taking the Indian Territory from his jurisdiction. They cut off his tail close up, — bully for Congress. I don't care what they do with the tariff, Hurrah for the Supreme Court, the most incorruptable court of the history of the world. Of course the Judge was to dispose of all criminal cases pending, and after that was finished only violators of internal revenue came under his control.

How our good Old Uncle Sam got stuck up, shook down and double-crossed by that court at Fort Smith. Court never adjourned — one term ran on 'til another was due, and let it also be remembered that witnesses came as far as 300 miles and received mileage and $1.50 per day for expenses while at court. A marshal got so much per each witness subpoenaed, and not one witness out of every four was used, while often 30 to 40 witnesses in one case would remain two months, and then the case would be continued. If tried, not one witness out of five knew a material fact. Of course we could expect a host of professional witnesses; the same men were called from term to term, stool pigeons of the deputy marshals, who grew fat haunting the saloons and low dives which flourished in Fort Smith. Naturally this swarm of witnesses promoted such industries as saloons, houses of ill-fame, and cheap boarding houses.

It is not my intention or desire to cast the remotest reflections upon the good citizens of Fort Smith; far from it, for during my stay there in durance vile, of four years and six months, I came to know most everybody in town; and I would be an ungrateful wretch indeed if I failed to remember and be thankful for the many kindly favors and expressions of sympathy and cheer proffered by many of the best citizens in the town, who loved fair play, and knew my case was one of 18 karat shanghi.

I stayed there so long that these good people almost looked upon me as a native son. I wish to add that the guards and keepers treated me with the greatest consideration, and were always willing to do me a favor. I spent most of my time during those long years reading good books supplied by my attorneys and friends. I was eager for knowledge, and was also allowed all and any newspapers and periodicals, and I bought many. I figured that if they did hang me, the information acquired wouldn't make their job any easier, and if they didn't, such knowledge would help me earn an honest living when they released me.

Soon after Congress took the jurisdiction of Indian Territory from Fort Smith, Judge Parker seemed to lose interest in life; the proud head drooped, and soon the gang of fawning syncophants, true to their hyena instincts, sneaked away when they should have stayed to cheer and condole. But such action is as old as history; Kings and Emperors have experienced the same "requiescat in pace."

In less than a year Judge Parker was no more. Of the 13 men under conviction for murder with the death penalty, in jail at the time of his death, 4 were acquitted, 2 given life sentences and 7 found guilty of or pleaded guilty to manslaughter. These facts speak more eloquently than words concerning the justice or injustice of the Federal Court at Fort Smith. Hon. John R. Rogers, a former member of Congress from Arkansas, was appointed to fill the place of Judge Parker, and soon disposed of all criminal cases pending. The leading business men of that town saw Fort Smith had a commercial future, and wished the bloody past to be obliterated. In a speech by Senator Vest of Missouri, on the floor of the senate, he said that the place was a shambles, a butcher's domain, a stench, and a disgrace to civilization and humanity.

The old gallows, which had for so long been one of the show places of the town, and the jail walls were removed in January, 1898. I came before Judge Rogers for sentence and was given three years for manslaughter, five years for the two train robberies, and four years for the Pryor Creek affair, and one year for the Nowata robbery, making a total of 13 years. Considering the number and gravity of the charges, this was a light sentence. Alf Cheney and Kid Wilson got 24 years for the Pryor Creek affair, and poor Cheney was innocent.

Judge Rogers gave me a kind and fatherly talk, and said if my future conduct was good and that the court would in a reasonable time join in a recommendation for a complete pardon. I don't know what the judge thinks of me now, or if his feeling would be a bit kind if he knew some of the facts of my later life; but my sentiment toward him shall always be one of gratitude and deepest respect.

On January 23, I left Fort Smith for Columbus, Ohio, to

begin my sentence, having spent four years, six months and 10 days in jail. I withstood the sudden change from the sunny South to the cold and frozen North in the dead of winter remarkably well, but many of the poor fellows from the Indian Territory succumbed to the rigorous climate, bad blood, and hard work put upon us. There were over 500 United States prisoners in Columbus at the time I entered. I had my neck bowed to do that sentence and do it well, irrespective of conditions, and my record as a prisoner was perfect; only the rankest of fools and imbeciles give trouble in prison. Hon. E. G. Coffin was warden, and through the intercession of friends granted me many important privileges. I can't think he ever had cause to be sorry for doing so.

My sentence read that no part of it should be spent at hard labor, and my work was piece-meal and easy. I learned the trade of glovemaker and after two years of steady work was considered by outside men who knew, to be competent to work in any shop. I also worked as assistant butcher and bread cutter. Since coming to Canon City I have mastered the trade of breadmaker. It is a good trade and I am glad I know it; but I often have been fearful, if the time comes when I am again reunited with my family, that my wife will make me do the pastry cooking. Shades of Tecumseh and Sitting Bull! Think of it! The swift and humiliating change . . . of an Indian warrior being forced by a masterful squaw to come to the low and menial drudgery of a pastry cook.

With little to do while in prison many incidents came to mind in which Kid Wilson and I had participated. One especially I recall when we visited a farmhouse way out in the boondocks. The owner was a kind man with heavy mustache tinged with gray, and there were unnumerable wrinkles around his shrews, kindly blue eyes. He wore blue overalls and top boots, and a flannel shirt open at the throat. He was as fine a type of manhood as I ever have seen in my life. "Fall off, boys," he said, as he walked to the kitchen door and bellowed, "Two more for breakfast, mother, and hungry ones, too, if I'm any judge."

While stabling our horses, I learned that he had settled on this farm the day of the big land rush, April 22, 1889, and had also been on the place long before the opening; he showed us the dugout he had lived in when the United States soldiers moved in beyond the Kansas border, but on the opening day he was first in the rush, and got the very land he had so long wanted. I congratulated him on his staying qualities, and that it paid is proven by the fact that he now owns 320 highly improved acres, well stocked, and has refused $16,000.00 for it. We spent a pleasant two hours with our boomer friend and his family. For genuine, unaffected, all-wool and a yard wide hospitality, the Oklahoman may be equaled, but not surpassed. Noon that day found us at another farmer's house, and he was equally hospitable; we sat down to a fine chicken dinner, and after the repast we were regaled with piano music by one of the farmer's charming daughters.

That night we put up some miles west of El Reno at another farmhouse. The next day we crossed the South Canadian River into the Caddo Reservation, a rather hilly country. We never missed a meal and everywhere we went we were cordially welcomed. We continued our journey to the home of some friends near Hobart, where we stayed several days. We had traveled about 350 miles, and when we left there we went north about 200 miles to see another friend. I didn't know exactly where he lived, but found him after four days' ride, and making only one inquiry. We were now in that little strip of land known as "No Man's Land," but I want to tell you that it is filled with No. 1 people. After a few days' rest we started west for Central New Mexico, some 400 miles away, with but one chance to stop at friends' homes some 165 miles west. We took our time, riding from forty to fifty miles a day. We were near Hooker, Okla., one Sunday evening about 4 o'clock, when a storm came up and we took refuge with a farmer. His family consisted of a wife and three fine daughters as one would care to see. Now, I was never an up-to-date Lothario and had never been much of a "lady's man," but, like all natural and vigorous men, enjoy the companionship of the opposite sex. And strange, too, it may seem to other people, I always looked for girls of education and refinement. I admired these girls for their refined and mirthful ways, and they did their best to entertain us. The oldest girl had a beau in attendance, and before supper he and she entertained with some music; the poor chap's fiddling was excruciatingly wicked and I was certainly glad when supper was announced. The foxy oldest daughter must have said what Napoleon said about winning a man's heart by pleasing his stomach, for that supper was one of the finest I ever ate in my life.

Our host was an honest old Texan and, of course, a Democrat, while his wife was a Republican and a lady of superior intelligence. During the meal we were discussing the merits of both parties, and our hostess asked me if I knew anything about socialism; said he thought from what she had heard of Socialists that they were about as bad as anarchists. Stumpy (Kid Wilson) was an 18-karat rampant Socialist, and to check any bad breaks I told her Stumpy was of that faith, and she apologized most sincerely for her remark and we had a laugh all around; but I could detect a grin of keen satisfaction from the Texan at seeing his wife so neatly taken in. Stumpy hinted that I could play the violin and after supper, accompanied on the piano by the best-looking daughter, I played with considerable flourish and aplomb. After several selections I started in on that old-time melody known by every fiddler, "The Texas Quickstep," which evoked roars of mirth from the old man.

Having told them that we were going to Hooker that night, we were really going to a friend's that lived west of Hooker, and were sure we could find him that night. Our old friend assured us we were welcome to stop with him, but we declined with thanks, and at 9 o'clock that night we left. We stopped by the road-side till morning, then fed our horses and had breakfast, before proceeding some twenty miles to reach friends.

The Teuton as a financier. A boy about 15 came to the door. I said: "Can we get some breakfast and get feed for our horses?" The boy put his head in the door and spoke in German, answering: "My father say how much you pay?" "Oh," I made answer about the price. The boy then replied: "He say $2.50." I said: "No, that is too much; tell him $1.50." Another lapse of time and he again put his head out of the half-open door. "He say two dollar." I then offered him $1.75, telling him that if that did not suffice we would go on. Another three minutes' conversation in German and the boy said: "Get down, it is all right."

After feeding our horses we went into the house. The old man was a fine-looking fellow about 60, with clear-cut features and intelligent face, and did not speak English. The good frau was over 50, but of tremendous bulk; a slovenly girl of about 14, who kept her old fashioned bonnet on in the house, helped to throw our breakfast together, which was soon ready. Here is the bill of fare: Light bread, black coffee, two eggs each and corn syrup. The chilly night air had given me the appetite of a mother coyote, and taking out the $1.75, I gave it to the cook and, laying another dollar on the table, I said: "Bring up six more eggs apiece." This was indeed a windfall and the whole family got busy. Even the head of the house condescended to poke up the fire.

The next few days brought us into New Mexico, where we stayed with a friend for a month and a half. Late in June we came to Colorado and pulled off the Amity affair, which was tame and featureless; the pursuit "amateurish", the worst I ever saw. The nearest the officers got to a hot trail was when they arrested a prominent cattleman who knew me a few years previous in Oklahoma.

After returning to New Mexico, Stumpy decided that he could not come back; said he wanted to quit for good.

Late in July I started back to Eastern Oklahoma from Central New Mexico, a distance of something over 800 miles, alone. I traveled northeast about 250 miles, so as to strike that 168-mile strip originally called "No Man's Land," and which also joins New Mexico, to rest a few days at a friend's who lived there.

One night late I arrived at Perry, a small station on the Rock Island railroad about thirty miles from Tucumcari. I put up at the only hotel in town and unsaddled and tied my mount to a fence in lieu of a livery stable. I arose early next morning (at 6) and made inquiries about horse feed and was told that Mr. Perry, the owner of the townsite, was the only person from whom I could get feed or water. Despite the fact that I had not eaten in twenty hours, I went at once to forage for my horse. On reaching the house I could see through screens that the family were at breakfast. I asked if I could get water and feed for my horse. Someone from inside replied: "Yes, sir, you certainly can, and something to eat yourself." Now, this was western hospitality with elaborate trimmings, but I soon saw why, for the speaker was Rod Perry, an intermarried citizen of the Cherokee Nation, and up to a few months before living in Eastern Oklahoma. I stayed with my old friend Perry for a couple of days.

This happened twenty-five or thirty miles west of Guyman, in Western Oklahoma.

I stopped at a windmill to water and asked if I could stay for the night; three or four men were filling barrels with water, and one said that he lived a mile to the north and that I might stop up there. A heavy-set man with him carried a shotgun, also a couple of prairie-dogs. We walked on together and on his missing an easy shot, I said: "H--- Let me have that shotgun." On arriving at the house we had dogs, some old, some young. Learned things fast! — that's what I did. I learned that my partner was a minister of the gospel and had been a missionary across the deep salt; but the knockout jolt came when he and another preacher began skinning those dogs, young and old, for supper. No doubt some of those older dogs had stood on their hind legs and barked defiance to the antelope and buffalo before the days of the Santa Fe Trail. Their bushy tails and hides were thrown to two skinny curs, who proceeded to chew with industrious perseverence thereon. The portion for supper was passed in to fry. The aroma of a genuine dog stew not only tickles an Indian's risibles, but stimulates his olfactory nerves and saliva to acute possibilities. Soon the smell of these ancient pups frying was neither fragrant nor edifying. At supper I ate one piece. Soon we were ready for church, which was one mile northwest, and being among the first arrivals, took seats near the front.

There were five ministers present besides the missionary's wife, who was something of a haranguer herself. The first half-hour was something of a quiet one, but after that things got warm, with a few fervid testimonials and a sure-enough revival was on tap [tab]. You know, the kind that makes all the boys and girls holler "Halleluhah," during dogdays and kick their heels up at the country-dances as soon as Jack Frost cools off their foolish heads. I saw I was in for it and at first pretended to look the other way (for after each testimonial an all-around handshaking took place), but I soon saw that I was losing out; for the older, bolder and more enthusiastic dames were grabbing me anyway; the timid and prettier ones passing me up. I saw this would never do; I must play the game. This shouting continued until 12 o'clock; the energy of these people of the plains, was past normal. I ("the stranger within our gates," as the most noisy of the parsons dubbed me) was called upon for a testimonial; an old Union soldier had just spoken and closed up by saying that we all had sinned and come short of the glory of God. I said that the sentiments of the brother preceding were my sentiments, that the associations of the evening should ever remain in happy retrospect, that the ministers were doing a great work in that community. I still stick to that testimonial. I will tell you why: First, I endorse what the old soldier said about everybody falling short of perfection. Secondly, because I was sitting by the prettiest girl present — not a bad retrospect. Thirdly, if the preachers hold true to form on eating prairie dogs, they will do the community a great favor by cleaning out these pesky creatures.

The second day after, I was passing near the little town of Hardesty on the Rock Island railroad, and not being able to get horse feed from farmers, went by town to feed. As I rode up the only street in town, someone quite a ways down waived me. I rode down and shook hands with my missionary friend, who had driven another route, and was there to dedicate a church. I was taken around and introduced to the family he was stopping with; was invited to the house and introduced to the family; was invited to dinner and my horse fed. They would not accept a cent; I did not like to sponge, so I donated one dollar to the church. I have forgotten my friend's name, but he certainly was a good sort and a thorough good christian gentleman. A few days later, I pulled up at a farmhouse for dinner about six or seven miles from the northeast corner of the Panhandle, but in Oklahoma. This farmer was from Minnesota and just returning from pasture; said one of his

Jerseys had screwworms from a wire scratch; and, no doubt, seeing that I was mounted on a fine horse and saddle, asked me to go out and help. Ordinarily, I could not throw a rope in the Atlantic Ocean, but always being willing to take a chance, and with the firm belief that if chances are even, I have the best of it, I run my bred horse, Jeff, up by the side of that little Jersey, dropped my rope on and turned off with professional ease. My friend was enthusiastic over my cleverness; said I must have been to lots of roping contents. I told him I had, which was true — but as a spectator.

I stayed over night, I think it is five miles north of Gage, Oklahoma, with a man named Grummett, or Grimmett. Anyway, he was a fine man, and I always regret lying to a fellow like that. I told him I was off the Cheyenne Indian Reservation about eighty miles east and that I had been over in the Panhandle country after some horses. It don't take the second look at me to see that I am not a Swede, hence, I always find out where a man is from first, when I know just about how far I can string him. If my host was from Eastern Oklahoma, I was from the Kiowa Reservation in Southwest Oklahoma. If he was from Southwest Oklahoma, of course, I naturally was a Shawnee from Northeast Oklahoma. If they were just a year or so from the states I was a native son, going over to the next town to match a horserace or buy a bunch of polo ponies or collect for a number of horses I had sold the year before. I admit that traveling across the country under cover is not highly conducive to veracity.

I stopped one day at noon not far from Woodard, Oklahoma, and the farmer, who was rather too talkative, asked me too many questions. So I told him that I was riding a few days in advance of a bunch of horses that I was selling on one year's time without interest. The fellow swallowed the bait, hook and all; was in such high hopes of getting a new team on a year's time that I was sorry that I had told him anything. He did not want to charge me anything for dinner, but I gave the little three-year-old girl a dollar for conscience money.

As I came through the Cheyenne Reservation and by the postoffice and store named Fonda, I stopped at Indian's Camp to buy my son a pair of moccasins. Being out with Wild West shows has strengthened the theory that the Indians were one of the lost tribes of Israel for these Cheyenne, having all the trading instincts of the "Ikies" (Jews.) I finally got one pair that suited reduced from $3.00 down to $1.25, and had just paid for and tied them on my saddle, when an Indian boy of about six came up and began to yell, jump and point at the moccasins. The general belief is that Indian children do not cry, laugh or have the common sentiment of paleface children, belongs to the "Mother Goose and Little Red Riding Hood" shelf, for this child certainly had all the attributes. The mother gave him that $1.25, but he threw the money on the ground, and, seeing that I was ready to mount, got louder. I could not see the justice of my course in taking this little Indian boy's moccasins for my own boy, especially under such sincere protestations, so I sold them back for 75 cents, and it was worth 50 cents to see this little fellow sit right down with such satisfaction and put them on and start on a trot for a clump of timber 300 yards north of the camp; and as I rode east, I saw a little black head peeking over the high grass at the edge of the timber.

At noon on the same day I stopped at Cantonment, which is a misnomer, as the only thing I saw of a mili-appearance was a squinty-eyed Indian policeman with a faded uniform and hungry look. However, up at the school building, where a few teachers, an interpreter and a clerk ate — was called mess — about ten of us sat down to table — an auburn-haired woman of about thirty, who seemed to be mistress of the management; two old-maid school teachers, who did their best toward dignified conversation and deportment; two other teachers, two Indians of perhaps 25 or 30, who tried to ape the ways of the white man by small table talk and manners whose pale cast of talk stripped them of all natural dignity and common sense. Men are no more born equal than they are born the same size and complexion, and you can't make them so by writing it in laws and constitutions.

When we finished dinner I gave the Titian-haired lady a ten-dollar bill, out of which to take the price of my dinner, but she could not get the change in town, so she gave me back the bill, saying that I could send the amount by postoffice order. She seemed satisfied I would, or maybe she was a game loser. Anyway, I rode five miles out of my way that evening and through the burg of Longsdale and bought a 25-cents postoffice order and mailed it to her.

The next day I got to a friend's house within a few miles of Guthrie, Oklahoma, and stayed all through August, 1908, to dodge the heat and rest my horse and self. Later on I went to Eastern Oklahoma for about five weeks and started west again, coming through Tulsa at night about the 5th or 6th of October of the same year. The second evening for supper I pulled up just west of Ripley, at what is known as the Morehead plantation, where a thousand acres of cotton is grown every year, and to see the swarms of negroes necessary to grow and pick this cotton, one could easily imagine themselves way down south, instead of a day's ride from "Bleeding Kansas."

I had heard of the Morehead home and hospitality. I found Mrs. Morehead preparing supper, and on inquiring if I could feed self and horse, she said I could, and with a strong Irish brogue, asked my name. I replied "McCoy." That name made a "hit" and the good lady called a man to care for my horse and gave me the latest paper. Of course, it was an imposition, but when one is on the jump you could scarecely expect him to be a stickler for hair-splitting truths. The father and son came soon, both fine gentlemen, the younger Morehead being a college man, also of vast practical knowledge. After supper we had a couple of hours' conversation. While I am satisfied he was too shrewd to swallow all I told him, he was too well-bred to evince any surprise when I left at 10 o'clock at night. On offering to pay for hospitality, he would not think of taking a cent, but gave me a hearty invitation to call again.

As I came on west, it happened that I crossed the South Canadian where Stumpy and I crossed that spring. The river runs about north here. On the west bank and about a mile north of the crossing is a fine pool of water about 75 by 50 feet and very deep. We had camped there in the spring, and seeing two ducks, killed one and ate it; and on this trip, as I rode up I saw that duck had a mate, and by a little waiting, got to kill them both. As well as other conveniences of campers, a stout springboard faced southeast, showing that people had used this clear pool for ablutions during summer.

Quite a cornfield to the northwest, but no houses in sight from any direction. It is perhaps 600 yards north to the mouth of Little Robe. It was here, at the mouth of Little Robe that happened one of those regrettable and cowardly tragedies of the plains. A party of Comanches — not a "war party", as evidenced by the presence of their women and children — was engaged in the unpardonable crime of killing and drying buffalo meat. An armed expedition from Texas, accompanied by a horde of traitor and renegade Indians, surprised and killed every Indian in camp. According to their own account, they spared neither age nor sex; and as I rode up the valley, I could see in my mind's eye women and children being ridden down and butchered by those cut-throats, both white and red.

The former owner had cut and stacked the coarse, rank grass which, within the memory of living men, was stained with innocent blood. What excuse, what military necessity, required that these Texans march four or five hundred miles to attack a peaceful Indian village? If we believe in the law of compensation, then the white folks of these United States are sure in for some bad luck; if not, then the meanest and strongest get the biggest loaf, with no fixed immutable laws, but a haphazard conglomeration that is liable to skid into oblivion.

I passed the evening previous where Custer trained his artillery on the Cheyenne lodges on the north bank of the Washita, about twenty-five or thirty miles southeast. Appreciating the fact that the red man seemed in hard luck in that locality, I lost no time in getting several miles away.

Within about 200 miles of Clayton, N.M., at a sort of a stage stand, I stopped for water. A small boy, seven or eight was standing by the windmill, and a fine-looking Mexican woman and shikepoke-looking cowboy were coming from cowpen to house with milk. I asked my young friend if that was his parents. His replied that that was his mother. Then I asked: "where did your father go?" He answered: "He killed himself about a month ago. I don't know where he went." A country lad of eight years answered what prelates and infidels wrangled over for centuries.

I spent the latter part of the summer and fall of 1908 in New Mexico with a friend. Nothing of note happened. I rode a little every day to keep my horse in trim, practiced shooting with the same regularity, and occasionally went and tried my gun on an antelope, and if I missed getting an antelope I would knock down a good, healthy-looking two-year beef. One day I was doing a little scouting around the country, some sixty miles from where I stayed, and came up to a sheep camp and made a request for dinner. The fellows in charge was a fine looking Mexican with very white teeth and a long mustache. He said the boss said not to feed anybody. Now, to not feed anybody was something new to one acquainted with the spirit and customs of the West. In fair English, he told me that he was willing, but that the boss, only a month from England, was an awful grouch and bulldozer. I said, "Why don't you knock his head off?" "Oh," he replied, "I am not afraid, but when I do I would lose my job. He always comes by here right after noon."

I told him to go ahead and fix me some dinner; that I would wait for Mr. Johnny Bull, and teach him something of the proprieties and habits of free born Americans. I had not long to wait. I saw the Englishman riding toward us with the up-and-down seat they effect. A stack of millet was fanced nearby. I led my horse over, threw the gate down and let him into it. Of course, this was done to exasperate my English cousin. Shortly he trotted up with a loud bawl about my horse being in his stack. I observed a gun on his saddle, so as I stepped over, I brought my two automatics where I could use them quick. He said, "Your horse is destroying my stack." I said, "Who the hell are you?" "I am the boss of this ranch." To which I said, "I don't give a damn if you are the boss of ten ranches."

The dude said nothing more after that and I politely up and left, thanking the Mexican for his hospitality.

The reader will have to remember that I wrote this in 1912 while at the Canon City Prison so some of my recollections may seem a bit hazy and my English not too good. But I think this work stands as an effort on my part to detail as best I can the experiences I have encountered while on the run.

While a prisoner at Columbus I had ample time to read from the prison library, and all papers and magazines I could afford. I made no attempt to make special study, but tried to get an intelligent comprehension of what the best minds in all history had thought. I soon realized that it was not worth while for me to try to remember language, style, dates, but to grasp the ideas in concrete. What caused me to come to this conclusion was, after I had finished reading Patrick Henry's Defi to the English and was trying, with closed book, to repeat some of its thrilling passages, I found I was too thick headed for that sort of thing and gave it up in disgust. I realized and consoled myself with the fact that Mr. Henry had intended to convey the fact that "We'll kick the damned English into the sea or get ourselves killed," and that was all the facts necessary for me to know.

In 1902 I was pardoned by President Theodore Roosevelt; quite naturally I am one of the most ardent admirers of the Lion Tamer, and as a practical and living evidence, I offer Roosevelt Starr, my only son and heir, now 9 years of age. But I am getting ahead of my story again, and it might be well to say that in September, 1903, I married Miss Ollie F. Griffin, a part Cherokee, and a girl of much refinement and culture. Hence the young Roosevelt Starr, now 9, and weighing over 80 pounds.

After my pardon I went back to Tulsa where I engaged in the real estate business, and resided there until 1907; then we moved to a small town, Skiatook, only six miles from my allotment. I took my wife and young Ted to the inauguration of Hon. C. W. Haskell. I am never blase when there is something of interest happening. It was a perfect day, just enough military to lend color to the scene. Crack bands from all over the state were in gala attire. We made our way to the Carnegie Library where the inaugural exercises were to be held, myself and family standing near the front where the governor and party would stand.

As the governor stepped forward to take the oath of

office and deliver his address, I held my small son high above the crowd to see the first governor of Oklahoma. Altho' not of the same politics, I had voted for Haskell because the Republicans had the effrontery to ask decent people to vote for a carpet-bagger, and I had enough of that tribe. And when Governor Haskell spoke so feelingly of the state's duty to the Indians and gave the Indian Orphan Band the place of honor in the parade at the exercises later in the day, I was glad I had voted for him; racial pride and welfare triumphed over political faith. In addition, Robert L. Owens, himself a Cherokee, took oath of office for United States Senator from Oklahoma; and all around the governor and his party were dark-haired men and women, prima-facie evidence that the red-man intended to help guide the ship of state. I'll admit I went away feeling rather proud and chesty, for I was living an upright, honest life, — proud of my home and family, and interested in all things pertaining to the welfare of my fellowman.

A few days later I learned from what I believed to be a reliable source, that the state of Arkansas had made requisition to the governor of Oklahoma for my person for robbing the Bentonville, Ark., bank in June, '93, over 13 years back. Having had some experience with Arkansas juries and courts, and feeling that a community that would hound a man for a past offense after years of proper conduct, could scarcely be expected to give him justice, I made up my mind that I would never take the chance of having to go back, and took to the "tall and uncut." I preferred a quiet and unostentatious interment in a respectable cemetery than a life on the Arkansas convict farm where the lash and bloodhound are the primary accessories of gentle persuasion.

After a time spent in bitter meditation on the scurvy trick Fate had played on me, I proceeded to dig in and break the law. I can see now what a foolish thing it was to do, but at the time I was hostile, and bitter against fate. All the past wrongs seem to rise up and cloud my better judgment. My reason seemed to leave me, and I simply went to pieces. Imagine my shame and humiliation, and utter dejection when I learned a couple of months later that Governor Haskell had absolutely refused to give me up, and had I stayed to face the music, I might now have held a place of honor and influence with my own people instead of occupying a prison cell.

Influential friends had convinced the governor that I simply could not get justice if extradited. This period of my life I shall always be bitterly ashamed of; I betrayed the confidence of my friends and the governor, but I did not know that friends were working for me, nor did I doubt but what the requisition would be ignored, until after I had again broken the law. Of course, I then had to stay a fugitive from justice. My friends used poor judgment in telling me anything at all about the requisition; however, I shall always feel just as grateful as if their efforts had brought about years of honorable life, instead of the present condition of things.

During the fall and winter of 1907 and the early part of '08, I stayed under cover in Oklahoma. I still had many friends who would shield me. In the spring of '08 the papers credited me with having got off the reservation with forty kinds of war paint on, — of course we must always allow our newspaper friends considerable latitude. Hell had broke loose, and somebody had to be charged with the crimes; what more natural than that I should be the fall guy, since I was at large, and my whereabouts unknown? The same old story of giving a dog a bad name. Two banks were robbed in Kansas and Missouri, and two in Oklahoma, — all happened in the daytime and within a few days of each other. I deny these charge in toto, and in three of these cases the bandits have since been apprehended and convicted. The papers claimed that I was in all of them, and had me in four different places at the same time. Special correspondents were rushed to these scenes and large bodies of armed men were supposed to be close on my trail. I suppose there were a lot of men looking for me, since I was the "only man loose who could rob a bank," but they were a lot of four-flushers of the rankest type who knew that whoever the outlaws were, they had ample time to get away. I was not in any of the three states where the robberies were committed at that time, but a lot of foolish people said if I was, I could not get away on account of my marked appearance and personalities.

I have nothing but respect for a sworn officer of the law that does his duty, but for the volunteer faker, I haven't even respectable contempt; and if through a mistake they ever got too near to me, I made 'em break the underbrush getting out of range.

In April '08 I left Oklahoma on horseback in company with a party I shall call Stumpy. Our start was made from near Muskogee, and we rode about 50 miles that day. The next day we stayed in the mountains in the Creek country. This was about three weeks after the big uproar, and we were both carrying a rifle apiece, and a 45 colt automatic. The second night we made a light ride, and grass being short, I invaded a farmer's cornbin for feed for the horses. The third night put us out of the country where people knew me, and we decided to ride the balance of the trip in daylight. The third morning at sunrise we were about 12 miles north and 10 miles west of Oklahoma City, and close to the little town of Edmond in one of the finest farming countries I ever saw. A pretentious looking dwelling and huge red barns stood off the road to the left, and I remarked to my companion that right there was a good place to feed; for no doubt the owner was an old timer with plenty of country hams, eggs, and oats. As we reached the house, out came a typical Oklahoma boomer of about fifty, white cowboy hat sideways on his head.

Most of the day was spent with this prosperous farmer. He was good to us and gave us several of the best meals we had ever eaten. This farmer wanted us to stay several days with them but we had to move on, not being too safe to linger long in one spot. We made a trip into New Mexico and laid up for a while in a nice hiding place.

I went from New Mexico to Arizona in January, and on May 11, 1909, at a little mining town named Bouse, some sixty miles from the line of Old Mexico, I was arrested. My arrest was effected through the treachery of a resident of Tulsa, and at that time a resident of Bouse. I asked this so-called friend to dispose of a land allotment for me back in Tulsa, but instead he gave the authorities my address. It was not long before the Colorado police had me in tow.

Of course, the newspapers got their usual food for big

headlines. I was returned to Colorado to stand trial for bank robbery. The Colorado sheriff was just newly elected. As a matter of fact he was forty miles away. He and one Fenton actually got within forty miles of me. They, through the newspapers, told all about how they drew their guns and leveled them at my heart, and a lot of that stuff. Personally, I think it pretty hard to point a gun at a man's heart forty miles away, but that particular sheriff and whiskey detective said they did. I understand that Fenton has got numerous promotions and credit for effecting my capture. Fact is, the traitor who was a former city treasurer of Tulsa had some money of mine. I sent for it and he told Fenton that I was at a certain town in Arizona, awaiting this money. Fenton went to Colorado and brought the sheriff down with him, but stayed forty miles away while the Arizona officers arrested me. The sheriff of Colorado, who won his office by less than ten votes, got re-elected because of his ability to trail me all the way to Arizona and arrest me. It's remarkable how such frauds and hypocrites can get by with that brand.

On my return to Colorado I waived preliminary hearing and employed as counsel Hon. Granby Hillyer of Lamar, Colorado. I have never regretted my selection, for I regard him not only as a good lawyer, but a conscientious gentleman. Again the Colorado sheriff showed his little cowardly nature. Prowers County had just finished a new jail at great expense to the taxpayers, but for fear of the consequences if I escaped while under his care, Mr. Cold Foot Simpson got an order from the court and had me transferred to Pueblo, with strict orders to let me see nobody, the reason was that I was put in the solitary condemned cell and kept there from June 8th to November 24th and my bond fixed at such an exorbitant figure too, I had no chance to give.

Several friends from Oklahoma came to Pueblo to see me, but were denied admission to the jail. The sheriff at Pueblo said he had strict orders from the sheriff in Lamar not to let me see anyone. It didn't make any difference what I had done, they had no right to put me in solitary confinement and the condemned cell before I had a trial; not apt to increase a man's respect for law and order nor that intangible thing they call society. No fair person will hardly blame me if I feel a little peeved over such treatment.

I was brought to Lamar about the last of November and pleaded guilty. Received a sentence of from seven to twenty-five years at Canon City, a very beautiful, charming summer resort, but not a nice place to go with a penal sentence hanging over your head.

As I entered the prison a squarely-built man with a broad forehead and friendly eyes, said: "Henry, come over here. I want to talk to you for a minute." His manner invited confidence; he introduced himself as the warden. We had two or three minutes' conversation. I felt that if a man treated Tynan square, he had nothing to fear, and my relations with him since have been more than justified my first impression. Thomas J. Tynan has done more practical good toward solving the great problem of penology than all the reformers of all time. Why? Because he starts in while a man is in the penitentiary. He builds up their minds and bodies. He appeals to their sense of fairness and manhood. Every intelligent person knows you can't make a man better by harsh treatment, bad food and foul air. I said Tynan started in while the men were under his care. That's precisely his way. His honor system, at first ridiculed by the newspapers and sneered at by the police, has long ago passed the experimental stage. It's a success, and those who knocked it now have to admit the warden knew what he was about. Seven states that I can recall have adopted his honor system. It's easy to say "Me too," but it took a brave soul to say to the world: "I am going to give these poor devils a chance," and he did and the men under him have amply upheld his contention.

A word about the honor system. A prisoner is allowed to go many miles, yes, often 200 miles, from the penitentiary without armed guards, to work on the roads. All between him and his liberty is his word not to run away. To the ordinary person it would seem a joke to send a man with many years to serve, where he could walk away at will, but it's a fact that the percentage of runaways is so small as to be negligible. I worked on the road for over two years and the last sixteen months acted as night man of the camp with a gun, horse and saddle at my disposal. To the average person who has gleaned opinion of me from the newspaper writers, it would mean murder, bank robbery and every crime in the calendar. Truth is, I stayed it out.

A lot of people will be curious to know about certain things, so I'll ask and answer. What is your politics? Haven't any. Your religion? Same. Do you think you have led a correct life? No, but it's as good as some others that are holding office. Don't you think society is going to the dogs? No, I don't; it never was away from them. Don't you feel that it's a great crime to take people's money? Yes, I know it's wrong, but I am only a small thief; the lawyers take it all away from me, and still I go to the penitentiary. The big thieves never go to the pen, and besides, they keep what they steal. For that reason I feel much abused.

BIBLIOGRAPHY

Benedict, John D., Muskogee, *S. J. Clarke Co., Chicago, 1922.*

Breihan, Carl W., Outlaws of the Old West, *John Long, Ltd., London, 1959.*

Breihan, Carl W., Badmen of the Frontier Days, *McBride Company, New York, 1957.*

Breihan, Carl W., Great Gunfighters of the West, *Naylor Company, San Antonio, 1952. Paperback, New American Library, New York, 1977.*

Chapman, Berlin Basil, Founding of Stillwater, *Times Journal Publishing Co., Oklahoma City, 1948.*

Davis, Clyde Brion, The Arkansas, *Farrar & Rinehart, Inc., New York, 1940.*

Glascock, Carl Burgess, Then Came Oil, *Bobbs-Merrill Co., New York, 1938.*

Graves, Richard S., Oklahoma Outlaws, *State Printing Co., Oklahoma City, 1915.*

Harman, S. W., Hell on the Border, *Phoenix Publishing Co., Fort Smith, Arkansas, 1898.*

Harrington, Fred Harvey, The Hanging Judge, *Caxton Printers, Ltd., Caldwell, Idaho, 1951.*

Newsom, J. A., Wild and Modern Indians, Harlow Publishing Co., Oklahoma City, 1923.

Nix, Everitt Dumas, Oklahombres,*Eden Publishing Co., St. Louis, Mo., 1929.*

Rascoe, Burton, Bandit Queen,*Random House, New York, 1941.*

Russell, Jesse Lewis, Behind These Ozark Hills,*Hobson Press, New York, 1947.*

Starr, Henry, Life of Henry Starr,*R. D. Gordon, Tulsa, Okla., 1914.*

ABOUT THE AUTHOR

Carl W. Breihan is a former St. Louis County Police Commissioner, Deputy Sheriff, Deputy Constable, and Deputy Marshall. Presently he is serving his fourth 4-year term on the St. Louis County Council, the Legislative body for that political subdivision. Mr. Breihan resides with his wife Ethel in the Concord Village area of suburban St. Louis. His daughter Janis also resides in the area. He also has a son, Carl, who lives with his family in Franklin, Indiana, and a married daughter Carol Ann Willey whose family resides in Detroit.

Colonel Breihan is an historian of note and a universally recognized authority on the James and Younger Brothers. He knew the sons of Frank and Jesse James and Bill Doolin, as well as close relatives of the Youngers and other noted outlaws. He had published eighteen books dealing with various outlaws, lawmen, and badmen of the Old West, and hundreds of magazine articles. Some of his books were also published in England and in Germany. *The Day Jesse James Was Killed* was done in Braille for the Royal Academy for the Blind in London.